Trade Unions and Arab Revolutions

This book traces the role of the UGTT (the Tunisian General Labor Union) during Tunisia's 2011 revolution and the transition period that ensued— Tunisia being the Arab country where trade unionism was the strongest and most influential in shaping the outcomes of the uprising. The UGTT, from its role as the cornerstone of the nationalist movement in the colonial era, has always had a key place in Tunisian politics: not so much as a labor union but as an organization that has always linked social struggles to political and national demands.

The book examines the role played by the UGTT in Tunisia's revolution and more generally in the restructuring of the Tunisian political arena during the three years following the popular uprising,this book asks searching questions such as: How did UGTT interact with the popular uprising that led to the departure of Ben Ali? What was the role played by the UGTT in the "political transition" leading to the adoption on January 26, 2014 of the first democratic constitution in the country's history? How successful was the UGTT in neutralizing the risk of self- implosion caused by the different political and social crises? And what are the challenges that the UGTT faces in the new political landscape?

This volume will be of key reading interest to scholars and researchers of social movements, labor movements, organizational studies, political transitions and Arab revolutions and also likely to be of interest to practitioners especially among activists, unionists and advocates within civil society.

Hèla Yousfi is Associate Professor at Université Paris-Dauphine, PSL Research University, CNRS, UMR [7088], DRM, Paris, France.

Routledge Research in Employment Relations

Series Editors:
Rick Delbridge and Edmund Heery
Cardiff Business School, UK

For a full list of titles in this series, please visit www.routledge.com

Aspects of the employment relationship are central to numerous courses at both undergraduate and postgraduate level.

Drawing from insights from industrial relations, human resource management and industrial sociology, this series provides an alternative source of research-based materials and texts, reviewing key developments in employment research.

Books published in this series are works of high academic merit, drawn from a wide range of academic studies in the social sciences.

Trade Unions and Arab Revolutions
The Tunisian Case of UGTT

Hèla Yousfi

Routledge
Taylor & Francis Group

LONDON AND NEW YORK

First published 2018 by Routledge

2 Park Square, Milton Park, Abingdon, Oxfordshire OX14 4RN
52 Vanderbilt Avenue, New York, NY 10017

Routledge is an imprint of the Taylor & Francis Group, an informa business

First issued in paperback 2019

Library of Congress Cataloging-in-Publication Data
A catalog record for this book has been requested

ISBN: 978-1-138-23205-1 (hbk)
ISBN: 978-0-367-88504-5 (pbk)

Typeset in Sabon
by Apex CoVantage, LLC

To my mother,
Naima Hammami Yousfi

Contents

Images and Map

Images

Map

Acknowledgements

Much like the story you are about to read, my journey with this book was anything but smooth sailing. I would like to express my gratitude to all those who helped me arrive at my destination.

The research and translation work required for this work were generously funded by the Université Paris-Dauphine, PSL, Research University.

My thanks go out to Sami Souihli, Choukri Hmed, Nouri Abid, Hichem Abdessamad, Isabelle Huault and Jonathan Murphy who believed in the project from the beginning and encouraged me at each step of the way.

I would also like to offer my sincere thanks to my colleagues Assia Boutaleb, Jean Pierre Segal and Jérôme Heurtaux, who agreed to read the early drafts and gave me insightful, supportive feedback. I would like to thank Hajer Bouden, Romain Costa and Besma Ouraïed, who helped guide my ideas while writing the manuscript, as well as Montassar Akremi and Thierry Brésillon, who provided the iconographic illustrations that appear in this book. I am immensely thankful to Ethan Footlik who did the translation of this book.

I would like to express my profound gratitude to my brothers Kais and Nadhem for their unfailing support throughout this journey.

Thank you to my friends for their encouragement: Rim Tlili, Thouraya Amamou, Hosni and Hassanine Krid, Amina Ben Fadhl, Maher Hamdi, Bahija Ouezini, Faiza and Wejdane Mejri, Nahla Chahal, Moncef Taleb, Sonia Djelidi, Habib Ayeb, Ahmad Ben Massoud, Nejma Bouakra, Emmanuel Gras, Khansa and Myriam Ben Tarjem, Ines Vehlo, Ghassen Amami, Chiraz and Nawel Gafsia, Maha Ben Abdeladhim, Azza Chaabouni and Afef Hagi.

A special thought goes out to my parents Naima Hammami and Mohammed Lamine Yousfi, who introduced me to the UGTT. I hope to be a worthy recipient of the invaluable legacy they passed on to me.

Lastly, I cannot overstate my gratitude to the UGTT members who graciously gave their time despite the difficulties the organization was experiencing. The hardest part for me was having to leave out some of their accounts, but I did my best to reproduce their words as faithfully as possible. Although I was an outside observer, I shared their desires and disappointments and hope to have honored the faith they put in me.

That which is written in blood from the heart cannot be written in ink.

Gibran Khalil Gibran

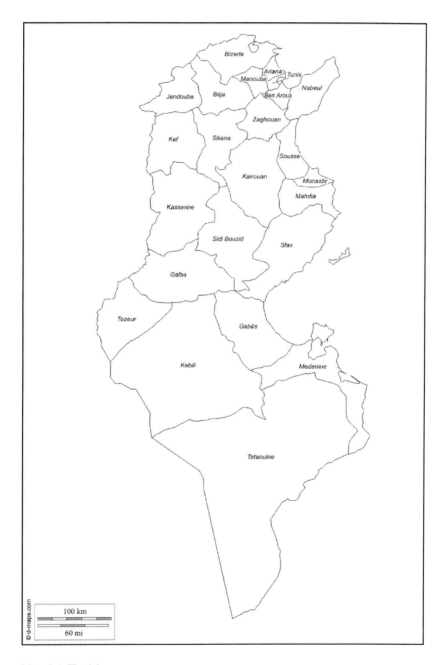

Map 0.1 Tunisie.

Introduction

> Today you can be proud of the Tunisian General Labor Union [UGTT] and the role it played before and after the outbreak of the revolution for freedom and dignity—and that which it continues to play now. Just as Farhat Hached and his comrades fulfilled their destiny during the colonial period by taking charge of the Tunisian liberation movement, rallying support and leading the fight, the UGTT is again rising to the occasion. The union is utilizing its previous experience as a counterbalance and pressure group to play an integral part in political reform and the democratic transition. O defenders of our homeland and knights of liberty, you can be proud of your UGTT. Just as the union supported the revolutionaries on December 17, 2010, and helped transform activist slogans into political and civic demands, it has worked with all the other political elements and civil society stakeholders over the past three years to lay the groundwork for a participatory democracy and a society founded upon civic rights and equality.

This is how UGTT Secretary General Houcine Abbassi described the organization's role at a ceremony commemorating the 61st anniversary of the assassination of political leader and UGTT founder Farhat Hached on December 5, 2013.

Let us start from the very beginning. Spurred on by a powerful popular uprising that began on December 17, 2010, the Tunisian General Labor Union, the country's oldest and most prominent national organization, became firmly entrenched in the political action. The union's ability to rally support enabled it to influence the course of Tunisian politics, but its true intentions have remained subject to interpretation. The UGTT clearly does not have designs on governing the country, instead choosing to alternate between and/or combine—depending on the situation—negotiating strategies, support for rebellious social movements and attempts to radically break with the past. Many questions have been raised about where the UGTT's role as a union and social actor ends and its political activism begins. Those who view the UGTT as a political entity are quick to point out the organization's vital contribution to the national independence movement and construction of nationhood. They heap praise on the union, which some believe saved the Tunisian revolution. Those who take a more critical view of the UGTT's role in the country's political upheaval subscribe to the more commonly held idea of a labor union, namely that it should focus exclusively on advancing workers' causes. This simultaneous glorification and condemnation leaves little room for a nuanced, disinterested study of the UGTT and its role in the fast-changing Tunisian political landscape. As such, there is a significant risk of addressing the relationship between our idea of what a trade union should be and the actual situation in Tunisia only as an echoing refrain. To move beyond this incantation, we have to bid farewell to the world of conjecture and come back down to earth to select a vantage point for observation: the UGTT itself. The goal is to observe, analyze, seek to understand and delve into what really occurs when unionists jointly define and develop the UGTT's actions in the midst of a historic turning point that sparks tensions inside and outside the union.

How did the UGTT interact with the popular uprising that led to Ben Ali's fall? What role did the UGTT play in the political transition that saw Tunisia adopt its first democratic constitution on January 26, 2014? How was the UGTT able to offset the risk of being torn apart by the country's successive political and social crises? What is the UGTT's true objective: take power, impose some sort of dictatorship of the proletariat, or help the economic and political elite hold their grip on power? What challenges does the UGTT face in the new political landscape?

These questions cannot be answered via a classic political approach that treats each crisis as a battle to retain or acquire power. Gaining a real understanding of what is at stake requires exploring both the internal dynamics of the UGTT and the union's interactions with the various social and political actors in Tunisia. To that end, we must examine how the unionists themselves tell the story of the UGTT's actions, interpret its stances, speak about its role in Tunisia's political and social transformation, and react to the attacks targeting them and to the public's lack of understanding about unionism.

The goal of this book is to provide insight into the role played by the UGTT in the Tunisian revolution and, more broadly, in reshaping Tunisian politics over the three years that followed the popular uprising.

The focus is less on giving an account of three years of social and political changes in Tunisia than on understanding the attributes, methods and evolution of Tunisia's largest national organization. More specifically, this work reframes the UGTT's place in the protest movement and revolution and analyzes its positioning as a "counterbalance"—to use unionists' preferred term—negotiating unstable power relationships between the social movement, successive transition governments, national organizations and political parties. The aim is to lend a voice to the UGTT, not only by presenting its official positions and statements by its leaders, but by analyzing the perspectives and remarks collected during my interviews and discussions with UGTT members over the past three years.

To that end, I adopted a classic method in sociology of organizations: studying a system of interdependent actors—the UGTT members—and seeking to understand the parameters of their organizational and political environment, as well as the strategies they employ therein. This involved a combination of direct observation, analysis of official documents and a series of interviews. One fundamental aspect of this method is to compare the actors' strategies with their interpretation of the situations they are in and what they are likely to achieve.[1] I therefore chose to conduct the study using an ethnographic approach, which consisted of frequent, extended fieldwork. These visits enabled me to conduct interviews and gain a first-hand understanding of local perspectives on the UGTT's role and the strategies pursued by the actors at various stages of the revolutionary process.

I conducted some 60 interviews with the most diverse group of unionists possible in order to study the pivotal moments in the UGTT's actions over the course of three years, from January 2011 to January 2014. The unionists interviewed belong to different levels of the UGTT hierarchy in various regions of Tunisia, in particular areas at the center of the popular uprising, such as Sidi Bouzid, Sfax, Gafsa and Tunis. They are affiliated with unions in a variety of sectors, including education, the postal and telecommunications service, healthcare, and textiles.

They hail from diverse political backgrounds, from the extreme left to Democratic Constitutional Rally (RCD), the former ruling power. Additional interviews were conducted with civil society actors both critical of and favorable to the UGTT: human rights activists and members of other organizations such as the Union of Unemployed Graduates (UDC) and the Tunisian Human Rights League (LTDH), as well as members of political parties such as the Islamist party Ennahdha. In addition, I had the opportunity to attend the 22nd UGTT Congress, which was held from December 25 to 28, 2011. I was able to observe both the formal meetings and informal negotiations regarding the union elections, which offered a window into the process leading to the development of the UGTT's political and social agenda during the transition period.

This sociological approach has the advantage of addressing both the events that took place and how they were experienced by my interviewees. This provides insight into how the unionists interpreted the changes underway, viewed the political and social situation in Tunisia, tackled the issues at hand and devised practical means of action. The challenge in preparing this work was to reproduce the conflicts, settings and situations that I observed—among critics, laymen and specialists alike—as faithfully as possible with regard to the organization and unionists' actions.

Three main considerations guided my research:

First, I sought to depict the recent events described by the unionists as accurately as possible by factoring in the fact that, at the outset of the popular uprising, the outcome known today could not have been predicted or expected. My goal with this work was to identify the ways in which the series of events set in motion by the revolution affected the preexisting forms of continuity in protests organized at the UGTT. Instead of approaching the revolutionary process as a movement that overthrew the political order and established another in its place, I attempted to make sense of the dynamic within the union organization—a space for organized, collective action and a physical and symbolic refuge for social and political activists—during the revolutionary period, in terms of its contribution to rebuilding Tunisian politics and its interactions with organizations and social movements with varying degrees of structure. Among the key points of inquiry are the various crises that shaped life in Tunisia from December 17, 2010 to January 26, 2014, during which negotiations were held that would transform the political sphere.

Through ethnographic observation of the UGTT over an extended period of time that included this series of crises, I avoided teleological pitfalls and was able to reconstruct the flow of events and contradictions that defined this time of uncertainty, as well as the strategies that shifted constantly to reflect the fast-moving conditions and balance of power (Dobry, 2009).[2] A brief detour into Tunisian history rounds out the observational approach by situating the UGTT's actions in time, space and the country's prevailing political and social order. This study is unique in that the interviewees spoke retrospectively about the uprising while also commenting on various ongoing crises. Pairing the retrospective interviews with descriptions of current events provides a means of pinpointing the synchrony and diachrony in the unionists' complex relationships with the history of protest movements, the union as an organization and the revolution. I feel that this approach offers a greater understanding of the interrelated permanence and change in the unionists' practices and their interpretation of the challenges the UGTT faced amidst the sea change taking place in Tunisian politics. It identifies the surviving elements from the UGTT's traditional operating methods and the forms of differentiation that are beginning to emerge as the political sphere continues to evolve.

The second consideration that guided the work was a focus on understanding the unique aspects of the UGTT's identity in order to comprehend the intricacies of the union's role in transforming Tunisian politics. The UGTT's central role in the crises that have rocked Tunisia over the past three years has raised many questions. Is the UGTT a union whose top priority is to defend workers' rights? Or an organization that resembles a political party and imposes its political will? Is it a flexible institution that bends to meet leaders' demands? The lack of consensus about the UGTT stems from the fact that there is truth to all these ideas. The fight for workers' rights and continued efforts to influence political and national decisions are present in equal parts. As we will see throughout this work, the UGTT strives to defend individual and collective freedoms but two tendencies coexist within the union: a tendency to submit to the ruling power, on the one hand, which can lead to the union practically becoming part and parcel of the state apparatus, as was the case with the union's bureaucracy; and, on the other hand, a tendency to resist the ruling power, which gains the upper hand during times of crisis. The lines grow even blurrier when one considers the opposing views with regard to the UGTT's role. One group believes that the UGTT should focus solely on its social role as a trade union that defends its members' interests, oversees strikes and refrains from wading into national politics. On the other side are those who back a political role for the UGTT and view the organization as a counterbalance that defends radical positions in order to impose its political will.

Given this situation, the UGTT's emphasis on broad-based solutions that reconcile divergent interests is perceived as the expression of a conservatism that bridles the union's power. This separation of roles ignores the fact that the UGTT was founded at the crossroads of the worker's movement and the national liberation movement. The UGTT is more than a traditional union confederation—it's a political organization that shelters social movements, a staging point for resistance against single-party hegemony for an entire set of social groups, and a venue for the continual negotiations to achieve political and social balance. Understanding how the union's two main missions coexist is a prerequisite for understanding the nature and limits of the UGTT's influence on Tunisian politics.

The third consideration integral to the work is analysis of the union as a unique forum for collective movements. The UGTT is not solely a political and social force that lent broad support to the popular uprising and influenced the direction of Tunisia's political transformation. It is also the only space for collective organized action in Tunisia that managed to resist the authoritarian regime's attempts to eradicate all forms of resistance. The very existence of the UGTT refutes the belief that members of societies subjected to an authoritarian regime become a shadow of their former selves and succumb to apathy and demotivation. Analyzing the organizational culture that underpins this union with hundreds of thousands of members—from a wide range of social strata and political backgrounds, as well as regions and sectors—is key to understanding what it means to organize in a society dominated by an authoritarian system. In this context, organizational culture refers to the set of social norms and values accepted and shared by most members of the organization and which make it unique, in a manner of speaking. In sum, a set of characteristics that separate the organization from all other organizations. This culture provides signposts that guide unionists' actions and gives them a sense of identity and unity rooted in members' participation as a group. We can find out more about the prerequisite conditions, practices and success factors of collective movements in fast-shifting political landscapes by exploring the development of the UGTT following the fall of Ben Ali, the organizational strategies that define its actions, and its relationships with government institutions, political parties and social movements.

Without overlooking the classic difficulties faced by all countries in the throes of revolution as they attempt to establish a new, stable political and social order, this work intends to study, via the singular example of the UGTT, the means by which this challenge can be met. As I will attempt to demonstrate, one important factor to be taken into account is the unique political culture that governs the structure of social relations in Tunisia. Indeed, the UGTT is akin to a microsociety that brings together a wide range of political views and social categories, offering an exceptional laboratory for exploring the conditions required to establish viable democratic institutions.

The interviews with the unionists—who are often active in associations and political networks outside the organization—are all the more valuable for their insight into issues related to the revolutionary process and the conditions for regime change, above and beyond issues pertaining to the UGTT. This has led me to develop the hypothesis—rooted in my professional experience in other private- and public-sector settings in Tunisia and other Arab countries—that the meanings the unionists assign to the organizations' various political positions and the manner in which they dealt with so many internal conflicts and outside attacks result not only from the organization's unique culture, but also reflect the expectations shared by many Tunisians with regard to good government.[3]

The unionists are the central figures in my narrative. I followed them for three years, lending an ear as they expressed both optimism and discouragement, with a consistent focus on shedding light on the dynamics of an organization that is anything but ordinary. Their invaluable input served as a window into the UGTT and its role in the political sphere, on topics that included the internal conflicts the unionists faced, the doubts they raised, the attacks they suffered, and the public's lack of understanding with regard to the union. I gained privileged access to the inner workings of the political decision-making process, listening to everyone from base-union members to high-ranking officials speak about the divisions and points of agreement within the union.

What is more, the UGTT is recognized as a place where the memory of the union movement and the struggle for independence are passed on to others, offering union members a means of contextualizing the revolution within contemporary Tunisian history. At the same time, the UGTT is a longstanding major organization with a strong organizational culture and, as such, has its own specific vocabulary that can obscure the true dynamics at play. Comparisons with different segments of public opinion (some more prevalent than others, depending on the subject) and the critical views of political actors were introduced in order to avoid preplanned, repeated remarks and encourage the unionists to better describe the motivations and issues that drove them to take action.

At the same time, I directed my attention to the metaphorical aspect of the unionists' everyday language, which is free of what could be viewed as linguistic constraints or union jargon, enabling me to gain access to the unionists' political culture. In the work, I put forward the hypothesis that all Tunisians share this culture. In addition, the interviews were conducted either in UGTT offices or cafes near the protest sites (Avenue Habib Bourguiba or near Place de la Kasbah in Tunis, downtown Sfax, etc.), in order to establish a connection between the interviews and these symbolic, emotional settings. That choice allowed me to comprehend what meaning the interviewees ascribed to the revolutionary process as well as the emotional aspect of the events. This dual focus on cognitive and emotional elements provides greater insight into how my interlocutors experienced the revolution, their hopes and fears, how they viewed the challenges the organization faced, and the reference points they used to assess strategies for individual and group mobilization.

It is important to note that the goal was not to determine whether those interviewed had a positive or negative opinion or were telling the truth—some of their remarks were formulaic or manipulative. Instead, I attempted to look beyond the discrepancies and finer details within my interlocutors' individual opinions and viewpoints—or between their remarks and those of individuals outside the union or other unionists—to pinpoint the commonalities in how the union members formulated an opinion. While variations plainly exist in my respondents' comments, all their remarks nevertheless denote the presence of an organizational culture and the use of specific categories within this culture to give meaning to their experiences. These similarities occurred with extraordinary frequency in the materials collected, despite differences among the interviewees in terms of rank, region and sector. This information is a valuable tool for dissecting how specific characteristics of the organization influenced the strategies adopted by its members. More broadly, the interviewees' descriptions of the complex relationships between the UGTT and political parties, between the UGTT and the social movements, and internal power struggles, implicitly convey, in one manner or another, their shared vision for Tunisia and their idea of good government and the prerequisite conditions for establishing lasting, viable democratic institutions.

All these methodological considerations serve to avoid depicting a generalized vision of what a trade union "should be" or any related misinterpretations. Another means of grasping the complexity of the UGTT, in addition to the unionists' shared organizational culture, is the internal and external divisions regarding what role the union should play. This empathetic approach is in no way apologetic. Respecting the UGTT means revealing its weaknesses and wavering as well as the reasons for its effectiveness and the true outcomes of its emancipatory mission. Understanding the UGTT and its role in contemporary Tunisian politics means understanding its bright spots and gray areas and reframing the union within the context of its social, cultural and political history.

These considerations led me to present the analysis in an original way. I chose to publish the interviewees' full accounts, with the exception of some ellipses mainly required for translation purposes, in order to provide readers with the interviewees' highly nuanced descriptions and analysis of their experiences. Rather than quote the unionists in order to illustrate my own points, I attempted to develop a narrative using their own analyses, paired with background information, and to illustrate how this narrative improves our understanding of the UGTT's role in the revolutionary process. I employed a narrative style, setting aside my own analysis until the end of each episode in the story. I also specify the relevance of the quotations to my analysis and the topic at hand. The unionists' words underpin the work from start to finish; the block quotations from interviews are complemented by boxes containing a selection of summaries and arguments by union members. I also chose powerful quotes as epigraphs for each chapter. My aim was to show my gratitude to the unionists by giving them a voice and clearly presenting their contributions.

The work is presented as a narrative in five episodes:

In the first episode, to shed light on recent events, I will take a brief look back at the history of the Tunisian labor movement by addressing the emergence and development of unionism in Tunisia and its impact on how the UGTT operates today.

I will endeavor to describe how unionism on the Tunisian mainland during the colonial period evolved as workers and the local economy grew more organized, giving rise to a trade union that stands out in the Arab world for the role it plays in politics and its ability to rally support. This historical overview will also provide an opportunity to delve into the internal organizational dynamics at the UGTT as well as its relationship with the single-party state and various social movements. At the same time, this foray into the past will help readers grasp how the radical changes that emerged from the uprising belie the continuity of the union's practices.

In the second episode, we will embark on a journey with the unionists to the very heart of the revolution. I will draw from union members' detailed description of the events that took place between December 17, 2010 (the date of Mohammed Bouazizi's self-immolation) and January 14, 2011 (the date on which Ben Ali fled) to analyze how they view their contribution to the protest movement. My intention is not to address all the questions and issues surrounding the revolutionary process, which will remain in the background of this narrative. I will focus, rather, on the various contradictions and tensions that the UGTT faced as an intermediary between the popular uprising and the apparatus of power. In particular, I will look at the dynamics at play between the unionists and the UGTT leadership and between the UGTT and the various groups of actors in the uprising.

I will seek to elucidate the strategies implemented by unionists in situations involving stark organizational constraints (pressure from the Executive Board, regulatory provisions, police repression, etc.) that afforded limited room for manoeuver, which defined the areas of critical uncertainty and the potential for cooperation/conflict with various actors. I will analyze unionists' methods for adjusting and reacting to often-unexpected events as well as the meaning they attributed to the strategies employed, whose consequences were often impossible to predict at the time. My aim is to convey, as faithfully as possible, unionists' views and experiences during this experimental period that turned the Tunisian political order on its head.

The starting point for the third episode is the fall of Ben Ali. The chapter describes the unionists' initial enthusiasm and ensuing hesitation and conflicts as the UGTT negotiated its role in the transition phase leading up to the National Constituent Assembly (ANC) elections on October 23, 2011. I will devote special attention to the UGTT's role in setting up the mechanisms for managing the transition period. We will see that the UGTT was a point of convergence for the issues raised by the revolutionary process. Not only did the UGTT face a series of attacks after the fall of Ben Ali, the union also had to contend with the overhaul of the traditional union system, with the arrival of two new trade unions: the General Tunisian Labor Confederation (confederation general des travailleurs tunisiens, or CGTT) and the Union of Tunisian Workers (Union des Travailleurs de Tunisie, or UTT). I will show how the uncertainty and fear felt by the "characters" in our story, who were very concerned about the place they had been granted in the political and union sphere, stem from competition between political actors. I will analyze both the manner in which the unionists reacted to campaigns against the UGTT as well as the resources mustered by the union as an organization to survive internal divisions and outside attacks.

In the fourth episode, readers will delve into the 22nd Tunisian General Labor Union Congress held in Tabarka from December 25 to 28, 2011. The theme of the UGTT congress—the first to take place after the uprising on December 17, 2010, and the National Constituent Assembly elections on October 23, 2011—was "I love you, O People," a posthumous homage to former UGTT leader Farhat Hached. The congress was held during a time of profound political and social upheaval. This chapter will draw from the interviewees' descriptions of the proceedings to detail the main challenges facing trade unionism at the national level and how unionists decided to address these issues. I will analyze the various processes that determined the congress delegates' voting behavior. I will also examine the ways in which the delegates attempted to adapt as best they could to the trying demands of the political and economic crisis—a period that raised incredibly thorny, crucial questions regarding the organization's ability to form a unified front. Lastly, I will look at the conditions required for Tunisian unionism to forge a new path amid all the political upheaval, in light of the outcomes of the congress described by the interviewees.

In the fifth and final episode, I will turn to the various political crises that shook the country in the run-up to the ratification of the first democratic constitution on January 26, 2014. The National Constituent Assembly elections on October 23, 2011, established some democratic legitimacy, but did little to command respect for political decisions and foster the emergence of a set of common rules accepted by all political and social actors. The political and economic instability during this period was exacerbated by political assassinations and created competing sources of legitimacy that gradually developed a new political lexicon and brought new issues to the fore in the debate over the new institutions to be established. Backed by its reputation for independence and impartiality, the UGTT took pride of place in the interactions between the different sources of legitimacy and systems of power. I will focus on the nature of the interactions between the UGTT and the other political and social actors in Tunisia, which dictated the process for reaching a political solution that the actors found more or less acceptable. I will home in on how unionists viewed the UGTT's role in the national dialogue with the employers' organization UTICA (Tunisian Union of Industry, Trade and Handicrafts Tunisian Union of Industry, Trade and Handicrafts), the National Order of Lawyers and the Tunisian Human Rights League (LTDH). This dialogue led the Islamist-majority government to be replaced by a technocratic government whose primary goal was to isolate itself from the political clashes and prepare for the next elections.

I will then expound the broader lessons that can be learned from this episode. I will do so by comparing the various institutional experiments implemented by the UGTT to manage successive political crises with how the unionists interviewed interpreted these initiatives, with a view to identifying the conditions and processes by which abstract democratic concepts were translated into local rules that met Tunisians' expectations for legitimate, fair government. I hope to provide a greater overall understanding of the forms of legitimate power by describing the methods for handling conflicts both inside and outside the UGTT. The UGTT and other organizations involved in the political battle formulated and conveyed messages that reflected not only political positions, but also a specific relationship with the political and the collective. A further goal of this work is to help expand the knowledge of Tunisians' local expectations in terms of good government.

In addition to relating the history of this momentous period in Tunisian politics, this work intends to provide in-depth analysis of the unique characteristics and development of one of the largest trade unions in the Arab world and an investigation into the social movements that set the Tunisian revolution in motion, which will largely determine Tunisia's political future. This insight into the UGTT can help improve our understanding of the impact of spaces for organized collective action, on changes that affect politics. More generally, this work sheds light on the new social and political dynamics afoot in Tunisia and raises questions—via examples of continuity and change—about the region's ability to reinvent politics.

Notes

1. One notable example of this method can be found in the paramount sociological research conducted in Poland in 1981 on the trade union Solidarnosc by a French and Polish team led by Alain Touraine, cf. Alain Touraine, Michel Wieviorka,

François Dubet and Jan Strzelecki (1982). The researchers adopted a sociological working method in which they assisted the participants in analyzing their own actions. My work on the UGTT is similar to the Solidarnosc study in that it shares the interviewees' analyses, but differs in its focus on the history of the Tunisian labor movement and the impact of the organizational environment that grew from the unionists' strategies.

2. My work falls within the tradition of research developed by *Gestion et société* (Management and Society), a research team at the French National Center for Scientific Research (CNRS) led by Philippe d'Iribarne. The main research focus of the team is developing an ethnology of modern societies through the comparative study of organizations. The results of this research can be found in a number of publications (Iribarne, Henry, Segal, Chevrier and Globokar, 1998; Iribarne, 2003a). For research specific to Arab countries, cf. Hèla Yousfi (2014; 2010; 2008; 2007).

3. To maintain anonymity, I also changed or deleted all terms, references, locations and names that could be used to identify the unionists and other interviewees. I did, however, choose to publish the names of public figures such as UGTT Secretary General Houcine Abbassi, union movement leaders like Adnene Hajji and Mohamed Trabelsi, and UGTT experts such as Mongi Amami and Abdeljelil Bedoui. When introducing direct quotations, I systematically include the interviewee's position (union activist or union official), sector and region. I kept the interviewees' spoken style, including repetition and verbal tics, in order to reproduce the liveliness of the interviews as best possible, giving an idea of the type of interview setting.

1   The Tunisian General Labor Union

A Uniquely Tunisian Organization

Historically, the UGTT has always played and occupied an important role in the country's turning points. You always find the UGTT at the center of historic moments, going all the way back to the war of independence. Hached paid the ultimate price—he was assassinated. When the state was being built, there was unity between the UGTT and the first constituent assembly during the drafting of the constitution, which was a fundamental historic moment. During the state-building period, the UGTT lost all of its top officials, who became ministers, mayors and governors. . . . For a time, the ruling power alienated the UGTT. Later, during the period of economic liberalism under Nouira, the UGTT was compelled to establish a contractual relationship with the regime based on negotiations and dialogue, which made the union the regime's main partner. The UGTT was among the founders of the new era in the 1970s, before being subdued, subjugated and domesticated yet again. After November 7, the regime sought to alienate the UGTT but we were able to resist, as evidenced by the efforts of the local and federal sections during the December 17, 2010 revolution.

                              Hédi, union activist, Secondary Education, Tunis

With 750,000 members,[1] the UGTT is the largest trade union in Tunisia and for many years was the only union. Predominantly present in the public sector, the UGTT comprises 24 regional unions, 19 sector federations and 21 general unions.[2] A number of different political movements are present in the UGTT, which has members from all regions of the country and social backgrounds, including manual workers, civil servants and doctors. The union was founded in 1946 by Farhat Hached and other Tunisian unionists[3] following a split with the French General Confederation of Labor (Confédération générale du travail, or CGT) near the end of World War II, when the French Communist Party and the French Section of the Worker's International (SFIO) refused to support independence for Tunisia. As the cornerstone of the independence movement during the colonial era, the UGTT has always played a vital role in Tunisian politics. The purview of the UGTT extends beyond that of a traditional trade union—throughout its history, the labor organization has paired social initiatives with political and national aims. Unlike its counterparts in other Arab countries, the UGTT has always enjoyed a certain amount of independence—more so during some periods than in others—from the state apparatus. After Tunisia gained independence in 1956, two factions coexisted within the union. The first, known as the "union bureaucracy,"[4] submitted to the will of the regime, while the second resisted the ruling power and gained the upper hand during times of crisis, maintaining control over certain federations in education, the postal service and telecommunications as well as some local and regional unions. Many social movements have been able to secure the support of UGTT federations and sections, despite the union bureaucracy's close ties with the government. As a result, the UGTT was able to play a decisive role in the rallies and demonstrations that led to the fall of Ben Ali. The UGTT continues to play a key part in the transformation of the Tunisian political landscape.

The UGTT has a unique organizational structure in relation to other Arab or French unions, leading some observers to speak of "two UGTTs" or to define the UGTT in terms of its structural and/or political ambivalence (Chouikha and Geisser, 2010; Gobe, 2008), while others see a reflection of the incomplete modernization of Tunisian society (Hamzaoui, 2013; Amami, 2008). However, a static or binary perspective that postulates direct competition—reified at its core between a bureaucracy guided by impersonal rules designed to uphold "modernity" and local social practices that must be overcome—does not suffice to fully explain that unique structure that emerged from the colonial trade union tradition. The primary aim of this chapter is to retrace the history of the Tunisian trade-union movement and its impact on the development of the UGTT. The chapter will follow the

Image 1.1 Bourguiba and Hached in the Early 1950s.

Image 1.2 From Left to Right: Ahmed Ben Salah, Habib Achour, Habib Bourguiba, Abdallah Farhat and Khelifa Houas in Kerkennah.

advance of the national union movement—framed in its proper economic, social, political and cultural context—taking into account the historical processes and prevarications among Tunisian social movements at the root of the negotiations that imposed the colonial union model, which led to the emergence of a uniquely Tunisian union organization. I will then endeavor to describe the mechanisms that govern relationships within the UGTT and the union's unique position in Tunisian politics, as explained by the UGTT's past relations with the single-party state, which were characterized by compromises as well as dissidence expressed via confrontation and avoidance strategies.

The Emergence of the Tunisian Labor Movement

The Tunisian labor movement took root at the start of the 20th century. The movement continued to develop in reaction to capitalist colonial exploitation and the arrival of foreign workers and union organizations that predated the formation of the Tunisian working class. How did the union movement born in Europe, which arrived in Tunisia along with colonial capitalism, affect local labor conditions? How did the working class inter-act with the national independence movement? How did social and politi-cal struggles play out in the battle waged by the Tunisian working class? What alliances did Tunisian workers form to break free from French dom-inance and join the fight for independence? The answers to these questions do much to explain the UGTT's current structure and role in Tunisian politics.

The spread of French colonial capitalism greatly intensified following World War I, permeating all economic sectors, from agriculture to mining and infrastructure. This growth was reliant on imported labor from Europe (France, Italy and Malta) for skilled positions and from North Africa (Libya, Algeria and Morocco) for low-skilled and unskilled infrastructure and min-ing jobs (Yousfi, 1983). Union work was initially reserved for Europeans, who were in the majority in all working-class sectors, including mining, construction, transportation and the food industry. As Tunisian craftsmen and farmers' (*fellahs*) situation grew increasingly unstable, Tunisian work-ers gradually began to take jobs at colonial companies. They joined French union confederations such as the CGT[5] and CGTU,[6] which provided an organizational model and a place to become acquainted with union cul-ture, but also perpetuated their marginalization and discrimination. Tuni-sian workers were underpaid in relation to the Europeans and especially the French, who benefitted from the "colonial third"—a 33% wage premium (Bessis, 1974). Tunisian workers quickly realized that the French unions were failing to defend them adequately and that they were mainly used as a bargaining chip to win concessions for French employees, compelling the Tunisians to create their own independent union.

The first independent Tunisian union organization, the General Con-federation of Tunisian Workers (Confédération générale des travailleurs tunisiens, or CGTT), was established by Mohamed Ali Hammi on Decem-ber 3, 1924, four years after the birth of Destour[7] and the Tunisian Commu-nist Party (PCT). Authorities from the French protectorate moved swiftly to suppress the CGTT and, after a series of labor strikes and protests, arrested Mohamed Ali Hammi and his comrades. In 1937, Belgacem Gnaoui founded the second incarnation of the CGTT, but conflicts between the union and the Neo-Destour Party[8] enabled the colonial authorities to curb the national movement and nip this second attempt at unionism in the bud. The third initiative was initiated by transportation-sector employee Farhat Hached, who created the UGTT with other Tunisian unionists on January 20, 1946, following a split with the French CGT. The UGTT launched a two-pronged campaign for workers' rights and national independence, forming an alliance with Neo-Destour. When the political party's leader, Habib Bourguiba, was arrested in January 1952, union chief Hached took charge of the national liberation movement. Hached would lead the movement until December 5, 1952, when he was assassinated by colonialist far-right elements abetted by the French secret service.

Two fundamental characteristics emerged from the origins and development of Tunisian unionism that would greatly affect the structure of the UGTT and the role it plays in Tunisian politics.

First, the Tunisian economy comprised two superimposed structures during the colonial era: a capitalist structure prevalent in industry, which was dominated by the French, and a structure with traditional relations of production that had long governed the peasantry and handicrafts (Ben Hamida, 2003). Thus, capitalist employer-employee relations based on salaried work became intertwined with pre-capitalist social relations organized by local communities. This model gave rise to a highly diversified proletariat. Ethnic and professional diversity became enmeshed with local, regional and tribal forms of solidarity that had a considerable influence on how the union confederations took shape. This unorthodox path to economic development was chronicled in several colonial works that stigmatized Tunisian workers, who were depicted as lacking balance or, at best, lagging behind western workers. One such example can be found in the memoir written by Louis Morel, Civil Inspector[9] for the Gafsa region, on the Gafsa miners (1949) (quoted in Amami, *op. cit.*, 77):

> In this case, the major error would consist, for example, in believing that the working masses standing before the trade union are similar or at least comparable to its followers in western countries. The union has to contend with the tribe, a group that is older, more homogenous and sturdier than itself. It even has to pursue a policy of selecting leaders based on their local stature. The end conclusion is that there is a clear gap between the Gafsa miners' technique, in the broadest sense of the term, and their customs, which lag several centuries behind.
>
> (Morel, 1949, 225–7)

For his part, Max Pellé (quoted in Amami, *op. cit.*) expressed amazement at the persistence of a form of dualism among Tunisian workers, which reminded him of laborers from the early 19th century. In a letter to the minister of foreign affairs dated November 6, 1907, Pellé wrote:

> The union movement is confronted with groups of workers who experience a sort of dualism with regard to their conscience and sense of belonging. On the one hand, they belong to a community of workers who share the same interests; on the other hand, they belong to a national or ethnic tribal community. And while work at large capitalist and colonial companies fosters communication with other communities and brings them closer together, because they share the same working conditions, each day after work the workers return to their neighborhood, family, tribe or ethnic or national community—a world that is almost completely closed off.[10]

The union movement worked to build a sense of unity among workers in specific trades and sectors in order to overcome these community, tribal and ethnic divisions. However, colonial companies treated Tunisian workers in such a way that it was difficult for them to identify solely as working class. Viewed from this perspective, the classic theory that "archaic" relations stifled the emergence of "modern" social relations (Tabbabi, 2006) appears less valid. The colonial ethnic hierarchy was more responsible for Tunisian workers' refusal to trade their tribal/community support system for pseudo-working-class unity that did not afford them any form of protection. French business owners exploited these community ties extensively as a means of eroding workers' unity, but these clans also served as a resource that helped Tunisian workers withstand the alienation caused by the colonial capitalist system. This type of solidarity played a formative role, as demonstrated by the presence of individuals from the same region or even the same town in the leadership of the first independent union organizations. Each new trade union provided an opportunity for members to formalize new regional and sector-based ties.[11] The first independent unions were created by groups on the fringes of urban society—the most impoverished subset of the emerging working class. Notably, migrants from the South working as dockworkers in the port of Tunis were the first to hold a wildcat strike, in August 1924, causing the split with the local section of the General Confederation of Labor (CGT) that led to the creation of the CGTT. Kerkennah Islands natives in Sfax would go on to form the core independent unions in the South, which helped bring about the founding of the UGTT in 1946 (Ben Hamida, 2001). The Gafsa mines offer a good example of the extent to which geography and community influence union practices (Hermassi, 1966). The workers and union leaders' shared geographic and social origins strengthened cohesiveness as the workers' movement continued to spread.

Thus, the Tunisian union movement, a product of colonialism and an ethnically diverse working class, comprised communities of workers with multiple allegiances—to workers' groups that share the same interests and to tribal, regional and national groups—whose propensity to take action varies in relation to the political and social climate. This vacillation between the imperative for workers' unity and community/ethnic priorities shaped the birth and development of the Tunisian union movement. The system in place at the UGTT would come to reflect this history, once strictly formal union relations could be paired with other political, regional and local affiliations that extended beyond the scope of the organization. This array of communities was matched in diversity by the social backgrounds of UGTT members. Highly qualified workers were joined by others who had only recently entered the ranks of the working class, many of whom small-scale farmers, craftsmen and shopkeepers. Teachers, office workers and public-sector officials rapidly became central to the union, particularly in supervisory roles.

Traditional hierarchical relations, social differences and regional and professional diversity combined to form a unique bureaucratic apparatus and organizational culture (Khiari, 2003).

Second, tensions gradually rose in the Tunisian labor movement between economic and political initiatives. The union movement was torn between focusing mainly on economic issues and remaining a minor player in the struggle for independence, or becoming "nationalistic" and abandoning the class struggle. On the one hand, the social struggles enlisted Tunisian workers in a form of class warfare that spurred them to join forces with European workers in order to gain leverage over employers, which pushed national independence into the background. On the other hand, the political struggle for national independence required Tunisian workers to cut ties with the existing European union movement, which paid little regard to the national anti-colonial aims of the Tunisian working class.

The contradictions in the universalistic language employed by the CGT illustrate this point. At times, the CGT would excoriate colonial policy, but the union also often proclaimed the French presence in Tunisia as an opportunity to "civilize the Tunisians" and transition from "feudal" relations to "modern" relations. Moreover, the CGT's defense of equal work for equal pay was far from sincere, given the disparity in wages for workers of different nationalities. The fact that Tunisian workers suffered from both social and political oppression gave substantial impetus to the independent union movement, whose main goal was to merge the struggles for social rights and independence in trade union action (Yousfi, *op. cit.*; Bessis, *op. cit.*).

Meanwhile, the national liberation movement suffered a long series of leadership crises. The nationalists (Destourians) and communists fought violently for ideological and political control over the movement. The Franco-Tunisian Agreement signed in 1954 specified that France would retain authority over Tunisia's domestic and external security for ten years, opening a deep rift within Neo-Destour between the two leaders of the liberation movement, Salah Ben Youssef[12] and Habib Bourguiba. Unlike Bourguiba, who advocated negotiating "phased-in" independence and making compromises with France, Ben Youssef supported Pan-Arabism, gave pride of place to Islam and wanted full independence immediately (Bessis and Belhassen, 2012). The conflict provoked violence and divided both their supporters and the country as a whole. Within the UGTT, the upper-class nationalist elite that belonged to Neo-Destour and the working class, who mainly came from disadvantaged areas, had a complicated relationship. In the end, the UGTT, including a number of Destourians, joined the liberation campaign led by Bourguiba and played an active role in the fight for independence.

The Neo-Destour Party Congress, held in Sfax from November 15 to 19, 1955, was a momentous event that cemented the UGTT's place in the struggle for independence and set the stage for the union's future relationship with the single-party state. The congress spelled the end of Ben Youssef's dissident movement and saw Bourguiba forge an unprecedented alliance with the various union factions present within the party, including the Neo-Destourians and those led by UGTT Secretary General Ahmed Ben Salah and Mustapha Filali, chairman of the union's economic and social commission (Ben Hamida, 2012, 50–1). In exchange for union support, two top UGTT officials—Ahmed Tlili and Abdallah Farhat—were named to the political committee formed at the congress and Neo-Destour accepted most of the union's economic and social demands. This coalition of diverse groups—the capitalist petty bourgeoisie, the new "westernized" elite and the unionized working class—strengthened the national movement and laid the foundation for an organic relationship between the UGTT and the ruling power. In time, it would become difficult to tell which was dependent on the other.[13]

Some of the issues facing the labor movement were resolved when Tunisia gained independence and the political order shifted, but the tensions between the social struggles inherent to union work and national political challenges—and the consequent vacillation between an independent working class and alliances with political parties—continued to play a defining role at the UGTT. This period of history formed the basis for both how the union operated internally and its relationship with the single-party state. The UGTT was founded in reaction to the political and ideological direction taken by the CGT, but retained many of its predecessor's practices and techniques for organizing union initiatives. As a result, the fledgling union embodied an unprecedented combination of traditional regional and tribal segmentation and procedural bureaucratic hierarchy. At the same time, the UGTT could not be considered a classic labor union, because its main sectors have members from the working class *stricto sensu* and the "new petty bourgeoisie": teachers, office workers, government officials and bank managers.

On the political front, the fight for independence required the UGTT to maintain an often-fragile balance between its independence as a union and cooperation with the party leading the liberation movement. This gave rise to unique power relations between the UGTT and Neo-Destour; the interplay between the two would greatly influence the development of Tunisian politics and the country's economic and social model.[14] As a result of this configuration, the UGTT established and spread the trade-union model imported from France, while continually readjusting its principles. The French model was grafted onto endogenous social relations but did not supplant them; the model endured and adapted until it finally fell apart and left in its place a uniquely Tunisian form of union organization. The UGTT, therefore, is partly a product of French colonization, yet the manner in which the union interacts with local forms of social and economic organization reflects a specific identity rooted in Tunisian history. The UGTT developed alongside the groups that form its ranks, which maintained, to varying degrees, relations that were unequal, corporatist and community-based. The union grew from compromises that reflected social activism at certain points in time, and interaction with the national liberation movement and the preexisting social structure at others, as well as the dominance of workers defending their own interests.

The UGTT and the Single-Party State: Willing Partners and Fierce Rivals

Soon after the UGTT was founded, in 1946, the union found itself at the forefront of the struggle for national liberation in a leading role cemented by its unconventional alliance with Neo-Destour. Through a balancing act of unionism and politics, the UGTT quickly rose to prominence as a preeminent organization in Tunisian politics. The union's statutes and motions at its annual congress demonstrated a commitment to social issues and a dedication to "progressive" individual and democratic political liberties. The alliance between the UGTT and the government proved to be a complicated relationship that alternated between unified commitment and controlled rivalry (Zeghidi, 2001). The ruling power continually sought to control the UGTT in order to maintain its dominance and foist its policy upon the union. The UGTT has nevertheless always retained a certain degree of independence—more so during certain periods than others—from the government (Hamzaoui, *op. cit.*). The union's post-independence history has been punctuated by a series of crises with the government that erupted in 1965, 1978, 1984 and 2010. In the next section, I will examine how the relationship between the UGTT and the single-party state evolved over time in terms of the dueling social and political issues at stake, the division of power between the two political actors and the resulting effect on the UGTT as an organization.

The UGTT and the PSD Jointly Undertake to Build the Tunisian State

After Tunisia gained its independence, on March 20, 1956, the UGTT, Neo-Destour, Tunisian Union of Industry, Trade and Handicrafts (UTICA)[15] and the National Union of Tunisian Farmers (UNAT)[16] formed a "national front" that ran in the 1956 constituent assembly elections and the 1959 parliamentary elections. The constituent assembly abolished the beylical monarchy and established a republic with a presidential system. Habib Bourguiba became the country's first president. Once in power, Bourguiba "put down" Ben Youssef's dissident movement and then sought to use the UGTT's prestige to strengthen his grip on power. Union members feared repression from those in power at the union, while the party leadership and government officials, seeing the ability of union leaders to rally support, were afraid they would have to fight or contain a protest movement. At the time, such a battle could have caused the demise of the state, which was still recovering from the Ben Youssef movement, with limited financial resources and no economic plan. In 1956, Ahmed Ben Salah, UGTT Secretary General from 1954 to 1956, accused the Tahar Ben Ammar government (which Neo-Destour had joined) of "serving the interests of the haute bourgeoisie." Between 1956 and 1961, the government partially broke free from colonial domination[17] and adopted a handful of social reforms, but the UGTT believed the country was pursuing liberal economic policy that benefitted the local bourgeoisie. At the 6th UGTT Congress in September 1956, the union's economic report stated:

> One would have thought that the Tunisian government would regard introducing the economic changes required to establish policy that meets people's needs as its most urgent priority. . . . Quite the contrary, we are witnessing a sort of faint-heartedness with regard to economic problems. . . . The government appears to be constantly searching for excuses to postpone the moment when it turns its attention to this issue. . . . The haute bourgeoisie is willfully diverting attention away from the social struggle. It is unacceptable that the government is doing nothing to stand in the way. The UGTT must act without delay to solemnly call the country's attention—that of these leaders, in particular—to the dangers of taking such a severely delusional view of the difficulties at hand. . . . Workers and the common people are not the only ones who have lost their patience with the vicious excesses of capitalist exploitation and who are ready to take a stand. The country cannot accept the risk of losing its real independence due to poorly planned economic policy.
>
> (UGTT, 1956, 7–8)

Ahmed Ben Salah gradually succeeded in establishing himself as the leader of Tunisian unionism and the non-communist left. The UGTT and its 80,000 members began to exert an increasingly strong influence on Neo-Destour, especially with regard to economic and social issues. Ben Salah's strong personality and the UGTT's growing ability to rally its members—in primary and secondary education, in particular—led to fears within Neo-Destour that the UGTT could become uncontrollable or even form its own labor party (Hamza, 1994, 277). In an effort to maintain unity, Bourguiba warned that social demands aimed at reducing inequality shouldn't result in the poor bullying the rich, and stated that the top priority was to build the Tunisian state. A Neo-Destourian group quickly formed within the UGTT to remove Ben Salah.[18] This chain of events laid the foundation for the authoritarian system of government that endured under various guises until January 2011. Neo-Destour was the only authorized political party throughout this period, apart from the pseudo-multi-party system that appeared in the 1980s.

Relations between the UGTT and the single-party state have alternated between alliance, subordination and competition since this period. The Bourguiba regime functioned in an alliance between its Neo-Destour party and the UGTT leadership from 1956 until the 1970s. The union played an active role in building the state, in particular with regard to social and economic reforms. To give one example, the UGTT's 1955 platform resulted in the 1958 healthcare plan, the 1958 education plan and the 1964 industrialization plan. Ministers who had previously served as UGTT secretary general were appointed to implement the plans. The call for unity to achieve independence was replaced by rhetoric emphasizing the importance of national unity to build the nation, further strengthening the organic relationship between the government, the party and the union. Bourguiba made the leadership decisions for both the party and the union and even ruled on issues at lower levels. He could replace secretaries general, have them transferred, or appoint and then fire them, as he did with ministers. Another aspect of this organic relationship, alongside Bourguiba's direct involvement in internal matters at the UGTT, was the widespread presence of union officials in the party and machinery of government. Most union officials were drawn from the Destour ranks until the early 1970s and political officials approved candidacies for union positions based on party loyalty. Several UGTT officials went on to become ministers or head an economic institution.

What is more, the state controlled the UGTT's purse strings by collecting its membership dues directly from wages and allocating subsidies for the union from the national social security fund. The government was effective at using the UGTT's financial dependence on the state as leverage for blackmail and corruption, making it difficult for the union to claim any sort of independence. The system that took root consisted of entangled union, Destour and government bureaucracy with Habib Bourguiba at the helm (Khiari, *op. cit.*).

On an economic level, Tunisia moved in a socialist direction in the 1960s, establishing an import substitution scheme with significant government intervention. Neo-Destour, which became the Socialist Destourian Party (PSD) in 1963, accepted the economic and social plan put forward at the 6th UGTT Congress in 1956. On the basis of that plan, UGTT Secretary General Ahmed Ben Salah, a co-opted member of the Neo-Destour political committee, was appointed Planning and Finance Minister and given the task of designing a "Destourian socialist" economic reform package. Ben Salah prepared a plan for 1962 to 1971 entitled "Perspectives décennales," or "ten-year outlook," which aimed to "decolonize the national economy" by integrating the colonial sector and "tunisiafiying" foreign-held economic enclaves. The government introduced a raft of measures during Ben Salah's tenure, including the creation of farming, handicraft and business cooperatives as well as many state-run companies. The country's policy focus shifted from agriculture to industrialization and, by 1964, industry accounted for half of domestic production. Farming collectives were established on nationalized colonist land in 1964 and the collectivization process accelerated from 1967 to the end of 1969. This era is referred to as Ben Salah's "decade of cooperatives" (Ben Salah, 2008). The subsequent failure of the cooperative system signaled the demise of the socialist experiment, which ended with Bourguiba abruptly firing Ben Salah in November 1969.[19]

The developmentalist doctrine that took hold in the decades following independence helped shape Tunisia's patrimonial, authoritarian welfare state through the use of modernist rhetoric as a means of legitimization (Camau, 1987). The government acted as a job provider by expanding access to public education and healthcare and implementing initiatives to boost consumer spending and social welfare. The UGTT's involvement in Tunisia's economic development in the decades that followed independence took the form of a participatory approach to unionism that remained active as long as the government provided employment and social services (Catusse, Destremau and Verdier, 2008).

The first major crisis between the UGTT and the PSD occurred when the union campaigned for pay raises in 1964. Then UGTT Secretary General Habib Achour defied the orders of the party and political committee—of which he was a member from 1964 to 1966—and publicly opposed the government's cooperativist policy. Meanwhile, employees began to form trade groups loyal to the ruling power, as a rival power to the UGTT. In an open letter to Habib Bourguiba written in 1966, member of the resistance, unionist and Bourguiba opponent Ahmed Tlili[20] offered an interesting perspective on the various crises that affected the relationship between the UGTT and the single-party state:

> In less than nine years of independence, Tunisian unionism has endured three crises that have hampered its development. The first dates back to 1956. The fledgling government openly provoked the crisis by intervening in an internal dispute in order to brazenly encourage and incite discord. There was little justification for these actions; the dispute could have been settled within the union by its members. The second occurred in 1963, when the government intervened again to replace members—using so-called democratic methods—of the organization's steering committee. Finally, in 1965, the UGTT lost its outward appearance along with all freedom of action. A detailed explanation of these crises—origins, root causes, sequence of events and guilty parties—over the past nine years would require recounting the most eventful period in the history of Tunisian unionism. It would be best to remain concise and note only that the transformation of Tunisian unionism reflects the broader lack of discussion—even at the highest levels—of the country's political leaders. These crises and other major events in the nation are rooted in the counsel of self-serving clans that change often but share a common denominator: personal interest in defiance of the greater interest of the nation. There is no other valid explanation, as one could easily demonstrate when addressing the issue at length. Thus, the public criticism directed at Tunisian unionism does not stand up to scrutiny. . . . All the other judgments do not conform to reality. The reality is that the UGTT took part in the struggle for national liberation, worked tirelessly to provide independent Tunisia with a modern government, and

played an effective, positive role in building a national economy that is as democratic as possible. The union has consistently endeavored to bring about well-being, peace and liberty for all without distinction of any kind. It's also for the youth of Tunisia that unionism has maintained peaceful labor relations, in spite of the lack of negotiations with employers and the government's economic errors. Comparisons of the UGTT to so-called revolutionary unionism that seeks to establish a dictatorship of the proletariat are meritless and bear no resemblance to the UGTT's philosophy. This type of argument is only valid for those who want to reduce the UGTT to the role of a go-between, such as that which exists in the country where this supposed dictatorship of the proletariat reigns. The UGTT, which was the nation's second vital spark after the party, has also been left on the sidelines. The consequences will be dire, because the fate of these two powers is creating a massive void. Nature hates voids and could fill this one at any time.

(Tlili, 1966, 27–30)

Salah Hamzaoui (2013) explains that when Habib Achour was arrested in 1965, he drew up a new strategy for the UGTT: support the political authority but resist whenever there is a perceived threat to workers' interests. This new approach coincided with the arrival on the job market of the "generation of independence"—educated young people who opposed both the policy of establishing cooperatives and the total dominance of Neo-Destour over the state apparatus, and hoped for a new relationship between the government and its citizens as well as more openness to the world (Ayari, 2009; Naccache, 2009). The main opposition movement of the 1960s and 1970s emerged during this period with the creation of the Tunisian Socialist Study and Action Group between July and October 1963.[21] Other factors also came into play that altered the relationship between the UGTT and the single-party state: the Tunisian Communist Party was banned and third-world movements gained prominence on an international scale. The omnipotence of the Socialist Destourian Party and the lack of room for organized political opposition led the UGTT to serve as a staging point for protests and gradually become the main counterpower to the single-party regime. In the next section, I will describe the series of crises that took place between the government and the UGTT during each wave of economic liberalization. I will illustrate how these crises—in particular those in 1974 and 1984—instilled a desire in unionists to break with the past and gain independence from the regime.

Economic Liberalization Frays the "Social Contract" Binding the UGTT and the Regime

Tunisia changed course after a decade of cooperatives, establishing a free-market economic regime open to the outside world and foreign investment.

The transition was led by Hédi Nouira, a former Central Bank of Tunisia governor who became prime minister in 1970. Nouira's first act after taking office was to bring Habib Achour back into the fold. The new internationally oriented plan implemented by the Nouira government marked a drastic departure from the economic policy of the 1960s, when the priority was on the domestic market. From the outset, Nouira was clear with regard to the new direction of Tunisia's economic policy. The core sectors of the economy would remain public, but the rest would go to private companies. The country's economic focus shifted to developing agriculture as a means to secure growth; in industry, major projects and heavy industry were eschewed in favor of processing industries. Tunisia made a steadfast return to a market economy and private property during this era. An industrial backbone protected by customs barriers erected to restrict foreign competition enabled the economy to post strong growth. Companies flourished in this favorable business environment and dynamic domestic market, spurred on and regulated by the state. In addition, the narrow confines of the market fostered a business development model with highly diversified companies, first in commercial ventures and later in industry.

Tunisia also opened the door to foreign investment. A law passed in April 1972 offered incentives to foreign companies that established operations in Tunisia. The government granted significant benefits designed to help exporters import raw materials and export finished products. This new export-driven development model was responsible for a radical shift in the economy caused by a massive influx of investment from European countries, especially in the textile industry. These investments and exports boosted Tunisia's growth to the highest levels the country has ever seen (Ben Hammouda, 2012). However, the state would remain Tunisia's primary economic player despite the increased openness to the private sector compared with the previous era. For example, the government limited competition through a system of price controls on many products, the financial sector remained entirely under state control and the economy was substantially protected by customs duties.

Crisis first hit the era of modernization at the end of the 1970s. There were both economic and political consequences when the modernization model began to run out of steam. Tunisia's financial standing began a precipitous slide, both in terms of the public deficit and trade deficit, leading to a rapid rise in international debt and debt servicing. The country's debt situation continued to worsen following the international economic crisis in the early 1980s. Meanwhile, a dearth of agriculture investment resulted in a sharp increase in food imports. This period also saw a rise in regional disparities, due to the fact that exporters were mainly located in coastal regions. These economic problems combined with political problems to spark the Tunisian authoritarian model's first major crisis (*id.*).

Tunisia's fast-changing society began to challenge the single-party's monopoly on power. The regime would no longer be able to draw legitimacy from its leadership in the struggle for independence or economic development. Tensions began to flare due to mounting opposition from large swathes of Tunisia's youth, who were educated and had gained political awareness in the student movement. These young people with left-wing ideals suffered retaliation from the repressive state machinery and filed several major lawsuits in opposition to Bourguiba's authoritarian regime. At the 18th UGET Congress[22] held in Korba in 1971, opponents of the student union's subservience to the PSD took the majority for the first time and rejected the government's control over the student organization. A student revolt erupted on February 5, 1972. Meanwhile, the failure of efforts to expand the PSD's political horizons, initiated by Ahmed Mestiri[23] and Bahi Ladgham[24] at the Monastir party conference in 1971, spurred dissidents to join the union movement.

At the same time, the government's disengagement and free-market economic policy put strains on the "social contract" binding the union and the regime. New sectors developed—education, metalworking, electrical and mechanical industries, banking and healthcare—and their employees joined the ranks of the union movement alongside those from declining traditional sectors such as mining and ports. The new younger, more qualified working class that had emerged with the industrialization sparked by the 1972 investment law strengthened the UGTT as an organization and began to demand their fair share of the profits from the capital influx and foreign trade.

The union movement was the strongest voice of protest against authoritarianism and the UGTT began a long struggle for autonomy. The union launched several strikes in specific sectors that cemented its leading role in the fight for social progress and freedom as a union. The UGTT's offensive expanded beyond socioeconomic issues to tackle political grievances and gradually forged ties with democracy and political freedom movements. The UGTT's independence paradigm took hold amid a social climate of general discontent. (The term "independence" has multiple meanings in this context: the union's independence from the party; the regional and sector-based sections' independence from the Executive Board; and broader individual and political freedoms.)

The party, press and, at times, the UGTT Executive Bureau chose to label the largest strikes as political and manipulated by foreign interests (Hamzaoui, *op. cit.*). The UGTT's criticism of the regime grew harsher and the union was accused of inciting disobedience. The UGTT and the authoritarian regime clashed in a bloody showdown on January 26, 1978, ushering in a period of heavy repression against unions, social movements and the political opposition. These years of repression were also an era of great social activism and resistance among political actors. Each protest would result in the police or party militia damaging or destroying UGTT buildings and facilities. Top and mid-level officials at the union were arrested and given harsh sentences by the justice system, which was under the party's thumb, and replaced by an imposed leadership team picked to keep the union in line. However, the fairly elected union bodies resisted, sometimes in secrecy, and often got the better of the repressive government and forced it to back down. These defeats represented the first chinks in the armor of Bourguiba's authoritarian model (Cherni, 2011).

Tunisia embarked on a series of economic reforms to counteract the effects of the crisis which revised the redistributive role of the state. The country experienced a second wave of liberalization aimed at developing a new growth model even more economically liberal and open than the last. As in other countries in the Global South, Tunisia's financial institutions pushed for more liberalization and integration into the international markets. The government implemented a series of reforms in the early 1980s in order to reduce financial imbalances. According to Hakim Ben Hammouda (2012), these reforms were based on the assessment that excess demand and inelastic supply had caused deficits to rise. The new economic policy in the early 1980s sought to remedy the perceived deficiencies of the Tunisian economy by reducing demand and public spending. The policy also rolled back the role of the state by privatizing major state-run companies and giving them a greater role in managing the economy. Finally, the policy fostered a more open economy through exports, further integrating Tunisia into the global economic system. This resulted in immediate cuts to the welfare state and large swathes of the Tunisian economy became marginalized.

The reforms failed to live up to expectations in terms of economic performance. Growth remained weak and the financial reforms decreased investment and caused interest rates to rise. The policy proved unable to improve the trade deficit or reduce the debt. In addition, the deficit reduction policy led to a decision to reduce state contributions to the General Compensation Fund, which subsidized staple goods (*id.*). For Tunisians, the result was mass social exclusion that mirrored the social divide between the inland regions and the coastal cities. In December 1983, the decision to double the price of bread was met with outrage among the country's poorest citizens in the South, who converged on the capital, leading to the "bread riots" of January 3, 1984.[25] The Bourguiba regime immediately resorted to force, calling in the army for aid. On February 3, 1984, General Zine El-Abidine Ben Ali was appointed as head of national security; a year later he would become chief of national security at the interior ministry. The weeklong revolt on the streets ended only when the President rescinded the price hike. A diminished Bourguiba announced the decision in a wavering voice during one of his last public speeches. The imminent "changing of the guard" and the maneuvering among different PSD factions to succeed the depleted, illness-weakened president heightened the sense of uncertainty and concerns about the future. It was in this chaotic environment that Zine El-Abidine Ben Ali, who had since become prime minister, carried out the "medical" coup d'etat that removed the "father of the nation" from power in the early hours of November 7, 1987.

During the 1984 riots, the UGTT was once again at the center of the revolt, divided between those who appealed for calm, embodied by the leadership, and a more radical camp that took up the cause of the social movement and supported the rioting by marginalized groups. The leadership had accepted the plan for a price increase with the caveat that compensation for the country's poorest be included as part of the deal. UGTT officials instructed unionists not to take part in the strikes and called on the government to end the state of emergency. Undermined by infighting and pressure from creditors to open up the economy, the regime took an increasingly hardline stance with the UGTT. In February 1984, the postal service and primary and secondary education unions held strikes without the approval of the UGTT Executive Board. The far-left unionists who had organized the strike action were expelled from the union. According to Olfa Lamloum (1988), when Habib Achour called off the general strike scheduled for May 7, 1984, without first consulting the relevant bodies in the union, his unilateral action marked the beginning of the end for the union leadership. Achour was placed under house arrest in November 1985.

This period also saw the emergence of a strong tide of Islamist opposition.[26] The development of protest movements against the authoritarian regime in the 1970s and 1980s and the resurgence of social inequality coincided with the politicization of the Islamist movement in Tunisia. In the mid-1970s, Islamists became highly critical of Habib Bourguiba, but did not speak out against economic liberalization. Nor did they lend support to the protest movements as the UGTT developed into the most powerful opposition force in the country. The Islamist movement, which had a large following in high schools and universities, did not turn its attention to economic issues until the 1980s. In a tactical move designed to expand its sphere of influence, the Islamic Tendency Movement (MTI), the forerunner to Ennahdha, attempted to infiltrate the UGTT's base and intermediate branches, but to little avail (Alexander, 2000).

The protest movements gained momentum at the end of the 1970s, surprising both the regime and the union bureaucracy and putting strains on the pact between the two parties to maintain the peaceful relations they had ritualized in annual collective bargaining. The UGTT was forced to reassess its collusive alliance with the PSD, which had been an important component of the initial years of independence. Under pressure from the protest movements, the UGTT gradually transitioned from an organic relationship with the party apparatus and the state in which the union channeled social and economic demands, to closer ties with the union's base. The UGTT increasingly defended workers' interests against employers and the successive governments of the era, which were intent on pursuing a policy to spur investment and accused of bias toward business owners. However, as Riadh Zghal (1998) notes, the UGTT's leaders, unable to cope with the intensity of the protests, threw their support behind the union's base due to the emergence of a new working class and more structured opposition rather than an ideological clash with the ruling power.

The UGTT, then, no longer bears resemblance to the labor union established in 1946. Sociological and political developments have made the union an umbrella group for individuals from the entire political spectrum and all social categories, where intellectuals commingle with managers and technicians. In a country without democracy or freedom of expression, the UGTT became one of the country's rare forums for opposing the economic and political hegemony, gradually attracting activists of various, chiefly left-wing political persuasions. The union developed into a refuge where one could be political without being exposed to the same risks as in the outside world. These changes led the UGTT to begin defending itself both against the regime's attempts to tighten its grip on power and the risk of being swallowed up by one of the political groups under its wing.

What impact did these various economic and social crises have on the UGTT's relationship with the single-party apparatus and its interactions with Tunisia's social movements?

The UGTT Alternates Between Autonomy and Dependence

From the outset, the Tunisian union movement charted a unique path that set it apart from unionism elsewhere in the Arab world. A single organization has always dominated Tunisian unionism; experiments with union pluralism were often fleeting affairs orchestrated by the regime to weaken the UGTT's ability to rally support. Moreover, Neo-Destour (PSD from 1964 onwards), which enjoyed total hegemony over politics and society as a whole, helped completely obscure the issue of pluralism in union circles.

The regime had always sought to dominate the UGTT, but the various social movements that formed Tunisia's unionist heritage made preserving political independence and autonomy from the government and opposition parties into a rallying cry for union activism. Thus, unlike other Arab unions such as the General Union of Algerian Workers (UGTA) and Egyptian Trade Union Federation (ETUF), which became completely subservient to the government, the UGTT always had a certain degree of independence—more during certain periods than in others—from the single-party state (Gobe, *op. cit.*).

The UGTT leadership forged a unique relationship with the single-party state that entailed an often shaky balance between autonomy and dependence from both the union's base and the ruling power. The union's leaders were highly aware of their ability to counter the ruling power by drawing on the deep roots of the union machine and its local and regional sections across the country, albeit discreetly in order to avoid risking government reprisal. Then again, they could not obey the party completely and risk facing opposition from their base and betraying their principles and the "national duties" they have always claimed. As a result, the political strategy at the union's central office has always been to strike a precarious balance between falling in line behind government policy and legitimizing major economic and social decisions, on the one hand, and defending workers' interests and maintaining a modicum of independence, on the other. A culture based on exerting pressure and pursuing negotiations became engrained at the union. The leadership publicly backed the political authorities and let them intervene directly in internal affairs at the union, in large part because many of the union's members continued to follow the party's orders and could sway elections at the annual congress. The union publicly declared its allegiance to the state and party on a regular basis in the run-up to elections or other key political events. However, during times of social crisis when workers' interests were jeopardized, the leadership would assert its independence and leverage its base to influence negotiations with the government (Hamzaoui, *op. cit.*).

The new structure of the relationship—alternating dependence and autonomy in strategies that combined pressure and negotiations—marked a departure from the organic union between the UGTT and the single-party state during the first years of independence, but still served to maintain a certain degree of social and political order. This unorthodox configuration expanded political and union freedoms while also, paradoxically, protecting the authoritarian system and the long-term future of the UGTT. Mutual support between the ruling power, business owners and UGTT enabled each of the three partners to act as a dominant force. The party counted on the ability of top union officials to keep adversarial political expression within acceptable limits in exchange for certain privileges. For their part, the union officials tolerated members speaking out against authoritarianism and protesting against political dependence insofar as it enabled them to maintain their legitimacy and play a leading role in the political balancing act that propelled the UGTT to become a key stakeholder in state affairs (*id.*). Viewed from this perspective, it is easier to understand why the clash between the two institutions—the UGTT and the ruling power—never led to either a total breakdown in relations between the Executive Board and the union's opposition sections or complete freedom for the UGTT to protest against the government as it wished. This autonomy was limited by the tacit power-sharing agreement between the union bureaucracy and the Destourian government. In addition, the UGTT was reliant on the state financially and union officials were engaged in a sophisticated system of privileges that bound them to difficult-to-break alliances, adding to the ambiguity clouding their relations.

This method of operating—a combination of autonomy and dependence—could also be found in union leaders' relationship with their base. Although union activists could be highly critical of their leaders, their opposition never reached the breaking point (*id.*). It is important to note that the union's organizational system helped it to maintain unity throughout this succession of crises. The UGTT has a centralized hierarchical structure with four levels—local, regional, federal and national—forming a network that spans the entire country. The union's highest body, the National Congress, elects the national executive committee and the secretary general; the base unions and local union bodies comprise the lowest level. Two parallel bodies lie in between at an intermediate level: the regional unions, whose executive committees are elected by base-union representatives on a regional basis (by governorate), and the federations and general unions, which are organized by sector.[27] This centralized, hierarchical structure concentrates hegemonic power in the hands of the Executive Board and secretary general, who is able to further consolidate power by granting privileges and forming alliances with various levels of the union representation.

What is more, the UGTT is not a labor union in the classic sense of the term. It has a bureaucratic apparatus that comprises individuals from different social backgrounds, most of whom from the public sector, and draws strength from its deep social and regional roots, which rival those of the party. The union lacks a strict ideological framework, which has enabled several political philosophies to coexist and encourages a reformist approach aimed at adapting to social change. Union membership fees are garnished directly from wages, collected by the authorities and transferred to the UGTT—a system that helped increase membership among all categories of employees. In sum, a number of factors enabled the UGTT to remain Tunisia's only union and suppress all attempts to divide its members: the union's centralized, hierarchical organization; solid financial backing; a sophisticated system of privileges inside and outside the organization that bound members to quid pro quo agreements; and the UGTT's reformist culture.

To what extent did this organizational culture endure during Ben Ali's reign?

Was the UGTT a Party to the Ben Ali Decade?

General Ben Ali, Prime Minister, former Director of General Security and the man who put down the revolts in January 1978, took power on November 7, 1987, declaring that "the Tunisian people is ready for democracy." He arrived in office amid an extremely tense political and economic situation. Ben Ali sought to pacify the political turbulence by reaching out to associations and opposition parties through a series of symbolic measures, including abolition of the lifetime presidential appointment and exceptional courts of law, as well as a law authorizing political pluralism. He became leader of the PSD, parted ways with anyone who wasn't completely loyal to him, and rechristened the party Democratic Constitutional Rally (Rassemblement constitutionnel démocratique, or RCD) in 1989. Weakened by years of oppression, the opposition reacted favorably to Ben Ali's message in the hope of achieving a real democratic awakening.

The National Pact Ties Down the UGTT

Ben Ali's inaugural policy act was the joint signing, on November 7, 1988, of a national pact designed to unite the entire nation around certain overarching values of national interest in four areas: identity, political system, development and foreign relations. The signatories of the pact undertook to uphold gender equality, the rights granted by the Code of Personal Status, republican principles, and to refuse to use Islam for political ends. Another stated goal of the pact was to guarantee a fair distribution of wealth between different regions and social categories, as well as to improve workers' lives to the point where they receive their fair share of their contribution to the country's development. The pact tied development to the need to overcome political divisions and repair relations between the various stakeholders in the labor market. It urged workers and employers to work together to streamline manufacturing and maintain an open, honest dialogue so that each party could "have a clear vision of its affairs and wholeheartedly accept the necessary sacrifices" (Zghal, *op. cit.*). On a political level, the goal of the pact was to establish a framework enabling the political parties and all national organizations to cooperate and reach binding agreements. The national pact reprised Bourguiba's rhetorical approach of uniting all stakeholders behind the national interest while adroitly pushing social, ideological and political disagreements into the background.

This new policy direction led Tunisia to bow to pressure from international financial organizations and then hasten its adoption of a structural adjustment program in 1986, which completed the economic liberalization only half finished after the departure of Ahmed Ben Salah. The goal was to reduce state interventionism liable of hindering market mechanisms through a raft of macroeconomic measures: price liberalization for most products, reform and/or privatization of semi-public companies, liberalization of the financial industry, liberalization of importations, new competition law, etc. While the government did not abandon all social measures, it did begin to heed the calls from its financial backers to integrate Tunisia into the globalized economy.

The state did, however, maintain a strong presence in areas such as infrastructure, industry and banking, while continuing to play a major role in the economy through public investment. A free-trade agreement with Europe that took effect in 1991 was paired with a program to bring companies up to speed through restructuring, technology park renovations, skills development and vocational training. The new investment code adopted in 1993 added further policy planks: infrastructure development, tax incentives, bank credit facilities, the removal of red tape in a number of areas, etc. In labor relations, the government implemented a wage policy based on negotiations every three years between the UGTT and employers' unions, in order to help foster the strife-free environment essential to economic recovery and growth. In 1994, the labor code was amended to include greater flexibility for employers, which expanded the forms of precarious work on offer, in particular for new hires (Zghal, *op. cit.*)

On the whole, the new economic policy was designed to achieve one major goal—expand exports to bring in an influx of capital—which entailed greater dependence on the global market. This new economic direction had a short-lived time in the sun in the 1990s after core macroeconomic indicators such as inflation and the budget deficit recovered. The World Bank also reported that the policy had successfully spurred relatively strong growth above the regional and global averages. This would later be touted as the "Tunisian economic miracle" and used by world powers to justify their unconditional support for the Ben Ali's authoritarian regime. This relative success did not, however, solve the structural deficiencies of the Tunisian economy, which suffered from a disproportionate amount of low-skilled workers flocking to a few in-demand sectors such as mass tourism and subcontracting (in textiles, mechanics, electronics and later call centers) that had little knock-on effect for the rest of the economy. In 1995, Tunisia signed a lopsided free-trade agreement with the European Union that greatly expanded this type of specialization. These pacts between Global South countries and EU Member States—especially France—offered paltry development aid, kept the ruling elite in power and delayed necessary changes (Mouhoud, 2011). Export revenues fell because Tunisian manufactured goods were not competitive on Europeans markets and trade barriers were still in place for agricultural products. The only means of compensating for this shortfall was tourism revenue, remittances from migrants and direct foreign investment, which remained very low.

Tunisia soon felt the consequences of this policy, as highlighted in various economic reports: persistent unemployment above 13% that hit educated youth particularly hard, low wages, insufficient purchasing power, agricultural production that was unable to satisfy local demand, and stagnation in industry, which resulted in the country importing 70% of its manufactured consumer goods. This downturn produced a lasting trade and balance of payments deficit, which forced the government to borrow and run up the national debt. And Tunisia's debt (and interest) payments further plunged the country into economic dependence. International financial organizations' injunctions and the limitations imposed by structural adjustment put heavy strains on the government's ability to perform its redistributive role. Tensions flared between social movements and the Ben Ali regime, dealing serious damage to the principle of peaceful labor relations that had legitimized the government's authoritarianism.

In the political sphere, the semblance of a democratic awakening quickly faded. In 1989, the democratic opposition parties began to adopt a critical attitude towards the government, which had demonstrated that it was not willing to share its authority. Ben Ali's new strategy of exploiting the polarization between the ruling power and Islamists briefly lent legitimacy to his continuing reign in the eyes of the Tunisian public and earned him the unconditional support of world powers. The Islamist movement was the first to suffer repression, which later spread to the entire political opposition. In this way, a firmly entrenched authoritarian regime[28] supplanted the traditional Destourian hegemony whose legitimacy, based on the social and political pact formed in the early days of independence, had been under-mined by the new social reality in Tunisia. This new authoritarian system relied on a repressive police force combined with criminal practices at the highest levels of government, leading to widespread arbitrariness and cor-ruption. The nepotistic "families" close to Ben Ali expanded their power through a large-scale scheme for dispossessing others that would become integral to the structure of social relations and extend throughout all the country's economic networks, including the parallel economy: drugs, con-traband cigarettes and alcohol and the arms trade (Meddeb, 2011). Mean-while, the economic interests of the local ruling elite aligned with those of foreign parties due to Tunisia's economic subordination to foreign capital, perpetuating mechanisms for pillage and repression. The continual focus on maintaining social stability—a key component of Bourguiba's model—endured for a period during the Ben Ali era through redistribution schemes such as the 26/26 fund,[29] but the system soon crumbled as the elites esca-lated their predation against a backdrop of economic liberalization (Ould Aoudia, 2006).

These political and economic developments made a definite impact on Tunisian unionism. In a departure from the previous arrangement, in which negotiations were held on an ad hoc basis and strike action was the UGTT's primary tool for winning concessions, the union was drawn into a contrac-tual policy that involved periodic, government-sponsored negotiations with the employers' organization UTICA. The "state mediator" strategy shifted labor disputes from the political arena (their venue in the 1970s and 1980s) to an associative approach that required the various stakeholders' full com-mitment to pursuing approved economic policy. As a result, the UGTT's legitimacy resided less in its representation of workers than in playing an active role that earned the union recognition as a partner in labor relations, without regard to the power relationships and unequal footing that dic-tated the decision-making process (Zghal, op. cit.). This concept of "associa-tive participation" subdued the fighting spirit of the union movement that had developed in the 1970s; key social objectives were brushed aside as the parties worked together to meet competitiveness targets (UGTT, 2006). The UGTT also helped to draft related laws which it then had to follow. Meanwhile, privatization programs severely curbed union action and the UGTT's low representation in the private sector structurally impaired the union movement.

The UGTT's quest for autonomy—the leitmotiv of unionism in the 1970s and 1980s—was increasingly compromised by the blurred line between par-ticipation and representation, as well as between partnership and negotia-tion. As this was unfolding, President Ben Ali pursued a policy of coopting the union leadership, whom he expected to approve all the government's economic and political decisions as a matter of course. However, it wasn't until 1989 that the UGTT voted in leadership loyal to the Ben Ali gov-ernment. Ismaïl Sahbani was elected UGTT Secretary General in 1989 and reelected in 1994 at controversial congresses controlled by the Ben Ali regime.[30] Sahbani was forced to resign in September 2000 in the wake of embezzlement and mismanagement allegations. Abdessalem Jrad took the reins of the organization and remained at the helm of the UGTT until the congress held in December 2011. Cherif, a teacher and unionist from Sfax, described the changes at the union:

> The issue of national independence was the backbone during the Farhat Hached era, for Ben Salah it was socialism, liberal reformism for Ahmed Tlili, populism for Habib Achour and the associative trade union for Ismaïl Sahbani. But now it's nothing. For members, the union's cause has become self-preservation; cronyism and lies are used to win votes and no one knows what they want.

This state of affairs at the UGTT led to a drop in support and influence on the national stage. It did not, however, prevent dissenting voices from speaking out within the organization or the emergence of regular social protests inside and outside the union (Khiari, *op. cit.*) against outsourced labor and unfair dismissals, in particular. Strikes were held in education, public healthcare and many state-run and private companies, while faltering negotiations in other sectors caused tensions to mount. In the political sphere, the UGTT endorsed President Ben Ali's candidacy for a fourth term in 2004, eliciting vehement criticism from certain regional and federal sections. The Executive Board barely gained approval for the motion supporting Ben Ali submitted to the Administrative Commission.

In July 2005, the UGTT openly criticized the invitation extended to the Israeli prime minister to take part in the World Summit on the Information Society and condemned the Tunisian Human Rights League being banned from the event.

The 2008 Revolt in the Mining Area of Redeyef Poses a Challenge to the Ben Ali Regime and the UGTT

The 2008 revolt in the mining area of Redeyef, in the Gafsa Governorate,[31] was the largest social movement in Tunisia since the bread riots of January 1984 and the first to deal a blow to the Ben Ali regime. At a time when all of Tunisia was fixated on the 2009 presidential elections, "hinterland Tunisia"—the part of the country that had felt the brunt of the regime's liberal economic policy and authoritarian excesses—stood up to Ben Ali with an uprising that came out of the blue. The economy in Redeyef and other towns in the Gafsa mining region (Oum Larayes, Metlaoui and El Mdhilla) and, indeed, that of Tunisia as a whole, have depended on the wealth produced by Gafsa Phosphate Company (CPG; founded in 1897) since the colonial era.[32] CPG has undergone a series of transformations throughout its history that are closely intertwined with Tunisia's economic development and have had direct repercussions for the local and regional economy. The company was the main job provider in the region until the late 1970s and developed much of its social and economic infrastructure.

The successive waves of economic liberalization in the 1980s resulted in a series of restructuring plans at CPG aimed at revamping operations and ensuring compliance with international financial and administrative standards. Like other state-run companies, CPG was subjected to the World Bank structural adjustment program in 1986, resulting in 10,000 layoffs in the region with the highest unemployment rate in the country (Allal, 2010). The consequences were soon felt and a major social and economic crisis broke out, further exacerbating corruption, environmental pollution and unemployment, especially among young people. Traditionally viewed as the "patron" of the local population, CPG became the "curse of Gafsa."[33]

The 2008 protests erupted against this backdrop of social and economic crisis. On January 5, 2008, CPG announced the results of a recruitment campaign—380 employees and managers hired out of more than 1,000 applicants—igniting anger among many of the region's unemployed, particularly with regard to the cronyism in the selection process. Recruitment at CPG was managed in coordination with local UGTT and RCD representatives.[34] Hiring decisions were made based on often-fragile compromises between the overlapping interests of tribes, families and those in positions of authority (Gantin and Seddik, 2008; Chouikha and Geisser, 2010, 419). The brunt of the criticism fell on Amara Abbassi—Secretary General of the UGTT regional union in Gafsa, Metlaoui tribal leader and RCD Member of Parliament for 20 years—who was accused of being at the center of a well-oiled, corrupt hiring scheme at CPG.

Unemployed young people formed the core of a large demonstration in Redeyef, which quickly spread to the other main towns in the mining area. Public anger swelled and various segments of society held protests: laborers, civil servants, craftsmen, high school students, mothers, miners' widows, etc. The six-month protest movement revolted against the corruption of local and national elites; called for the results of the unjust hiring campaign to be rescinded; appealed for fairer employment policy; and demanded that the state expand its development initiatives in the region, in particular with regard to public services like healthcare and education for the poorest citizens.

Local union leaders such as Adnene Hajji and Béchir Laabidi, most of whom from the primary education base union, openly clashed with the UGTT Secretary General and sided with the movement led by the unemployed. The Redeyef incident is an example of the longstanding tensions between the union bureaucracy, which was tempted to play into the regime's hands by condoning corruption, and the local and sector unions, which endeavored to wrest control from the regime at all costs by supporting the social movement. Communist Workers' Party activist Ammar Amroussia looks back on the revolt in the mining region (quoted in Chouikha, Geisser, *op. cit.*, 419):

> It may have been the first time that the public turned its rage against the Tunisian General Labor Union [UGTT] and the regional union and mining unions, in particular. People expressed their outrage (via marches, public statements and discussions) not only at the regime, but also at all those who symbolized union corruption. These figures hold responsibility for how the situation deteriorated, in addition to their acceptance of the results of the CPG hiring campaign, involvement in the herd mentality, personal relationships, corruption and direct exploitation of workers through subcontracting firms. Not only did the UGTT and the mining unions remain silent, they even refused to present objections from the region's residents at the last regional committee meeting.

The embattled government, concerned by the size of the uprising, was quick to react. The army violently suppressed the movement in the mining region, resulting in three deaths and dozens of wounded, as well as about a hundred arrests. The regime was able to put down the uprising, despite the fact that the protesters had received support from the opposition parties—especially the Tunisian Communist Workers' Party (PCOT)—and other civil-society organizations such as the Tunisian Association of Democratic Women (ATFD), the Tunisian Human Rights League (LTDH) and the Tunisian Federation for Citizenship on Both Banks of the Mediterranean (FTCR). Government repression, combined with the weakness of the opposition parties and internal divisions at the UGTT, kept the social movement in check and prevented it from spreading, but the mining region revolt still made some important strides. The events revealed the dark side of the economic miracle touted by the regime and international financial institutions, while also exposing the regime's weaknesses and potential means of exploiting them. The Redeyef incident in 2008 would come to be remembered as the "dress rehearsal" for the popular uprisings in December 2010 that led to the fall of Ben Ali.

In Conclusion

The UGTT is viewed as an exception in Arab unionism in that it never completely surrendered to the regime. The coexistence of different factions within the UGTT enabled the union to alternate between autonomy and dependence in both its internal organization and relations with the single-party state. The union had always contained a wing represented by the union bureaucracy that favored submission to the government and even near-integration into the state machinery. Left-wing political movements and Arab nationalist groups completely stripped of political expression made up the other wing of the union, which sought to resist the regime and took the upper hand when the crisis struck, bolstered by their control over certain federations in education, the postal service and telecommunications as well as some local and regional unions. This configuration enabled the UGTT to provide structural and political support to social movements in spite of the union bureaucracy's close relationship with the regime. The UGTT's centralized structure and its organizational culture combining dependence and autonomy saved the union sections from being co-opted by the regime during the various crises at the union.

Furthermore, the history of the Tunisian union movement and the UGTT, in particular, show that social and economic policy issues have not traditionally been the main points of discord between union leadership and the government. The union regularly exploited these issues as a means of pressuring the single-party state and maintaining its power in the political arena. As a result, union protests over socioeconomic issues were systematically diverted to address political issues deemed essential, such as the need for national unity or maintaining peaceful labor relations, thus downplaying the importance of social and economic demands. While there was much talk at the union about the working class and the disputes between employers and employees, this rhetoric never gave rise to a real class struggle and was often used as a tool in relations between the UGTT and the regime. Another factor was the unique composition of the UGTT, whose members mainly worked in the public sector, making the state its top employer as well as a mediator in conflicts between union groups and greatly restricting the reach of social movements at the union. In this way, the UGTT paradoxically served the cause of the successive waves of economic liberalization, in spite of its complex relationship with the single-party state and the concessions it won for employees. The UGTT and the regime worked in tandem to manage and oversee various social groups and control the distribution of wealth.

In a twist of fate or an instance of poetic justice, social issues came to the fore, debunking the myth of the "Tunisian miracle" and weakening the regime. The damage was dealt by the southern and central western regions, which had suffered the consequences of two-tiered regional development, namely widespread unemployment, unstable working conditions and a lack of infrastructure. The Gafsa mining region revolt in 2008, in the southern town of Redeyef, gave an indication of the severity of the situation and gained an echo in France via a movement led by immigrants' associations. Two years later, in the summer of 2010, a large number of young protesters clashed with the police during the Ben Guerdane riots. Internal divisions began to emerge at the UGTT over what approach to take. Certain left-wing national unions—education, the postal service and telecommunications, in particular—and local and regional union sections felt a desire to join the protest movement, but the central leadership had a close relationship with the regime and could only foresee a mediation role for the union, at most. As in 1978 and 1984, Ben Ali put down these protest movements forcefully. The revolutionary process that was set in motion on December 17, 2010, when Mohammed Bouazizi set himself on fire in Sidi Bouzid, drew a great deal of inspiration from the social movement in Redeyef in 2008. This time, the unionists were determined not to commit the same mistakes.

Notes

1. Cf. www.ugtt.org.tn.
2. A list of the UGTT's decision-making bodies can be found in Appendix B.
3. The founding members included Habib Achour, Sahbi Farhat, Béchir Ben Brahim, Béchir Bellagha and Salem Cheffi.
4. This term is employed both in a narrow sense in reference to the Executive Board and more broadly to describe all or part of the Administrative Commission.
5. A regional union led by French nationals at every level, which reported to the French CGT and worked under the aegis of the French Section of the Workers' International. Conflicts between political factions continued to plague the organization, which was torn between support for the French Communist Party and the SFIO.
6. Founded in 1892, the Unitary General Labor Confederation (Confédération générale du travail unitaire, or CGTU) reported to the central office in France and mainly represented arsenal, railway, postal-service workers and civil servants who were either communists or supported the movement, as well as Italian workers of all political persuasions.
7. Destour, which means "constitution" in Arabic, was a Tunisian political party founded in 1921 by a group of public figures—doctors, lawyers, journalists and certain members of bourgeois families and individuals close to the Bey—who sought to liberate Tunisia from the French protectorate. Abdelaziz Thâalbi led the party until 1944.
8. Neo-Destour was a Tunisian political party founded after a split with the liberal constitutional party (Destour) on March 2, 1934, by a group of young intellectuals that included Habib Bourguiba, Mahmoud El Materi, Tahar Sfar and Bahri Guiga. The party worked to liberate the Tunisian people from the French protectorate. It became the Socialist Destourian Party (PSD) in 1963.
9. Civil inspectors served as local representatives of the colonial authorities, with power over a specific district.
10. Archives de la Compagnie des Phosphates de Gafsa (ACPG), 1907, *Lettre de Max Pellé au ministre des affaires étrangères en date du 6/11/1907.*
11. For more information on the origins and development of the Tunisian working class and the social and regional components of the first experiments with unionism, as well as the historical conditions under which they were carried out, cf. the work of Claude Liauzu (1977).
12. Salah Ben Youssef led Neo-Destour from 1934 to 1955. He was supported by Ahmed Ben Bella and, for a time, by Gamal Abdel Nasser. He was assassinated in 1961 in Frankfurt, Germany at the orders of Bourguiba and others. In the official historical narrative, Youssefists are depicted as diehard resistance fighters and dogmatic Arab nationalists.
13. After a period as a member of the Moscow-aligned World Federation of Trade Unions, the UGTT joined the International Confederation of Free Trade Unions (ICFTU) in 1951, as the latter provided a forum for Tunisian nationalists to present their movement to an international audience (Chater, 2006).
14. Salah Hamzaoui has written about Sfax and Gafsa's continual perch atop the UGTT leadership and the weak representation of the Sahel region, which holds economic and political power. Hamzaoui asserts that there is a division of labor

within the union between those who handle political matters and those responsible for union matters (Hamzaoui, *op. cit.*, 282).

15. Founded in 1947, the Tunisian Union of Industry, Trade and Handicrafts (UTICA) is the country's main national employers' organization. UTICA is an umbrella organization for professional groups in various non-agricultural sectors, including industry, retail, services, handicrafts and small trades. Hèdi Timoumi (1983) explains that UTICA provided unwavering support to all Neo-Destour and Habib Bourguiba's political stances.

16. The National Union of Tunisian Farmers (UNAT) is an agricultural union that represents professionals in the country's primary sector. UNAT was founded in 1949 as the General Union of Tunisian Farmers (UGAT), then renamed the National Union of Tunisian Farmers in 1955 and, finally, the Tunisian Union of Agriculture and Fishery (UTAP) in 1995.

17. Mahmoud Ben Romdhane (1982) explains that French economic interests continued to dominate certain key sectors of the economy and Tunisia remained as economically dependent on France as it had been in the past. During the Cold War, Tunisia established another relationship of dependency with Washington, which provided significant financial aid between 1957 and 1961, aimed at making the country a beacon for the third world.

18. The government formed a rival trade union, the Union of Tunisian Workers (Union des travailleurs tunisisens, or UTT), in reaction to the UGTT's efforts to achieve autonomy. The two unions were "reunified" some time later and Ahmed Tlili replaced Ahmed Ben Salah.

19. Works by Christian Morrisson and Béchir Talbi (1996) and Hakim Ben Hammouda (2012) provided a great deal of the information on the Tunisian economy presented here.

20. Gafsa native Ahmed Tlili served as UGTT Secretary General from 1957 to 1963.

21. Known under the French acronym GEAST or as Perspectives, from the name of its publication, "Perspectives tunisiennes pour une Tunisie meilleure." An umbrella organization for various left-wing groups, GEAST charged that the government was impeding the freedom of political organization and pursuing an inadequate cooperative development policy. The collective drew a distinction between Destourian socialism and the "true socialist path," which it viewed as the only means of uniting Tunisia and achieving economic development without land collectivization by the state.

22. The General Union of Tunisia'Students (Union générale des étudiants de Tunisie, or UGET) is a student organization formed in 1952 in order to represent students and work with other national organizations toward Tunisia's independence and development. Neo-Destour had fairly tight control over UGET until the Korba congress in 1971, when left-wing students took over leadership of the student movement. Since, the ruling power has regularly attacked UGET, which was responsible for politicizing several generations of students and training several waves of left-wing and far-left groups. In 1986, another student organization with close ties to the Islamic movement was founded, the General Union of Tunisian Students (Union générale tunisienne des étudiants, or UGTE).

23. Ahmed Mestiri is a Tunisian lawyer and politician who was a founding member of Neo-Destour and served as a minister several times under Bourguiba. In June 1978, Mestiri founded the Movement of Socialist Democrats (MDS) and became the party's secretary general. In 1981, his party won the first pluralistic legislative election, but the PSD prevented MDS from taking seats in parliament and announced falsified results via the interior ministry.

24. Bahi Ladgham was an independence activist who served as prime minister in the third government formed after independence, from November 7, 1969, until he

was replaced by Hédi Nouira on November 2, 1970. He also helped found the
Tunisian army.

25. *Inthifadat-al-khobz* in Arabic.

26. Tunisian Islamism appeared in 1971 in the form of *Jama'a al islamiyya*, an
organization that became the Islamic Tendency Movement (*Harakat al-Ittijah
al-Islâmî*) on June 6, 1981, and, finally, the Renaissance Movement (Ennahdha)
in February 1989.

27. Cf. www.ugtt.org.tn.

28. A number of works analyze the authoritarian regime from Bourguiba to Ben Ali
from different perspectives, among which: Mahmoud Ben Romdhane (2011);
Sadri Khiari (2003); Béatrice Hibou (2006); Michel Camau and Vincent Geisser
(2003); Ahmed Mestiri (2012); Jocelyne Dakhlia (2011); Sami Ben Gharbia
(2011); Fathi Ben Haj Yahia (2010); and Ouejdane Mejri and Afef Hajji (2013).

29. A national solidarity fund endowed with approximately 0.1% of Tunisian GDP
for public investment in poverty-reduction programs and projects. Under the
Ben Ali regime, the fund was known by its postal account number, 26–26.

30. Zine el-Abidine Ben Ali opened the UGTT congress in April 1999, demonstrating the extent to which the government had tamed the union.

31. Gafsa is a traditional stronghold of the union movement. The first phosphate
workers' strike took place in 1937 and was put down violently by the colonial
authorities.

32. Tunisia is the world's second-largest exporter of natural phosphates and fifth-
largest producer of phosphates, with annual production of approximately 8 million
metric tons and significant reserves. Phosphates and their byproducts represented
4% of Tunisia's GDP and 13% of total exports in 2009.

33. Cf. the documentary *Cursed Be the Phosphate*, directed by Sami Tlili, Tunisia,
2012.

34. Open positions at CPG were allocated by tribe; 20% of available positions were
earmarked for the local union via an agreement between the UGTT's general
management and CPG.

2 Unionists Recount the December 17, 2010 Uprising From the Outbreak of the Revolt to Efforts to Organize the Movement

Through his act, Bouazizi expressed his refusal to be denied his existence. He stood up for his dignity. He had a hard time with the poverty and contempt, but when he was expelled from a public area, he took that as a negation of his existence; when he went to see the governor, the representative of state authority, he was treated in the same way. In reality, Bouazizi asked for two things, the right to work and the right to exist. This sentiment spread to the people almost instantly through media, without any actions on the part of intellectuals. The people had felt like foreigners in their own country for 50 years and he helped them re-emerge from the fringes. Unionists received the message loud and clear and lifted off the yoke of the union bureaucracy, which had put forward arguments about their fears for the country and fear of chaos and a political vacuum. But the unionists could only be convinced of one thing: the need to regain their dignity. That made the decision easier and that's the reason that we attended the regional strikes in Sfax, Jendouba, Gabès and across the rest of the country.

Cherif, union activist, Primary Education, Sfax

On December 17, 2010, images of Mohammed Bouazizi setting himself on fire spread across social media, eliciting intense emotions among Tunisians, which gradually transformed into a vast protest movement that led to Ben Ali fleeing on January 14, 2011. Beset by the same anger and indignation, unionists joined the movement, then called the *intifada*,[1] and played an active role as organizers. One unionist from Sidi Bouzid explained that Bouazizi's self-immolation wasn't the only factor behind the revolt, but it was the "straw that broke the camel's back":

The December 17, 2011, revolution started in Sidi Bouzid; Bouazizi's self-immolation was the straw that broke the camel's back, but that incident alone cannot be viewed as the main factor that sparked the revolution. The residents of Sidi Bouzid have long suffered from economic hardship—people experienced injustice and humiliation. Bouazizi was the sixth person to commit suicide in 2010; five people committed suicide before him but he was the straw that broke the camel's back. People gathered to protest in front of the governorate offices on December 17 and they gradually grew in number. The governor refused to leave the building and they started throwing stones at him. Afterwards he tried to speak to them twice, but they weren't convinced.

(Mohammed, union activist, Secondary Education, Sidi Bouzid)

How did this "straw that broke the camel's back" snowball into a large protest movement that led to the fall of Ben Ali? How did unionists react to this turn of events? How do unionists view their contribution to the protest movement? Did they act as individuals or UGTT members? How do they explain the discrepancy between the initial conciliatory official statements by the union leadership and the daily protests in the streets?

When answering these questions, my interviewees alternated between two different narratives. The first narrative, recounted by all unionists, depicts the fall of Ben Ali as the expected, foreseen outcome of an "accumulation of social struggles" over the past two decades. However, when called upon to

Image 2.1 Sidi Bouzid on December 17, 2011.

Image 2.2 The Fateful Meeting of the National Administrative Commission on January 4, 2011.

describe their actions in concrete terms, they spontaneously introduced a second narrative: their extraordinary missteps, improvisation and adjustments during this rapid chain of events, many of which unforeseen. In this chapter, I will attempt to shed light on how the individuals interviewed attributed meaning to their actions and those of their organization. In the first section, I will use their detailed description of the events that took place between December 17, 2010 and January 14, 2011, to gain perspective on their view of the role they played in the uprising. I will then focus on the organizational dynamic within the UGTT, to home in on the various contradictions and tensions that the union faced as an intermediary between the popular uprising and the state apparatus. I will describe how the organization, as an authority and communication system governed by a well-defined structure and precise assignment of roles, reacted to often-unforeseen events. I will also cover the process by which unionists adjusted to the circumstances and the organizational resources mustered to support the protest movement.[2]

The UGTT Serves as a Refuge (*Maljaâ*) for the Popular Uprising

As soon as the *intifadas*, or protests, broke out, a number of practical organizational issues quickly came to the fore, requiring protestors to devise concrete solutions that went beyond speeches and slogans. How did unionists react to the *intifada* that erupted in Sidi Bouzid? How do they explain the spread of the movement and the fact that it withstood the test of time?

All the unionists interviewed agreed that the protest movement took shape in a completely spontaneous manner without any specific leadership:

> The incident with Bouazizi, who was humiliated, sparked the revolution. The events unfolded completely spontaneously in the beginning, but the anger in the streets, the ferment and the rallies held by Sidi Bouzid residents—who were outraged and shocked by the incident—created a popular protest movement. There wasn't any political party, plan or clear goal.
>
> (Foued, union official, Primary Education, Sidi Bouzid)

However, most of the unionists interviewed also maintained that the UGTT welcomed and protected the protest movement, including this unionist from Redeyef:

> It cannot be said that there were political parties or clear political sympathies; demonstrators had them but they did not govern the protest movement. The UGTT welcomed [*moûhtadhan*] the movement. For our part, as unionists, we accepted and organized the movement.
>
> (Hassan, union activist, Mining, Redeyef)

Another unionist from Tunis adds:

> Social movements often take shape spontaneously, but as soon as these movements seek protection and refuge at the UGTT, unionists will fulfill their duties if they believe in the cause. That is how the movement, which started out spontaneously, was able to gain backing at the UGTT, a source of support that defended and adopted its positions. That's what happened in Sidi Bouzid and what happened in Tunis and elsewhere.
>
> (Azizi, union activist, Transportation, Tunis)

When asked how exactly the UGTT welcomed the protest movement (cf. Box 1), my interlocutors stated that this primarily involved serving as a physical refuge. Unlike in other Arab countries, where demonstrations depart from mosques, the UGTT was chosen as the ad hoc staging point for all the demonstrations and rallies:

> There weren't any political parties. There were people who had decided to protest and express their anger and those people spontaneously allied with the UGTT. They didn't depart from the mosques like they do in Egypt, for example. . . . In Tunisia, I see the UGTT offices playing the role of the mosques.
>
> (Thouraya, lawyer, Tunis)

For example, Place Mohamed Ali Hammi in Tunis, where the UGTT is located, was central to all the demonstrations:

> Remember that the January 14 demonstration on Avenue Habib Bourguiba could not have taken place if people had not been able to gather beforehand on Place Mohamed Ali Hammi. That gathering transformed into a demonstration that was able to break through the security blockade around the square.
>
> (Slim, union official, Health Care, Tunis)

The UGTT has offices across Tunisia which also served as sites where the various participants in the movement could plan and coordinate their actions:

> What does it mean to give structure to the movement? That there weren't any political party offices and there weren't any offices for the human rights league—the only place that served as a meeting point was the UGTT offices. Most of the meetings, protest movements and demonstrations were planned at the UGTT and then departed from the UGTT's square or were held in front the UGTT. Unionists from the base and intermediate unions and some members of the regional executive committee took part.
>
> (Mohammed, union activist, Secondary Education, Sidi Bouzid)

Sami notes the sacred, symbolic meaning attributed to the UGTT's square, which dates back to the colonial era:

> The UGTT offices are sacred and have been since the colonial era. No authority dares touch those who take refuge at the UGTT—the police aren't authorized to lay a hand on the demonstrators.
>
> (Sami, unionist, Information, Bizerte)[3]

Others add that the UGTT not only serves as a physical refuge that has given shelter to various social movements, it is also the only space where opponents of different political stripes can exercise political expression. The UGTT is one of the rare spaces that were able to avoid total domination by the regime. Mongi explains:

> The UGTT is the *hadhin*, or shelter, for all the political opposition groups and human rights activists. The opposition—legally recognized and otherwise—was persecuted and often sought refuge at the union to make their voice heard and exercise their right to free movement. The UGTT's open-mindedness and positions in support of dissidents enabled the union to develop an "immunity of the people" that helped it to withstand multiple crises in which it was

pitted against the conformism promoted by the Bourguiba and Ben Ali regimes.

(Mongi Amami, sociologist and former director of the UGTT research and documentation department)

In a similar vein, Fatma, a union activist in the textiles sector in Bizerte, describes the freedom of expression that she believes is a defining part of the UGTT:

> I remember that in the beginning, when I joined the union movement, I was at a meeting in Bizerte and I observed how the unionists spoke and expressed themselves. I was amazed—I didn't know that there was a place where we could express ourselves so freely. They spoke as if the political police didn't exist, as if Ben Ali didn't impose a reign of terror. The place surprised me. I had thought that the UGTT only defended workers and didn't realize the freedom they had. We were under the protection of the UGTT; the only place where I felt safe was at the UGTT offices, where I could express myself and feel at ease.

Box 1 The UGTT Shelters the Uprising

We have heard a lot of analysis that focuses on the fact that the movement emerged spontaneously, without a leader or chief. It's true that the UGTT didn't create the movement—it was spontaneous in the strictest sense of the term—but without guidance and activists who believed in and structured the revolution, it never would have happened. . . . The UGTT played a central role in the revolution. . . . First of all, you have to look at the UGTT's place in Tunisian society and what its mission was. In addition to its traditional role defending workers' rights, the UGTT had a social and political mission. It played a role as a refuge [*maljaâ*] for practically all the political movements. This was due, of course, to the lack of freedom for political work—even the political parties recognized that they were controlled and didn't have freedom of movement; the ones that weren't officially sanctioned even more so. . . . As a result, anyone who wanted to speak their mind took shelter at the UGTT. That's what happened on December 17, 2010: when people wanted to protest, they automatically went to the UGTT offices to take refuge and seek support. The spontaneous movements found activists who could help them express their demands. When the UGTT takes in a movement, it gets behind their demands. The UGTT was the staging point because people couldn't depart from anywhere else. The UGTT is a refuge that often provides a sort of protection, because when a protest takes place on its grounds or in front of its square, the police generally avoid confrontation. That is why people who want to express an opinion come to the UGTT for protection—they are looking for a place where they can convey a message to the public, a place where they can deliver their demands to the government and lay them out in concrete terms. The UGTT fulfills all these roles. . . . That's what happened on December 17, 2010, in Sidi Bouzid. In Tunis, all the demonstrations departed from Place Mohamed Ali Hammi and if the unionists there hadn't joined the movement, it would have remained limited to a small group. Demonstrations are only effective when they receive broad support from unionists.

Abdeljelil Bedoui, UGTT economist, expert and advisor

The UGTT offices are presented as a physical, symbolic and political refuge. These buildings also served as a site for several political actors to coordinate their actions. How did the unionists assist with this coordination?

Unionists Help Guide the Movement

One of the recurring themes in the unionists' remarks on their role in the popular uprising was "guidance."[4] The interviewees emphasized the spontaneous nature of the movement and stated that they joined early on, to provide guidance. Farid, a teacher and unionist in Sidi Bouzid:

It has become a mass protest movement, but unionists in the primary and secondary education unions, lawyers and a few political activists quickly stepped in to guide the movement.

A union official from Gafsa:

In 2011, the movement was spontaneous and the impromptu demonstrations departed from local unions, mainly in Thala, Kasserine and Sidi Bouzid. The unionists joined the demonstrations to provide guidance.

(Kader, union activist, Mining, Gafsa)

The interviewees used the term "guidance" to describe three types of actions: the politicization of the movement, coordination between different participants—especially the lawyers and the unemployed young people—and mediation with the various union and political authorities.

The unionists interviewed, most of whom had both political and union duties,[5] placed great emphasis on their important role in politicizing the uprising by pairing the social and economic demands with political aims. Early on, the protestors chanted slogans about the right to employment and equality in regional development. Gradually, political slogans emerged on issues such as clamping down on corruption and calling for the ouster of Ben Ali. Larbi, a nurse and union activist in Sidi Bouzid, offers his perspective:

From the outset, our inclination was to urge people not to view that act as a suicide, but as a political assassination. Bouazizi should be considered a victim of the regime. . . . Unionists played an important role in guiding the movement in its choice of slogans and demonstration routes, as well as in planning rallies and strikes. . . . There was uniformity in the slogans that were chanted; there was not, for example, one person yelling "God is great" and another yelling "the People is great." Purely ideological slogans were avoided as was anything that could divide people. The slogans were meant to unite people behind common political and social demands.

Later he added:

Early on, the slogans mainly had a social protest message. The slogan that was most chanted during the first few days was, "Employment is a right, pack of thieves!" and later "No to the Trabelsis, who stole the budget!" which was chanted in early January. Then, on January 11, the police responded violently the first time that "O great people, reject another term for the president!" was chanted. The police went crazy and the police chief came to tell us that he didn't like that. He met us in the café and said, "You are unionists, I like you and I respect you, but I don't want to hear that slogan. Let me be, I don't want to have any problems. . . . It was an Arabic professor who started that chant very loudly; he's a friend who ran the movie club.

Larbi's remarks indicate that the social and political aspect of protesters demands helped to expand the movement, as people from different regions identified with the sentiment. The fact that protesters in demonstrations and rallies across Tunisia chanted the same radical slogans enabled the movement to grow stronger and push on:

The revolution that began in Sidi Bouzid had broad slogans about development [and] the right to employment. . . . For example, many people had supported the Redeyef revolt in 2008 but that had remained local, with local demands, whereas each governorate and city identified with the slogans chanted in Sidi Bouzid, which fueled the revolt. When you talk about regional development, Kasserine is for regional development, Gafsa is for regional development, Siliana is asking for regional development, as is Jendouba. Those cities not only supported Sidi Bouzid, they adopted its demands, which were embraced by all of the country's regions.

(Hafedh, union official, Health Care, Sidi Bouzid)

The second aspect of the union's guidance was coordinating demonstrations. The unionists interviewed stressed that the UGTT served as the hub for communication between different groups of actors, especially human rights activists, lawyers and unemployed young people. One unionist from Sidi Bouzid gave particularly insightful remarks on the topic:

> The people who took Bouazizi to the hospital were unionists. On December 18, 2011, we formed a body called the Committee for Supporting and Monitoring the Sidi Bouzid Demonstrations. The committee, which was created at the UGTT, comprises political activists, human rights activists, young people and lawyers. Officials from the primary and secondary education unions and the Order of Lawyers led the committee. They oversaw the committee's work during the 12 days when Sidi Bouzid was closed off by the government and forces of repression.
>
> (Helmi, union activist, Postal Service, Sidi Bouzid)

Networks of activists established during previous movements were quickly reactivated during the Sidi Bouzid uprising. For instance, one unionist from Redeyef describes how the revolt in his city provided an opportunity for lawyers and unionists to forge ties that would be renewed in 2011:

> We coordinated our actions with the lawyers. The lawyers who stepped forward in 2011 are the same ones who defended us in 2008—they led a major offensive against the Ben Ali regime. The videos of lawyers that made the rounds on Facebook—lawyers who were on the front lines of the demonstrations—really energized the movement. I think that the 2008 movement had made a strong impact on them, because it gave them the opportunity to defend the right to employment and they sided with the people. They helped guide and supervise the demonstrations in Sidi Bouzid, Kasserine and Tunis, playing a very important role.
>
> (Adel, union official, Secondary Education, Redeyef)

Lawyers were among the major opponents of the Ben Ali regime in the 2000s. They did not lead demonstrations, but they often took a place near the front of the procession and were allies of unionists in all regions. They provided invaluable support to the popular protest movement (Gobe, *op. cit.*), organizing sit-ins in front of the courthouse and coordinating their actions with unionist protestors. Tunis-based blogger Ahmed explains:

> The Order of Lawyers was one of the civil-society organizations that truly worked as part of the opposition in the country, not at the grassroots level but at the top. The Order of Lawyers often stood up to the regime. . . . The lawyers really played a political role from December 17, 2010 to January 14, 2011. You would look at the lawyers who came out in Kasserine and see them in their imposing formal dress at

the Kasserine courthouse while the police was shooting everywhere! It was an incredible sight to behold and the same thing happened in Sidi Bouzid, where they also played an important role.

In addition, young people[6]—especially the unemployed, university students and high school students—demonstrated a great ability to resist and carry on with the demonstrations despite suffering brutal suppression. The unionists coordinated their events and faced down the regime with these radical, resistant young people.

> We consulted each other on everything and made decisions democratically. For example, the young people [students and unemployed], lawyers and everyone else had to be present when issuing a press release or organizing any kind of event. Decisions were made democratically— everyone had to be in agreement.
>
> (Adel, union official, Secondary Education, Redeyef)

For his part, Maher, an unemployed graduate, notes that a large number of activists from the Union of Unemployed Graduates (UDC),[7] who are generally former students and activists from the General Union of Tunisian Students (UGET), took part in the popular uprising from the very beginning. Accustomed to working in secrecy, they had experience partnering with unionists:

> Don't forget that the first slogan of the revolution—"Work is a right you pack of thieves"—had first been used by unemployed graduates. It's a slogan that became popular and did much to radicalize the protest movement initiated on December 17, 2010. The 2010 movement wasn't a first for us. We had campaigned for work, dignity and justice in secrecy since the end of the 1990s. We know all about prison and torture, but we never gave up on our wholly legitimate rights. The unionists have always supported us and even lent us their offices for our activities. The coordination with the unionists in 2010 was almost immediate.

The unionists and the young people who took part in the uprising also coordinated their communication with the media, which helped expand the campaign in support of the movement and, later, enable it to spread across the country. Activist bloggers were instrumental in delivering information to new audiences and helping it circulate more quickly, circumventing the media blackout imposed on the demonstrations. A unionist from Sfax explains:

> Young people filmed the events and we also interviewed them in order to defeat the media blackout. Then the young people posted everything

on Facebook and Twitter. They also helped us send videos to alternative Tunisian media outlets like Alhiwar Tounsi. And then Al-Jazeera started to cover us, before all the other international networks.

> (Mohsen, union activist, Postal Service, Sfax)

Helmi, a mailman and unionist in Sidi Bouzid:

> Young people took the initiative to share what happened on social media and us [unionists], we handled the interactions with Al-Jazeera, Al-Arabiya and France 24. If you look at the videos, you'll see that most of the interviewees in the international media were unionists.

The various actors established efficient methods and a meticulous division of tasks. During the day, the unionists would organize demonstrations and rallies for all social groups and ages. In the evening, the young people would clash with the police in what could be called guerrilla warfare. Meanwhile, the lawyers worked to defend the political prisoners. The unionists also took up a role as "mediators" between the young unemployed, who were particularly active and determined to continue with the protests and confront the police crackdown, and the regime authorities, who were resolved to put down the movement:

> As unionists, we wanted to prevent the young people from entering into a direct conflict with the people from the RCD. We had to keep the young people from being put in jail. That's what "guidance" meant to me—we served as an intermediary between the [unemployed] young people and the government.
>
> (Adel, union official, Secondary Education, Redeyef)

The unionists also put pressure on the UGTT's regional ruling bodies to intervene and help free the prisoners:

> The families of the young people who were in prison came to see us. We put pressure on the Executive Board to speak with the governor and have the prisoners freed.
>
> (Larbi, union activist, Health Care, Sidi Bouzid)

After the unionists, unemployed and lawyers came together, the spontaneous movement became more political. They combined their prior experience in activism with the disadvantaged young people's intricate knowledge of their urban environment. As the situation developed unpredictably, without local or national political leadership, inventive organizational methods emerged to counter repression from the regime and keep the movement alive. The unionists, who straddled the political and union worlds, found themselves at the center of an unprecedented partnership between traditional activist networks and young people from disadvantaged neighborhoods, who normally were kept out of such events. This cooperation was a key factor in the transition from riots into an organized movement and the supply of resources required to expand and sustain the efforts (Hmed, 2012; International Crisis Group, 2011).

> The revolution was spontaneous in the beginning—there weren't any political parties or forces behind it. That was true in the beginning, but when you look at the chain of events, you see that there were unionists who took action and organized the movement.
>   (Hatem, militant syndical, Primary Education, Sidi Bouzid)

Box 2   Unprecedented Cooperation Between Young People and Unionists

For 12 days, Sidi Bouzid remained blocked off and at the complete mercy of the police. The school on Avenue de la République turned into police barracks—they slept in the classrooms. They came from cities everywhere: Gabès, Gafsa, Sfax, etc. . . . There were rallies and demonstrations every day on the main street and on the square that would later be renamed Place des Martyrs [Martyrs' Square]. There were gatherings in front of the governorate headquarters every day. What was new and unique to Sidi Bouzid was the other revolution during the night, the [disadvantaged] young people's revolution, the young people of Facebook and the Internet—the Ben Ali generation that people said were apolitical. They organized themselves into groups in their neighborhoods, without any outside leadership. Oh, and I mustn't forget the role of the students who were on vacation and had experience organizing rallies and handling clashes with the police. . . . There were bloody clashes in the neighborhoods—Ouled Belhedi, Ennour, etc. and on the power and gas company's street—they used stones, set tires on fire, used Molotov cocktails. . . . The neighborhoods took shifts—they had an impressive system where they would use their cellphones and when one group was tired, they would call another and they would open up another "front" elsewhere. All that for 12 days straight. . . .

During the day, there were discussion groups in public places. There were even discussions with the police chief—people would ask questions about their strategies and freeing prisoners. The police asked us for a truce and if we could help them calm things down. For 12 days, there were battles in the night with the police and peaceful protests during the day led by adults, unionists, women, entrepreneurs—everybody. . . . For 12 days, the duration of the siege of Sidi Bouzid, before other regions joined the movement.

Foued, union official, Primary Education, Sidi Bouzid

The Spread of the Protest Movement

One of the key elements in the Sidi Bouzid *intifada* as described by the interviewees is the speed at which the protest movement grew—it reached most of the neighboring central cities in Sidi Bouzid Governorate in three days. The demonstrations quickly became regional in scale and appeared throughout the heart of the country. Unionists reached out to contacts across the region—in Regueb, Menzel Bouzayane and all the way up to Sfax and Bizerte—to "tone down the pressure" on those in Sidi Bouzid. "When we saw that the crackdown was focused on Sidi Bouzid and many reinforcements had arrived from Tunis, we decided to branch out and organize demonstrations in other regions," says Samir, a doctor and union activist from Sfax. The UGTT's offices across Tunisia and the unionists' backing proved decisive. Mohsen, a member of the postal service union in Sfax: "There were UGTT offices everywhere, which helped accommodate the expansion of the protest movement." The spread of the protests to new locales was a new development in relation to previous movements, which had remained restricted to a specific region. The government adopted a systematic strategy of surrounding protesters to wear down and extinguish the movement, as it had done in Redeyef in 2008 and in Ben Guerdane in 2010. Sidi Bouzid was able to break free from the blockade thanks to the swift support from the other regions, as notes a unionist from the city:

> The difference with the events in the mining area is that the government was able to block off Redeyef [for six months], restricting the *intifada* to a well-defined geographic area until the movement aborted. Sidi Bouzid, however, was able to break free from its isolation very quickly. How so? In Menzel Bouzayane, a small town 76 km from Sidi Bouzid—a governorate that belongs to Sidi Bouzid—they demonstrated in solidarity and that's where the first martyr died—Mohammed Ammari, a 26- or 28-year-old who held a master's degree in physics. There were two martyrs in the region. Then other delegations joined the movement—Meknassi, Jelma and Regueb—and broke the cordon around Sidi Bouzid. That's what upset the police.

On a similar note, Redeyef-based mining union activist Romdhane remarked:

> In the beginning, I thought that the movement would be restricted to Sidi Bouzid, like what happened with our movement in Redeyef in 2008. I was surprised by the speed at which it spread—everyone identified with Bouazizi and other [unemployed] young people also set themselves on fire in disadvantaged regions, until the movement reached Kasserine.

Samir, a mining union official from Gafsa, adds:

> Unlike in Sidi Bouzid, the other cities didn't follow suit in Redeyef in 2008. There were press releases and announcements in support of

Redeyef, but there weren't demonstrations or clashes in other cities, and that's why the movement remained restricted to Redeyef.

Certain left-leaning regional unions and national federations in education, the postal service and healthcare hurriedly spread the word about the base unionists' determination.[8] The UGTT's main interprofessional body, the Tunis Regional Union, called a rally on Place Mohamed Ali Hammi (located across from the UGTT headquarters) on December 27, 2010. This was met with a public repudiation from UGTT Secretary General Abdessalem Jrad, who chastised the secretary general of the secondary education union for his remarks and condemned the slogans hostile to Ben Ali. The UGTT did not release a statement in support of the movement until January 4.

The Turning Point: Repression Radicalizes the Movement

Police repression grew along with the movement, which helped radicalize those loyal to the cause. Hamdi, a doctor and unionist in Sfax:

> The demonstrations and rallies in Sfax were violently suppressed, especially when the police received outside reinforcements. That repression gave us even greater determination in the struggle.

Hafedh, a union official in Sidi Bouzid, adds:

> Sidi Bouzid was surrounded with cops, and then the army joined them. I thought that things would calm down but then the martyrs fell in Bouzayane. That's what inflamed the situation and when the martyrs fell in Regueb, we passed the point of no return.

However, all my interviewees pointed to the violent crackdown on the protest movement in Thala and Kasserine on January 8 and 9, 2011, as the point of no return that radicalized the protesters and hastened the fall of Ben Ali:

> When Thala and Kasserine joined the movement on January 6, 2011, the government felt that it was in danger, so it decided to change tactics and react very violently, with massacres in Thala and Kasserine. They had organized in the same way there—the demonstrations would depart from the local union in Thala and the regional union in Kasserine. . . . The government intervened very violently; police practices changed at that point, even in Sidi Bouzid, and protests were put down with live ammunition.
>
> (Farid, union official, Primary Education, Sidi Bouzid)

Others mentioned the role of the army in the regime's new offensive:

> The regime changed its strategy and the army arrived in Sidi Bouzid on January 6 or 7. After that point we had a new participant in the clashes—the army. There was a massacre in Regueb [near Sidi Bouzid] on January 9 in which six martyrs fell in a small town of no more than four or five thousand residents. Two women died, including Manal Bouallagui, a mother of two daughters.
>
> (Mohammed, union activist, Secondary Education, Sidi Bouzid)

The events in Thala and Kasserine touched off an unprecedented wave of support that reached most cities in Tunisia. Rallies were held in areas across the country in a show of solidarity and a rejection of the situation imposed by the government. Tunis-based UDC activist Rafik explains:

> When several people died in the massacres in Thala and later in Kasserine, a rally was called for January 10 on Place Mohamed Ali Hammi. It really was a special day that radically changed the situation. The slogans were no longer only social in nature—they attacked the regime directly. We had suffered savage repression—much worse than on December 25 and 27. We were surrounded by a police cordon and it was difficult to get out.

Imed, an activist from the postal-service union, has similar recollections:

> The protest movement in Sidi Bouzid spread to other regions, reaching Regueb and then Thala and Kasserine, which historically have been marginalized regions. The southwest region revolted [*intafadhat*] and there were two important occurrences: the police and what we call the "presidential guard" began to counter the protests with live ammunition and several martyrs fell, which meant that they had been given authorization to shoot at people. It obviously wasn't the first time in Tunisian history that people had been shot at. People were shot at in 1984 and army tanks were in the streets in 1978. But this time it was different; the police were exceptionally savage and took any excuse to shoot at people—several martyrs fell.

Ben Ali gave a second speech that was later dubbed "*bikouli hazm*" (with all due severity) in which he threatened to press charges against the protesters and punish them severely. He also announced the creation of three national commissions tasked with carrying out political reforms and investigating corruption and wanton acts during the protests. Unexpected, unpredictable events such as the savage repression and Ben Ali's menacing speech galvanized the protest movement. The Sidi Bouzid *intifada*, which had begun spontaneously, reached the point of no return. The protesters were more determined than ever to fight the ruling power and achieve their aims. Violent clashes between the police and young people from working-class neighborhoods like Hay Atadhamoun (City of Solidarity) erupted across the country on January 11, 2011, during which police stations were burned down. That is when the uprising reached the capital:

> The uprising had to reach Tunis to have a chance of undermining the regime. The handful of rallies that had been held on Place Mohamed Ali Hammi were not enough. The brutal repression in Kasserine and Thala fueled people's rage. Kids from working-class neighborhoods like Tadhamûn and Kram identified with the young people from inland regions. They were also poor and regularly subjected to police brutality. They started to burn down police stations and that is when, for the first time, I felt like something extraordinary was happening in the country.
>
> (Ghassen, unemployed, UDC, Tunis)

Regional Strikes Hasten the Fall of Ben Ali

Unionists from base and intermediate unions adapted their strategy in reaction to the rising violence on the part of the regime and the uprising swelled. They put all their effort into changing the prudent, wait-and-see attitude of the national leadership, which had only expressed tepid support for the Sidi Bouzid, Kasserine and Thala movements. The UGTT Executive Board's initial press releases had attempted to position the leadership in its usual role as a mediator, calling for the government to "free those who were arrested" and "take urgent measures to implement decisions regarding youth employment." Sami, a member of the UGTT Administrative Commission, believes that the tipping point for the central leadership was the violent crackdown on the protests in Kasserine. It was at that moment, he says, that unionists reached a consensus on the need to do everything in their power to force the UGTT leadership to end the mediation approach and seek to overthrow the government:

> For the first few days, we were there to listen to the demonstrators and request for the prisoners to be freed. But after the repression in Kasserine and Ben Ali's humiliating speech threatening the protesters, several of us in the Administrative Commission called for an end to the mediation approach and a clear entry into politics via a call to overthrow the government.

At that point, the UGTT Executive Board and Secretary General's Office had no choice but to back the protest movements—otherwise they would have lost all legitimacy in the eyes of their base and cut themselves off from the Tunisian people, who had been deeply moved by the self-immolation and suicide of several struggling graduates and the murder of dozens of civilians by sniper fire. On January 11, 2011, the members of the UGTT Administrative Commission issued a statement in which they:

- Condemned the use of live ammunition on demonstrators, which had resulted in a number of deaths in inland areas such as Thala, Kasserine and Regueb.
- Condemned the blockade surrounding the Kasserine regional labor union and the ransacking of its property and documents.
- Called for a commission to be formed to investigate the conditions under which live ammunition was used against protesters and to find those accountable.
- Emphatically called for the withdrawal of the army contingents in cities and main thoroughfares, as well as for the forces of order to call off their siege in certain inland regions.

The Administrative Commission gave local unions across the country the freedom to call regional and sector strikes.[9] Three regional unions—Sfax, Tozeur and Kairouan—called a general strike on January 12, 2011. The unionists depict the general strike in Sfax, a city of economic and historical importance, as a pivotal moment that did much to encourage and inspire the major demonstration that took place on January 14, 2011:

> I would like to concentrate on the Sfax regional strike, which was exceptional from both a qualitative and quantitative standpoint. The plan was for the demonstration to depart from the UGTT offices at 10 a.m., but the organizers were forced to leave earlier because the square was packed with people and we couldn't wait any longer. The slogans, which were very specific and mainly political, were based on two principles: dignity and freedom and the right to employment. . . . All sectors took part in large numbers: the private sector, civil service, etc. The Sfax demonstration was a turning point—it rattled the regime and scared them. The Sfax demonstration was a sign that the movement had spread from the inland regions towards the coast and the major cities. Tunis rallied and the young people from working-class neighborhoods in Tunis rallied. The Sfax demonstration created momentum for the January 14 demonstration.
>
> (Nejib, union activist, Primary Education, Sfax)

Larbi, a nurse and union activist in Sidi Bouzid, adds:

> There were several regional strikes in several cities after the [decision by the] UGTT Administrative Commission—Sidi Bouzid held a general strike on January 13. What can I say, the atmosphere was like what we had seen on TV, like Palestinians under siege—Gaza in Sidi Bouzid! Everything was closed off, there was a blockade. . . . More than 100,000

people attended the general strike in Sfax on January 12. It was a turning point. Some 30,000 people demonstrated in Sidi Bouzid, a city of 50,000.

In the eyes of Abdeljelil Bedoui, a UGTT economist, expert and advisor, the violently suppressed popular uprising became a revolutionary process when the UGTT's local and regional organizations took up the cause:

> How did the uprising turn into a revolution? The local and regional unions took up the cause. The police made a big mistake by using violence against the movement. The deaths and martyrs pushed the UGTT's regional organizations to call general strikes and hold demonstrations and rallies. The largest demonstrations were in Sfax on January 12 and in Tunis on January 14. That is what led to the fall of the regime. There never would have been a revolution without the support of the UGTT's local and regional organizations.

Mohsen, a union activist and postal-service worker in Sfax, offers his perspective:

> The National Administrative Commission makes the decisions on regional strikes. The commission met on January 12 and decided on the regional strikes, which were capped off by a general strike. The commission was responsible for coordination. The main unions, like primary and secondary education, started demonstrating on January 7. Six sectors took part from the start of the *intifada* and then other sectors joined the movement, which was capped off by a demonstration that departed from Place Mohamed Ali Hammi on January 14, after other major demonstrations in Sfax and elsewhere.

Several thousand people took to the streets for the regional strikes in the large inland cities, brandishing signs with unambiguously political slogans decrying "Ben Ali's dictatorship" and the corrupt, mafia-like clans. Ben Ali addressed the nation in a second speech on January 13, 2011, nearly a month after the start of the riots. In the speech, famous for the phrase *fhemtkoum* (I understand you), Ben Ali promised more freedoms for Tunisians, lower prices for staple goods, and to refrain from seeking another term in the 2014 presidential elections ("No lifetime presidency and I will not alter the age limit set forth in the constitution."). Many Tunisians were quick to react to these promises, which were delivered a tad too late. The regional union in Tunis called a two-hour general regional strike in the greater Tunis area on January 14, 2011. The Tunis demonstration departed from Place Mohamed Ali Hammi, across from the UGTT's longstanding headquarters, and continued toward Avenue Bourguiba, across from the interior ministry, a reviled symbol of the dictatorship. Several hundred thousand people—far more than just union members and activists—demonstrated under the slogan "Ben Ali out!" Ben Ali fled to Saudi Arabia that same evening.

One important point to remember is that according to the interviewees, no one had predicted that Ben Ali would flee. They all took action based on the sequence of events and adapted to new developments each day. They did not remotely suspect that their actions, combined with those of other actors, would change the face of the country completely:

> No one could believe that Ben Ali had left so quickly—no one could have predicted the speed at which he fled. At the same time, we all were expecting radical change in Tunisia.
>
> (Jilani, unemployed, UDC, Gafsa)

> Everyone was surprised. None of the political powers or leaders had predicted Ben Ali's fall. Everyone, including the radical parties, hoped that the ruling power would weaken so that they could grab more "territory," and then, suddenly, Ben Ali left and the conflicts began.
>
> (Mohamed Trabelsi, former UGTT Deputy Secretary General)

This turn of events suggests that the unionists, lacking the leadership required to organize the ad hoc movement due to the balance of power in favor of the regime, supplied the material, organizational and political resources needed to gradually transform the spontaneous *intifada* into the revolutionary process that hastened the fall of Ben Ali. They "guided" the uprising by coordinating various social groups, acting as a go-between with regime authorities and exerting pressure on the UGTT's decision-making bodies. As Hafedh, a union official from Sidi Bouzid, states:

> We organized the January 13 demonstration in Sidi Bouzid and it was a sight to behold. I'm not telling you that because I'm a UGTT official—it's the honest truth. Ben Ali would not have fled if the UGTT hadn't intervened; it would have been impossible. There was a large demonstration in Sfax on January 12 and others in Sidi Bouzid, Kasserine and Siliana on the 13th. Jendouba, the Tunis metro area and Bizerte followed suit on January 14. In the Tunis region, the general strike was supposed to last two hours and not a day, but the two hours turned into a whole day and you know the rest. That is how the UGTT made the final push that led to the fall of the regime.

Redeyef in 2008: A Dress Rehearsal for Sidi Bouzid in 2010

Many of the unionists interviewed described the movement in Redeyef in 2008 as a dress rehearsal for the uprising that began on December 17, 2010. Not only was the Redeyef conflict the first head-to-head confrontation between the Ben Ali regime and the social movement, it also served as a great inspiration to unionists, spurring them to become more proactive and providing the organizational strategies required to manage the crisis and a series of unpredictable events. The same set of circumstances occurred in Redeyef, namely violent repression of a social movement leading to a serious battle between the union bureaucracy and the intermediate and base unions, ending with a solution negotiated as a result of pressure from the latter:

> The UGTT Executive Board had a position that was completely at odds with certain general and regional unions in 2008. Members of the base unions turned up the pressure, forcing regional unions in areas such as Kairouan, Mahdia and Ben Arous, as well as sectors like primary, secondary and higher education, to support the movement in the mining area. For its part, the union bureaucracy suspended the term of Adnene Hajji and other unionists. . . . The Executive Board didn't change its position after the live shots fired in Redeyef and the large-scale campaign in support of the movement. At that time, after the shots were fired, the decision was made to hire lawyers to free the prisoners. At the urging of the base unions, a rally was held on Place Mohamed Ali Hammi in October 2008. . . . A few members of the Executive Board were in attendance. Houcine Abbassi was able to give a speech despite the tension among those in the audience, who considered the Executive Board to be complicit in the crimes in Redeyef because it had let the government put unionists in jail and Ben Ali fire on the protesters. . . . Abbassi was able to give a speech saying that the Executive Board was divided and only a minority supported the mining area protests. He added that the rally could strengthen the position of those who had sided with the mining areas.
>
> (Ali, union activist, Mining, Redeyef)

> How was there a change in Redeyef? Internal pressure from the base unions and external pressure from foreign union delegations caused the change. This internal and outside pressure is what caused the union leadership to shift its official position in support of the prisoners and to reinstate the terms of suspended union officials.
>
> (Najet, union activist, Health Care, Tunis)

The events in Redeyef appear to have informed the demonstration tactics of young unemployed people in Sidi Bouzid and the methods of coordination between unionists and various other participants in the uprising:

> Redeyef is two hours from Sidi Bouzid. There was urban guerrilla warfare between the cops and the young people during the night in Sidi Bouzid. Exactly the same thing had happened in Redeyef. The goal of the nighttime battles was to wear down the cops and the youth in Sidi Bouzid adopted the same strategy. There was daily coordination between the unionists, young people, lawyers and journalists in Sidi Bouzid, just as there had been in Redeyef.
>
> (Larbi, union activist, Health Care, Sidi Bouzid)

The fact is that, unlike the Sidi Bouzid uprising, the spread of the Redeyef movement was slowed down greatly by the internal conflict between the regional executive committee in Gafsa, which was supported by the UGTT Executive Board, and the local section in Redeyef. Ammar, a teacher and union activist from Gafsa, explains how the events unfolded:

> Amara Abbassi, the regional secretary for Gafsa, is among the most corrupt in the union. He was one of the people who were present at the most RCD parliament sessions and is one of the country's wealthiest individuals. He used every possible means: corruption, conniving with the government to get rid of dissident unionists—left-wing and Islamists alike. . . . The regional union and all its regional and sector bodies [including in mining] criticized and conspired against the Gafsa protest movement, doing everything in their power to destroy the movement. . . . Even the UGTT Executive Board didn't do anything for more than three months, failing to mention the mining area in its newspaper, Ach-Chaab. There were decisions and press releases from the regional administrative committee defending Amara Abbassi, but nothing on Adnene or Redeyef.

Adnene Hajji adds:

> In 2008, the Gafsa regional union and mining federation fought a battle with the unionists of Redeyef. The regional union was responsible for denying the residents' right to employment, liberty and dignity. You could say that the government, CPG management and the Gafsa regional union hit the region with a triple offensive. . . . The regional executive committee was the adversary in the conflict, so it couldn't take up both roles [adversary and supporter] at the same time. And the central union bureaucracy [the UGTT Executive Board] is a strategic ally of the regional executive committee, so it couldn't support the residents of the mining area, Adnene Hajji or anyone else. . . . That was the alliance among the union bureaucracy against the revolutionary forces within the union.

Several unionists who remembered the stalemate in Redeyef in 2008 quickly moved to frame the spread of the Sidi Bouzid movement as the main challenge in overcoming the regime. The members of the Sidi Bouzid base union were able to speak with one voice, which helped them to gain the support of intermediate organizations in Sidi Bouzid and other regional bodies relatively quickly. That, in turn, ramped up the pressure on the Executive Board:

> There was a great deal of support for the 2008 movement in Redeyef among the UGTT's base unions, which held demonstrations that

could have advanced the mining area's cause, but the regional executive committee did everything in its power to stifle the movement. . . . But the December 17–January 14 revolution was different, because the UGTT's regional committees and the Executive Board were forced to support the movement, for the simple reason that the intermediate bodies in Sidi Bouzid in all sectors [education, agriculture, etc.] had stood behind the movement from the beginning. That forced the Executive Board to send a delegation to Sidi Bouzid to try to find a resolution to the crisis.

(Souleiman, union activist, Secondary Education, Sfax)

Finally, the events in Redeyef provided more than just demonstration tactics for the unionists in 2011—they also pushed the UGTT Executive Board to react more quickly in an attempt to quell the conflict before it grew even more toxic:

There were many regions that defied the Executive Board's official position and left *bayt at-tâ'a* [the home or "circle of obedience"] in 2008—including Ben Arous, Sfax and Mahdia—and sectors such as primary and secondary education that spurned the Executive Board and held campaigns in support of the mining area prisoners. Consequently, the Executive Board, which is not used to giving in, finally caved in order to prevent the UGTT from imploding. In July/August 2008, internal pressure forced the committee to support the mining area prisoners, visit prisoners' families and offer material support. . . . You'll notice that the Executive Board learned its lesson in 2010, when two of its members visited the Sidi Bouzid regional committee to calm the crisis.

(Adnene Hajji, union leader, Redeyef)

The Internal Dynamics of an Organization in Crisis

The role of the UGTT as an organization in the revolutionary process remains highly controversial to this day. There are those who believe that the union played a central role in the revolutionary process and those who dispute that assertion. Those most critical of the UGTT point to the Executive Board's late showing of support and the official positions of the secretary general.

Kais, a journalist,[10] offers his perspective:

I don't understand people who say that the UGTT played a role in the Tunisian revolution. On January 13, after his meeting with Ben Ali, [UGTT Secretary General] Jrad told the press: "I found the President to have a deep understanding of the main problems and their causes, as well as a desire to solve them."

Amina, a blogger, stated:

> I don't understand it when people tell me that the UGTT played a role
> in the revolution. I will never forget how Jrad publicly condemned the
> anti-Ben Ali slogans chanted by demonstrators on December 27. It was
> infuriating to hear him say that.

Others put forward the theory that the unionists acted independently of the
union and that the UGTT as an organization did not deserve any credit for
the fall of the regime. A manager in a state-run company explains:

> The UGTT didn't play any role in the revolution. Don't forget that they
> put down the Redeyef movement in 2008, and in 2010, unionists took
> individual action in the base and intermediate unions but the UGTT
> can't be described as having played a role in the revolution. . . . Every-
> one knows that the Executive Board, with the support of most of the
> UGTT regional committees, sided with Ben Ali. They condemned the
> slogans chanted in certain regions up until January 11.

Another journalist and human-rights activist adds:

> We all saw how when the satellite channels broadcasted information on
> the revolution in Kasserine and Sidi Bouzid, most of their information
> came from unionists. That's something that no one can deny. The union-
> ists stepped forward to save the country, just like during the colonial
> era, but the union leaders had no part in it—they were with Ben Ali
> until the eve of his fall and afterwards.

These critical viewpoints raise questions about the internal dynamics of
the union during this period. Is there evidence that the unionists acted indi-
vidually, outside of the organization? How were decisions made within the
union during the uprising? How were roles and responsibilities allocated
among the UGTT's various decision-making bodies? What explains the disparity between unionists' actions in the streets and the Executive Board's
official statements?

   In the section that follows, I will home in on the chain of events and
actors involved using an intra-organizational approach, in order to shed
light on how the UGTT—as a group of individuals governed by a specific
system of authority and allocation of roles—reacted to internal pressure
from unionist demonstrators and external pressure from the regime and the
protest environment. I will focus specifically on how the actors derive meaning from the union's organizational culture and their strategies for taking
action and interpreting the course of events.

Regional and National Decision-Making Bodies Hesitate
Between Mediation and Confrontation

Many unionists rushed to join the popular uprising, but the regional committees and the Executive Board took a wait-and-see approach that bordered on hostility. This prudent attitude led the decision-making bodies to distance themselves from slogans critical of the government. One Sfax-based teacher and union member described the attitude of the regional secretary general for Sfax during the rally held on January 2, 2011, which was held in front of the UGTT regional headquarters, in solidarity with the people of Sidi Bouzid:

> The protesters chanted a lot of slogans. And despite the relatively large number of demonstrators, the secretary general of the regional union refused to lead the demonstration and chastised the people gathered there for ignoring his instructions. Individuals loyal to him chanted slogans reminiscent of regime propaganda. The demonstrators chanted back their own slogans: "Victims of the Redeyef uprising, show your solidarity!" "The movement continues—throw the traitors out!" "Oust the people's torturer!" "Down with Destour!" "It's our right to demonstrate!" and "It's our right to express ourselves!" Demonstrators spoke out to condemn the repression against the protesters by police forces called on to fight the popular movements and there were, in fact, a large number of police officers in the streets neighboring the regional union so that they could hem the protesters in.

The UGTT Secretary General took the same attitude toward the rally on Place Mohamed Ali Hammi on December 27, 2011. That could lead one to believe that the unionists adopted strategies for action that were separate from the organization. However, upon closer inspection, the unionists' remarks reveal that their actions were closely connected to how the union functioned. Union members were able to pressure the decision-making bodies into allocating carefully chosen roles to the unionists, regional executive committees and the national executive committee. At local and regional level, the unionists obtained material resources from the UGTT, which they used to hold demonstrations and maintain ties with the social groups that took part in the protest movement. Top regional union officials immediately began working as a go-between with the local authorities to free prisoners and protect demonstrators:

> Some people are trying to downplay the UGTT's role in order to get back at the union. . . . No, the UGTT was there. Different bodies within the union took part in the revolution and had a prominent place in the movement. They handled freeing the prisoners in Sidi Bouzid. . . . Obviously, the regional executive committee had a secondary role, but it

didn't attempt to block the demonstrations, it paid for the protest signs and played a central role in freeing the prisoners. You know, in Sidi Bouzid there were about 300 prisoners from Bouzayane, Meknassi, Regueb, Jelma, etc. It was the regional committee's job to free the prisoners, calm the situation and support the families. We held rallies in front of the UGTT to turn up the pressure and the regional committee negotiated with the *wali* [governor] for the prisoners. We even were able to hold a sit-in inside the regional union.

(Farid, union official, Primary Education, Sidi Bouzid)

The secretary general of the regional union in Sidi Bouzid explains:

December 18, 2010, was a very difficult day. It was a very intense day of clashes with law enforcement. It was a day when youths burned tires and threw rocks and law enforcement retaliated with tear gas. That made the situation even more difficult and a lot of youths were arrested. The next day, on December 19, the Sidi Bouzid regional union released a statement announcing its support for the demonstrators.

Later he added:

All the unionists met at the UGTT regional headquarters that day. The UGTT headquarters welcomed people from all social backgrounds and that evening the UGTT secretary general called us. After that day, he called us day and night asking for news from the region. As a regional union, people knew that our role is to appeal to the government to free the prisoners. We tried to do so at regional level but things grew complicated and we called the Executive Board so that they could intervene. . . . The regional union held demonstrations in the different governorates and worked to free the prisoners, who numbered in the hundreds. . . . We met with the governor in Sidi Bouzid along with a UGTT delegation to ask for the prisoners to be freed so that we could calm people down.

As the events were unfolding, the Sidi Bouzid regional committee kept in contact with its regional and national counterparts to monitor the situation:

I spent my time contacting local unions. I wouldn't go to bed until I had contacted the other regions, which I would call three or four times. Places like Bouzayane, Meknassi, Jelma and Ben Aoun. The Secretary General called me regularly and held several Administrative Commission meetings.

The members of all the base and intermediate unions in every region quickly moved to join the movement, but the regional executive committees held back, limiting themselves throughout the month of December to releasing statements of support demanding that the prisoners be freed and regional inequality addressed. The statements mirrored the official position of the national executive committee, demonstrating the discipline of the regional committees and the coordination that took place. On December 21, 2010, the national executive committee sent a delegation to Sidi Bouzid in an attempt to resolve the crisis:

> We received a visit from an Executive Board delegation—Mohammed Saad and Mouldi Jendoubi—on December 21, 2010. We met with all the union bodies in Sidi Bouzid, and the conclusion released in a statement was as follows: if there is any delay in freeing the prisoners or meeting the development demands, the regional union is ready to call a regional general strike.
>
> (Foued, union official, Primary Education, Sidi Bouzid)

The regional committee sent a letter with a list of prisoners to be freed to the national executive committee on December 31, 2010. National executive committee member Mohammed Saad sent a letter to the interior minister on January 2, 2011, stating that Sidi Bouzid would initiate a general strike on January 12 if the prisoners were not freed and the police presence reduced. The strike was called off a few days later after the political prisoners were released. The interviewees provided two competing interpretations of the wait-and-see attitude displayed by the Executive Board. Some believed that the central leadership had hesitated to act because they were completely subservient to the government:

> The Executive Board was part of the regime because it supported its economic policy, signed a pact for peaceful labor relations that established negotiations on pay raises every three years . . . and January 13 symbolized the Executive Board's support (in the person of Jrad) for the government, despite what had happened. Jrad visited the deposed president on January 13, in the final throes of his reign. It's easy to imagine what transpired between them, a president under siege and the secretary general of the country's largest trade union. They met to find a solution to the crisis, and that's when Jrad issued a statement saying that the president had expressed his solidarity with the workers. That means that the UGTT's official position up until the last minute was support for the regime, which completely contradicted the general position of the base. That forced the Executive Board to support the movement, but it would have acted differently if given the choice.
>
> (Cherif, union activist, Primary Education, Sfax)

On December 27, 2010, Jrad said that the UGTT would not assume responsibility for the slogans chanted on Place Mohamed Ali Hammi.

On January 8, Abid Briki tried to speak at a rally organized by the Tunis regional union, but wasn't allowed to do so. . . . I have a video of what happened but I didn't want to release it and harm the UGTT. . . . At the time, many unionists believed the Executive Board to be in league with the government and we were afraid that the mining area tragedy would repeat itself.

(Rafik, union activist, Mining, Redeyef)

Those more critical of the UGTT even asserted that the union was against the revolution, as one opposition unionist claimed:

The UGTT's official position in December 2010 was to oppose the revolution. When people demonstrated in front of the UGTT in December, Jrad announced in the newspaper Chourouq that we couldn't be held accountable for the slogans chanted. It was as if the UGTT had invited the regime to attack us. It was a very dangerous message implying that we weren't unionists, just bums. When the police hit us, he closed the door; later he would say that the UGTT was behind the revolution. . . . The UGTT [leadership] was under great pressure from unionists to reconsider and revise its positions a bit. . . . That was when the Administrative Commission came into play. Having both the government and the UGTT leadership against us was hard. The Executive Board was pushing us into a corner so that we would trip and fall, but if you start backpedaling then you lose credibility. It was very tough but we were able to achieve what we had wanted to politically.

(Najet, union activist, Health Care, Tunis)

Other interviewees tempered this view, explaining that the wait-and-see attitude stemmed from the Executive Board's role as a mediator between social movements and the government. This mediation role prevented the UGTT, as an organization that regularly negotiates with the government, from clashing directly with the regime. From this perspective, the Executive Board's apparent hesitation reflected constraints it faced as the UGTT's highest authority. A member of the Gafsa regional committee explains:

I believe there was a tactical division of roles. How else can you interpret the role of the UGTT as an organization in the revolution? The UGTT opened up its offices to demonstrators, provided moral and material support to the movement, and then expanded its role by holding regional strikes across Tunisia. The unionists obviously had a clear role but the Executive Board did not, which was a tactical choice, in my opinion. The union bureaucracy couldn't clash with regime directly. It didn't have a clearly stated position but its views could be seen in its support for the regional unions and in its various statements. A key turning point occurred when the UGTT held a general strike on January 14, which left from Place Mohamed Ali Hammi and ended on

Avenue Habib Bourguiba in front of the interior ministry. Certain members of the Executive Board announced on Place Mohamed Ali Hammi that they were with the people and couldn't let the people down. There was a division of roles. The Executive Board needed the pressure from the streets to be able to openly make decisions that opposed the regime.

(Belgacem, member of the regional committee, Gafsa)

Adnene Hajji viewed the situation along the same lines, emphasizing the sensitive nature of this mediation role and insisting on the importance of looking past the UGTT's official positions:

The UGTT mustn't be reduced to its official positions. It's one thing to talk about the UGTT's official position and another to talk about the UGTT as an organization and all its components. The unionists at the UGTT played an important role in the revolution as a segment of the Tunisian population and as activists. The Executive Board "held the stick from the middle" and waited a long time to officially join the movement. In the beginning, they didn't want to commit, but they ended up ceding to popular pressure.

This role as a mediator facilitating dialogue between the various parties— viewed as a betrayal by those critical of the union—is described in this excerpt from a statement released by the Executive Board on December 28, 2011:

In light of the organization's responsibility and national and social role, the UGTT Executive Board has quickly moved to manage the events underway through ongoing contact between the Secretary General and various levels of the national government, in order to free those who have been arrested during the incidents in the governorates. The Executive Board is pleased that the government has reacted positively and freed most of the prisoners.

At the urging of the intermediate and base branches, the UGTT Administrative Commission compelled the national executive committee to change course and release its first statement explicitly backing the protest movement. The Administrative Commission condemned the police violence against unionists and stressed the UGTT's national and social responsibilities, expressing its solidarity

with the people of Sidi Bouzid and all inland regions in their legitimate quest for a better life and a development model that guarantees equal opportunities, the right to a decent job and hiring opportunities that provide stable income that enable them to meet their needs. They also call for urgent assistance to repair the material damage in the Sidi Bouzid region.

The UGTT took its customary stance at the crossroads of social and political considerations. Seizing on the government's waning power, the union also issued its first call for political reforms aimed at "promoting democracy and securing freedoms, as well as ensuring a more dynamic role for the Tunisian League of Human Rights, an important national actor that works to establish the rule of law and institutions, which must be allowed to hold its congress without any interference in the decision-making process." Portraying itself as a key component of "peaceful labor relations," the UGTT expressed its willingness to seek out solutions via participation in regional councils, underlining

> the need to grant UGTT representatives permanent member status on regional employment committees and local employment commissions, and reiterates their request for an unemployment benefits fund that would protect workers laid off due to economic changes, the most notable of which is the policy of privatizing state-run companies.

The statement was designed to appease the intermediate organizations and win as many concessions as possible from the declining regime.

At what point and how did the UGTT's central leadership decide to yield to pressure from unionists and face the government head-on?

Pressure From Union Members Leads to a Breakdown in the Hierarchical Decision-Making Process

Unionists ramped up the pressure on the UGTT's ruling bodies following the events in Kasserine and Thala. Buoyed by the spread of the movement, the union members put all their efforts into pushing the Executive Board to shift from negotiations to an outright battle with the regime. The organizational system was such that the intermediate branches at regional level were subjected to the greatest pressure, as one unionist from Sidi Bouzid points out:

> We encountered a lot of difficulties and the confrontation with the government was particularly tough. Obviously, the government wasn't happy with what the UGTT was doing. Do you really think that the regime would give its blessing to the UGTT, which was holding demonstrations and strikes and calling for the fall of the regime? Of course the government wasn't happy. . . . As union officials, we went through a very difficult period. You would arrive at the UGTT square [*Batlâ*] in the morning and it was full of people, the anti-riot squads surrounded the square on all sides and the street was full of cop cars. How can you cope mentally? You can't, even when tear gas grenades aren't landing right next to you. We felt a lot of pressure from society to free the prisoners. There weren't any other organizations that could help us. We received

visits from everyone: truckers, farmers, craftsmen. . . . We received visits from people from all social backgrounds, people whose son was under arrest, people who were having problems at their company—it was a really tough time.

(Hafedh, union official, Health Care, Sidi Bouzid)

This pressure sparked a crisis at the UGTT that led to an immediate breakdown in the conventional decision-making process at the union and a disregard for the central hierarchy. The regional bodies ignored the regulatory provisions in the Tunisian labor code that required prior approval from the extended executive committee and ten days' notice to strike legally. The quick succession of events and the resurgence in violence pushed the regional unions to act independently, without waiting for approval from the Executive Board. In this way, the intermediate union bodies shifted from a mediation approach to a confrontation with both the government and the UGTT leadership.

There was a bit of coordination between the regional unions, but not enough, and each region was attempting to keep up with the onrush of events. The problem with our revolution was that there was no central leadership, only a series of general strikes . . .; the general strike in Sfax was planned long in advance and they didn't wait for approval from the Administrative Commission, which only recognized the legitimacy of the strike after the fact.

(Cherif, union activist, Primary Education, Sfax)

That historic event would not have taken place if the base and intermediate unions hadn't exerted pressure. In Sfax, for example, the regional executive committee had decided to hold a meeting on January 9, 2011, to review issues concerning retirement. They prepared everything needed to hold a successful meeting but we contacted the UGTT leadership on January 9 to refuse the meeting, because the country was going through a serious political crisis. The base and intermediate unions pressured the regional committee, which turned the meeting on retirement into a meeting to discuss the situation in the country. The conclusion of the meeting was historic: the decision to hold a large demonstration and a general regional strike.

(Moufida, union activist, Postal Service, Tunis)

Unionists freed themselves from the domination of the Executive Board and its hegemonic designs by objecting to the provision requiring ten days' notice for strikes, which had enabled the leadership to sign certain agreements against unionists' will and prevent the movement from spiraling out of their control. The crisis incited the unionists to set aside the "sanctity" of the hierarchy in order to make the decisions they deemed necessary to the needs of the protest movement:

> I would like to emphasize the fact that the true leaders of all these protests are from intermediate bodies, in particular the regional unions. However, the regional executive committees are tied down, by which I mean that even if they are democratically elected, power relationships have been established over the past few years that have led their members to hold the hierarchy as sacred. . . . You'll find progressive regional executive committees in regions like Sfax, but when it comes to major central decisions and political moves, the committees fall in line behind the central leadership's decisions in almost a military manner. The intermediate bodies are the only ones who can skirt these decisions.
>
> As a result, there is a large-scale battle between the intermediate bodies and the central leadership, which puts a great deal of pressure on all the organizations in order to curb their activist undercurrent. There are nevertheless protest movements that emerge from time to time, such as the conflict in Sfax last year [2010] between the Sfax executive committee and certain sectors, which ended with the suspension of union terms of office and firings. But in 2011, the Executive Board was faced with a difficult choice: either continue with its former policy of deferring judgment and promising to negotiate with Abdel Aziz Ben Dhia [special advisor to Ben Ali and official spokesman of the presidency] or join the protest movement, which had begun to bear resemblance to a revolution, especially after the police violence and the attacks on women and people in their homes.
>
> (Cherif, union activist, Primary Education, Sfax)

Consequently, in its subsequent meetings, the Administrative Commission provided legal cover for the unionists' decisions on the ground rather than serve as a decision-making body in its own right:

> Beginning on January 3 or 4, 2011, the Administrative Commission held a series of meetings during which it made decisions that gave the regions more freedom to make their own decisions to suit their needs. The Administrative Commission meetings became increasingly frequent and were very short. Why? Because the decisions were actually being made outside the Administrative Commission. The role of the commission changed; it sought to provide legal cover for decisions quickly and without any hang-ups. This radical change occurred because the movement from December 17 to January 14 stunned everyone—it was an existential movement. Unionists no longer acted based on union or electoral considerations or allegiances; they began to rely on their conscience. Unionists who had always made decisions based on the wishes

of the UGTT central leadership and would support the leadership without being prompted to do so, those unionists changed at that moment and began to do only what their conscience told them.

(Slim, union official, Healthcare, Tunis)

The power struggle between the intermediate sections and the Executive Board, which would definitely alter the course of events, played out during the administrative committee meeting held on January 11, 2011. The window for dialogue had closed and the UGTT called a strike. After having welcomed and backed the popular uprising, the unionists succeeded in pushing the Executive Board—via the Administrative Commission—to take a more offensive stance in support of the protestors and their demands. The negotiations ended with the decision to let the regions choose the date of their general strike. This compromise represented a success for the intermediate bodies, which were able to push through their decisions, but it also reflected the central leadership's continual focus on leaving room for maneuver in order to avoid cutting all ties with the government. Note that at the time, no one could have predicted the events that would follow or the fall of the government—the UGTT was not in any position to call for the government's demise.

A member of the Tunis Administrative Commission stresses this point:

> You have to evaluate the role of the UGTT from two perspectives: the first is from that of the central leadership and the second is from that of the local, regional and sector unions. You can't evaluate each in the same way. The intermediate sections—the local, regional, sector and base unions—played a leading role in the uprising, which was clear for all to see. Take the example of Sidi Bouzid. It was clear that everything was going through the local unions: the meetings, organization and protection. . . . Remember that the central leadership sent a delegation on December 20 to calm the revolution, so they didn't take the same attitude as the intermediate structures, which took part in the revolution. When I say "central leadership," I mean the Administrative Commission and not the Executive Board. The leadership was under pressure due to the events, which pushed them to decide in favor of a strike. But they wanted to avoid direct confrontation with the government and the responsibility of a general strike, so they opted for a series of regional strikes. . . . The leadership appeared to offload its responsibilities by delegating them to the regions and telling each to do as it pleased.
>
> (Raouf, union official, Energy, Tunis)

Redeyef-based teacher and unionist Adel expressed similar thoughts:

> The UGTT held an Administrative Commission meeting on January 11, 2011, to examine the situation. The idea was to organize a general strike across the country and the UGTT leadership felt the burden of

that responsibility and wanted to distance itself from it and negotiate. That is why they decided that each region would choose the date of its strike; each regional committee had to meet and decide which day to strike. By coincidence, the regional unions in Sfax, Tunis and Gafsa called strikes on the same day. They didn't plan it that way, it was an accident.

After the revolution, certain unionists reinterpreted the fall of Ben Ali on January 14, 2011, as a consequence of the Administrative Commission meeting on January 11, 2011, which they held up as a historic event—the culmination of a series of social movements spanning two decades, in particular Redeyef in 2008. The interviewees' detailed description of the organizational dynamics at the UGTT during the uprising suggests that there was no disconnect between the unionists' actions and the organizational framework in which they acted. Even the circumvention of the hierarchical decision-making process was quickly resolved by the central leadership, which covered for all the decisions taken at the local and regional levels. The political crisis led to unexpected events, such as violent police repression and the rapid spread of the movement, yet the codified system of roles and well-oiled procedures remained a source of inspiration for the unionists, who were charged with establishing coordination mechanisms and assigning roles to the various hierarchical bodies, as well as devising methods for pressuring the Executive Board into changing its stance. This formal structure, which drew from the union's unique historical trajectory, provided a framework for the various participants to interact, communicate, coordinate their actions and create a shared understanding that guided them in the strategies they pursued. The paradox often cited by the public—the divide between the official position of the Executive Board and that of the base and intermediate unions in terms of support for the uprising—can only be understood by accounting for the unique organizational dynamics at the UGTT.

The interplay between pressure and negotiation at the UGTT, which had a profound impact on the outcome of the Redeyef and Sidi Bouzid movements, in 2008 and 2010, respectively, appears to be rooted in the UGTT's unique organizational culture. What drives this dynamic?

The Organizational Culture at the UGTT Inspires Unionists' Actions

The interviewees' remarks reveal that they drew a great deal of inspiration from the culture at the UGTT. Two factions have long coexisted at the union: a "reformist" group capable of reaching compromises with the government, and another, more radical group which knows that, with sufficient pressure, it can make the leadership cede to popular demands. On that basis, the unionists were able to predict that the Executive Board would avoid a showdown with the government. They also knew that the Executive Board would only join the movement if they were able to exert enough pressure to tip the scales towards the people:

> The Executive Board has a classic strategy: it always studies the balance of power. If the base unions don't exert any pressure, they play into the hands of the government—the hands of the most powerful. The base unions play a key role in changing the direction of the union bureaucracy.
> (Najet, union activist, Health Care, Tunis)

> The UGTT has a unique position. The UGTT can't stand behind the revolutionary movement, it can't incite it, but it is unique in that its democratically elected leaders side with the social movements and the people's demands when social conflicts flare up. When that happens, the UGTT is forced to support the people's demands.
> (Mohamed Trabelsi, former UGTT Deputy Secretary General)

When describing the strategies used to pressure the Executive Board, the interviewees outlined three organizational relationships that underpin the culture at the union. The unionists' knowledge of these structural, regional/sector-based and political relationships greatly aided them in achieving their goals. The structural relationship signifies that the base and intermediate sections will always back social demonstrations, but the Executive Board acts based on the balance of power inherent to each demonstration:

> The strength of the UGTT resides in the base sections starting with the base unions. The base sections handle outreach. The unionists from those sections do volunteer work—they are the ones who sacrifice their family life and time to dedicate themselves to union work. They are always there; they are union workaholics. They are the only unionists who can protect the continuity and continued existence of the organization.
> (Ridha, union official, Postal Service, Bizerte)

> There is another distinction to be made, which is structural. You have to distinguish between the central leadership and the intermediate leadership, which has always been on the side of the working class. Under Ben Ali, the UGTT central leadership tried to exploit the working class by gifting peaceful labor relations to Ben Ali. There were few strikes under Jrad. From time to time, sectors would try to strike and the UGTT leadership would heed the government's request to convince them to give up on their demands. Those who refused to obey orders were systematically persecuted.
> (Fouzia, human rights activist)

In addition to the structural relationship between the various decision-making bodies, a regional and sector-based distinction came into play. The interviewees differentiated between the UGTT sectors and regions that have traditionally been bastions of resistance against the government and those with a more conciliatory, "reformist" approach:

> The UGTT is a mass organization and the members among its ranks are "yellow" unionists, but revolutionaries can also operate from within. A yellow union is a reformist union within the UGTT. There are two ideologies, the first being a left-wing, radical, democratic ideology that is most prevalent in the base and intermediate unions (as well as a few federations and a few regional unions). This faction believes in the importance of establishing democratic, activist practices at the UGTT and seizing positions of power democratically. On the other side is the bureaucratic faction that believes in the importance of a contractual policy in which the UGTT serves as a mediator between the working class and capital, an "intermediary." The UGTT leadership—the Executive Board and certain federations and major unions—belong to that faction. You find the radical ideology in primary and secondary education, tobacco, etc. and in certain regions like Sidi Bouzid, Gafsa, Sfax, Kasserine and Ben Arous. You find the contractual ideology in Tunis and on the coast.
>
> (Houssem, union activist, Postal Service, Sfax)

These two organizational relationships are closely intertwined with the political ties between the UGTT leadership and the ruling power. As mentioned earlier, the UGTT leadership alternated between periods of submission, consensus and confrontation with the single-party state. Ammar, a teacher and unionist from Gafsa, even describes the union bureaucracy as the ruling power's "Siamese twin":

> The union bureaucracy is the Siamese twin of the PSD [Socialist Destourian Party]. I'll give you three historical examples. During the battle between Salah Ben Youssef and Bourguiba at the PSD, do you know what played a decisive role in the battle and a decisive role in strengthening Bourguiba's hand over Ben Youssef? The UGTT Congress in Sfax in 1954. The second example is the bread riots [*intinfadhet elkhoubz*] in 1984. There were martyrs during that revolt, and what was the position of the union leadership at the time? It supported the decision to lower the compensation for the price of staple goods. And now, during the current revolution, what was the position of the UGTT leadership? It supported the government up to the last minute.

For his part, Rached, an activist and unionist, emphasizes the contentious nature of the relationship between the UGTT leadership and the single-party state:

> One may disagree with the UGTT leadership and the direction the UGTT has taken in politics and as a union, but we know that in its

history, the UGTT has played a decisive role in establishing policy in Tunisia, and has done so since Farhat Hached. The UGTT played a significant role in the liberation movement and had a hot-and-cold relationship with Destour, the Bourguiba regime and the Ben Ali regime. Sometimes they were enemies and sometimes they were friends. A relationship that oscillated between consensus and rejection. . . . The government's influence [on the UGTT] has been restricted to the Executive Board in recent years. There was a relationship based on negotiation and partnership with the UGTT. The relationship with the government resulted in double talk on the part the UGTT leadership: one message for the regions "on edge" and another in meetings with the government.

(Rached, union activist, Postal Service, Sfax)

Adnene Hajji notes the repercussions of this contentious relationship on the internal dynamics of the organization and the tensions between those seeking autonomy for the union and those who favored a conciliatory approach with the ruling power:

The 2008 conflict at the UGTT was not new—historically there has always been conflict at the UGTT. The UGTT is an organization with a highly diverse make-up and the only trade union in the country. Historically, the union played a role in the struggle for independence and building the nation. The UGTT leadership rivals that of the PSD and Bourguiba. All political camps in the country had members in the UGTT and there was a conflict because the government attempted to subdue [*tadjîn*] the UGTT. Historically, the PSD had the UGTT under its thumb following independence. For example, the series of secretaries general at the helm of the organization, including Ben Salah and Achour, all belonged to the single party. Achour was also on the PSD Political Committee and didn't leave it until 1977. In 1978, a push for independence emerged at the UGTT alongside the growth of the left-wing movement and the relationship between the union bureaucracy and the regional executive committees developed into a historic conflict. This could be seen in how the union's goals were expressed at congresses during different periods of union activism. They [the union leaders] were thought of as traitors, as people who had betrayed workers and exploited their cause, extending their slavery and misery in society.

All three of these relationships—structural, regional/sector and political—have produced a unique organizational culture based on pressure and negotiations, which governs relations between the Executive Board and the ruling power as well as those between the central leadership and dissident groups. This organizational culture, which is the product of the union's specific political history and culture (cf. Chapter 1), resulted in alternating periods of conflict and cooperation between the UGTT and the ruling power, as well as concurrent strategies for allegiance to/dependence on the regime and pockets of autonomy and resistance within the union. This is what enabled unionists to pursue strategies involving pressure and negotiation in order to shift the position of the Executive Board, achieve their aims and allay crises that could have caused a rift within the organization. As former UGTT Deputy Secretary General Mohamed Trabelsi so eloquently put it, "There has always been unity in the conflict and a conflict in the unity."

> The PSD and UGTT both had the same modernist plan for the country, but they sometimes disagreed on the issue of democracy, the independence of the UGTT, social justice and the redistribution of wealth. At times, the conflict would be more pronounced, and at others, there would be consensus, but there has always been unity in the conflict and a conflict in the unity.
>
> There is an Oriental proverb: the fish rots from the head. In Tunisia, we have an interesting phenomenon—the head can be rotten but the rest of the body intact. At the UGTT, even when the head is rotten, the rest of the organization is steadfast. While the union appears to have a pyramid structure where everything is supervised, in practice, there are several autonomous areas.
>
> (Fouzia, human rights activist)

In the past, this organizational culture has enabled the UGTT to maintain close ties with the working class without cutting the cord with the single-party state, giving the union what Tunis-based journalist and unionist Tarek terms an "intuitive political sense." He says that this sense is the reason why the Executive Board was able to correct its stance at the last minute in order to conserve its role in the political landscape:

> The UGTT is a dynamic organization, mainly thanks to its intermediate sections, which took brave stances under the dictatorship. But the Executive Board has always been a problem. Certain secretaries general of regional unions are great but when they become members of the Executive Board, they change their politics. It's as if when you join the Executive Board, there are things you can't say and lines you can't cross. . . . That being said, the central leadership can be criticized for many things but not for its political sense, which helps it know when to rethink its position. The leadership never jumped off the Ben Ali ship, but it set itself straight in time. It had a foot on each side.

Box 3 The Organizational Culture at the UGTT

The central leadership is always late to support movements, which is why some view its attitude as a form of hesitation. I'm not justifying the central leadership's position, only trying to analyze the situation objectively, in order to avoid basing our interpretation on subjective positions and analyses. The UGTT has to fulfill three roles that can be contradictory and difficult to reconcile, the first of which is to serve as a refuge [*maljaâ*].

The UGTT's second role is as an opponent of government decisions. There are many political dissidents at the UGTT, who influence general opinion at the union through their presence in several base unions, federations, regional unions and even the Administrative Commission. While they are not in the majority, they are influential, if only in terms of contesting the regime's economic, social and political decisions. Consequently, the UGTT is asked to be both the opposition and part of the government, because unionists "take refuge" there to solve their problems—and not only those that are union-related. For example, they may ask the UGTT for favors like retrieving a passport, obtaining a loan from a bank, or a job transfer. That role is not unlike that of the government.

The third role is the union's natural role as a partner in labor relations that achieves progress for workers in areas such as pay raises, social security, employment laws, etc. For the central leadership, this involves opposing the government—which requires keeping a distance—while achieving the traditional aims of a trade union and dealing with the government. It has to take part in the labor dialogue in order to achieve progress for workers. It takes a lot of acrobatics to maintain balance in all that. Managing these three roles is a very delicate and very difficult task. . . .

So the UGTT brought together several political camps and groups, each with their own expectations. There were those who wanted the UGTT to work toward social progress, and others who wanted to use the UGTT as a base for criticizing the regime and its decisions. And then there were those who used it as a place of power where they could fulfill their personal ambitions. As a result, experience has led the central leadership to never rush into backing social movements. The leadership studies the situation and checks to see if the demands are legitimate, if the Executive Board should support them or not. Generally speaking, when the central leadership sees that the various regional and sector-based unions have backed demands, pressure mounts on the Executive Board, which ends up doing the same. The committee obviously always tries to avoid political demands that oppose the regime—it always tries to avoid direct confrontation with the regime but when pressure mounts, it doesn't have a choice. It can't sidestep pressure from the base. That's what happened on Mohammed Ali Hammi Square the day when the Secretary General said that slogans like "The People want the regime to fall" and any other slogans that targeted the "ruling family" did not in any way represent the UGTT. The leadership always tries to avoid actions that push it toward direct confrontation with the regime; it has to take precautions to constantly maintain room for maneuver to be able intervene when it needs to sort out a situation or serve as a mediator. The central leadership is in a very delicate position and that is why it is always late to back causes—it studies and checks. . . . In the end, it has to join the movement due to pressure from its sections.

As a consequence, given the delicate situation of the Executive Board, there is always a divide between the base sections and the national sections.

Abdeljelil Bedoui, UGTT economist, expert and advisor

What is more, the union regularly returns to its collective memory of past struggles in order to give meaning to its actions and serve as a guide during moments of crisis, which further strengthens its organizational culture. Gafsa resident Jilani looks back on the unionists' demonstration against the Israeli attacks in Gaza, in 2009:

In 2009 during the war in Gaza, I remember it well: Mohamed Ali Hammi Place was packed with people. At the time, the Executive Board didn't see any problem with us demonstrating for Arab causes. They welcomed us back then and supported the movement for solidarity with Gaza. But the unionists—especially the left-wing ones—succeeded in bridging the Gaza protests with the mining area movement, which put pressure on the Executive Board. One of the slogans was "Undivided demands, Redeyef to Gaza."

(Jilani, unemployed, UDC)

Mohammed, a textile union official in Ben Arous, notes that various demonstrations were held at the UGTT, despite the regime's control over the Executive Board:

It's true that Bouazizi was the spark, but there were other struggles that laid the foundation, such as the battle within the UGTT over raising the retirement age and the internal conflict at the UGTT over the support for Ben Ali's candidacy in 2009. The Administrative Commission ended up supporting Ben Ali's candidacy—it was the last organization to do so and the support was conditional.

On a similar note, Béchir, a teacher and union activist in Redeyef, adds:

Our strength is the organization we have gained through an accumulation of struggles at the UGTT. We have devoted ourselves to several Arab causes such as Iraq and Palestine, we organize demonstrations, etc. In 2006, we started supporting the unemployed graduates that were holding a sit-in at the UGTT by protecting them and keeping their spirits up.

The UGTT's collective memory, which was long suppressed by the regime, has served as a key resource in movements ranging from the fight for independence to the crises at the UGTT in 1978 and 1984, as well as the recent demonstrations for Arab (Palestine, 2009) and national (Redeyef, 2008) causes. This memory, which is implicit in all the interviewees' remarks, shapes unionists' language and practices.

> In my eyes, Redeyef is the heart of the revolution because it laid the foundation for the revolutionary process. There wouldn't have been a revolution without the 2008 movement. I see it as a build-up of events over the course of history; the 2008 movement is the accumulated result of other struggles, which set the stage for the 2011 revolution.
>
> (Adnene Hajji, union leader, Redeyef)

> The UGTT played a central role in the success of the revolution throughout and provided guidance rooted in its historical legacy as a stakeholder in Tunisian society. The UGTT had human and structural mechanisms that enabled it to adapt to each period in history, from independence to the crises at the union in 1978 and 1985, up to the December 17 revolution. This historical legacy, an accumulation of past struggles, has enabled the union to overcome several crises. . . . Several unionists and national leaders took part in this series of struggles. It's true that the December 17 revolution against the oppressive regime did not have any leadership, but no one can deny that this accumulation of struggles, this legacy, was the catalyst that enabled several different generations to manage social crises and political differences. . . . It can be said, then, that the UGTT played a vital role in guiding the revolution, from the initial spark in Sidi Bouzid and the death of the martyr Bouazizi.
>
> (Omar, union activist, Education, Bizerte)

> I think that the revolution started a few years ago. I would place the start of the process in 1971 [the year of the Korba Congress] with the development of the student movement and the emergence of the first left-wing movements, which were repressed by the former regime. But the most recent event that set the stage for the revolution was in the mining area, where clear demands were put forward and guided by militant unionists. Unfortunately, however, the UGTT—via the Executive Board, which was in contact with Ben Ali—succeeded in putting down the movement and its activists were jailed and fired from their jobs, to say nothing of the martyrs that fell.
>
> (Chedhli, union activist, Secondary Education, Sfax)

It is not surprising that all the unionists interviewed have since reconstructed the events in a way that emphasizes an "accumulation of struggles."

While the idea ignores the unique circumstances of the December 17 uprising, it does have the virtue of revealing the extent to which unionists cannot help but uphold the identity of the UGTT. This social and political legacy, which is passed on from generation to generation and archived by the organization's formal bodies, both provided unionists with significant resources for the movement and fostered a strong sense of identity that later enabled the UGTT to maintain its place in the political landscape in the face of various political crises.

> The first secret of the UGTT is that its history is a series of events, which are archived and kept as part of a memory that is passed on from generation to generation within the organization through its bodies and meetings. That is what guarantees continuity. Mohammed Ali, Hached and others made their mark on the independence and union movements, influencing several generations. As I told you earlier, the UGTT has a great sense of national duty. Unionists have been loyal to the interests of the nation throughout the union's history, which shows that the UGTT's heritage is clearly one of the union's distinctive characteristics. In addition to national causes, the UGTT has also defended universal principles such as individual and collective liberties, independence and democratic practices. All of that forms part of the UGTT's heritage and strengthens it even further.
>
> (Ridha, union official, Postal Service, Bizerte)

In Conclusion

The unionists recognize that they are not the ones who instigated the popular uprising on December 17, 2010, but they all stressed that they had provided logistical and political "guidance" to the movement. The balance of power favored the popular uprising but the movement lacked leadership, so the unionists stepped in to provide the material, organizational and political resources required to gradually transform a spontaneous *intifada* into a revolutionary process that hastened the fall of Ben Ali. They drew from experiences in past movements and strategies for adjusting to unforeseen developments. The unionists' challenges, goals and expectations were regularly thrown into disorder by the unpredictable reactions of the regime and the shifting dynamics of the protest movement.

At the same time, the unionists' accounts reveal how they carried out all their collective actions within an organizational framework that provided a stable point of reference for the movement. The political crisis led to unexpected events, such as violent police repression and the rapid spread of the movement, but the codified system of roles, rules and procedures provided a blueprint for action for the unionists, who were charged with establishing coordination mechanisms and assigning roles, as well as devising methods for pressuring the Executive Board into changing its stance. The unionists' strategy appears to have resulted from both foresight gained from their intricate knowledge of the organization and the unpredictability of the effect their actions would have on the course of events and the other actors in the movement. The Executive Board, which had successfully controlled and refocused past social movements, was taken by surprise and, for the first time, was compelled to cede to pressure from the base and attack the regime head-on. The revolutionary process, which pushed certain regional unions and federations to distance themselves from the Executive Board and make decisions independently, set a precedent that paved the way for new relations between the intermediate sections and the central leadership. This created an opportunity for a more equal balance of power and an end to the hegemonic excesses of the Executive Board.

More broadly, the case of the UGTT raises questions about the role of organizations in transforming an uprising into a revolutionary process capable of establishing a long-term alternative to an incumbent political regime. There is no doubt that the UGTT's centralized hierarchical structure—several local, regional, federal and national levels with more than half a million people from all walks of life—gave the union political sway and an ability to unite Tunisians on an unparalleled scale. Backed by a long history of activism and a unique organizational culture that combined strategies for pressure and negotiation, the UGTT was able to both maintain cohesion despite internal tensions caused by the uprising and serve as the driving force behind a coordination network comprising several groups of actors that focused the protest movement and hastened the fall of Ben Ali.

Lastly, the collective memory of the UGTT's struggles supplied unionists with the resources needed to interact, communicate and attribute a shared meaning to the movement. This collective memory is also what led the unionists to depict the end of Ben Ali's reign as the expected, predictable result of an "accumulation of struggles." That rhetoric featured prominently in the events that followed, when it was used to negotiate the union's role in the fast-changing Tunisian political landscape.

Notes

1. *Intifada* is an Arabic term that means "uprising." Used to describe a revolt against an oppressive regime or foreign enemy, the word is often associated with the people's resistance movement against the Israeli occupation of Palestine in December 1987 and September 2000.
2. The quotes presented in this chapter are excerpts from interviews mainly conducted in January and February 2011. They serve to demonstrate that unionists, whatever their region, sector or position, employ the same classification to describe how the UGTT operates, reflecting the influence of the union's organizational framework on the strategies adopted and methods for coping with the various crises they encountered.
3. There is a notable exception to the sweeping opinion expressed by this interviewee. The police barged into the UGTT offices and arrested a large number of unionists during the incidents that took place on January 26, 1978.

4. Amor Cherni (2011, 198) notes that the expression "guidance" is used ambiguously in UGTT literature. The term may refer to the organizations that endeavored to keep the movement from overstepping boundaries in ways that would not benefit anyone. The expression was also used in relation to the experienced officials that the UGTT "lent" to the movement to lead activist initiatives and demonstrations in the street, in order to expand the protests and attain the goals that had been set. Within the context of my research, the word "guidance" pertains to the unionists' efforts to organize and politicize the movement.
5. The unionists who joined the movement at the outset mainly belonged to left-wing and far-left parties such as the Tunisian Communist Workers' Party (PCOT) and the Democratic Patriots' Movement (Watad) or Arab nationalist groups.
6. The term "young people" is polysemous; depending on the context, it may refer to an age group, cyber activists, young people from disadvantaged neighborhoods, unemployed graduates or sometimes all these groups together. Whenever possible, I specify whom the unionists are talking about when they use the term.
7. Founded on May 25, 2006, UDC is an organization that seeks to represent unemployed graduates in their efforts to actions to exercise their right to work. On February 18, 2011, the union obtained official authorization in the form of a visa from the ministry of the interior, which authorizes the creation of political parties, unions and associations. The organization now boasts more than 10,000 members and has a presence in all 24 governorates via its local and regional sections.
8. The union opposition within the UGTT held an initial rally called the "democratic union gathering" (*al-liqâ' an-naqâbî dimoqratî*) on Place Mohamed Ali Hammi on December 25, 2010.
9. Meanwhile, the executive board at the Tunisian Order of Lawyers called a general lawyers' strike in all courts on January 14, 2011, to show solidarity with the families of the victims and support the demonstrators' demands. For more information on the lawyers' role in the Tunisian revolution, cf. Éric Gobe, (2013, 295–308).
10. Most of the journalists interviewed work for national daily newspapers and cover Tunisian society.

3 The UGTT's Polarizing Role During the Transition

> The culture at the UGTT is such that when the leadership wavers on a decision and pressure mounts from the base, the leaders end up falling into line—that's what the public fails to understand. Some reduce the organization's initiatives to the work of individuals within the organization. Several anti-UGTT campaigns took place in the days after January 14 and people wanted to break up the UGTT. Only those who have done union work can understand the organization's culture. The UGTT operates like a tribe. It has endured several crises and paid dearly, it has been broken up and unionists have been imprisoned. This series of struggles is what gives unionists the energy and the means to take action and adapt to each new situation.
>
> Ridha, union official, Postal Service, Bizerte

The fall of Ben Ali on January 14, 2011, marked the start of a major political crisis in Tunisia characterized by political and institutional instability, which led to an explosion of different forms of demonstrations and demands across the country in various segments of Tunisian society. New battlegrounds emerged between political and social actors during this transitional period, which lasted from January 15 to October 11, 2011—the date on which the National Constituent Assembly (ANC) elections were held—upending the common conventions and rules that had dictated relations between the government and the governed. The stakes were decidedly high: a new political order was taking shape. The fundamental issue of how to carry out the "democratic transition"[1] dominated discussion during the period. The absence a democratically elected government led very heated tensions to arise between the proponents of a legalist approach advocating institutional continuity and their opponents, who sought revolutionary legitimacy and a radical break with the former regime. During this debate, the UGTT reprised the role it had played during the uprising on December 17, 2010, deciding to speak out and serve as a "key"[2] stakeholder in efforts to restructure the Tunisian political landscape. The union's political stance as an intermediary between the social movements and the government proved highly controversial during this turbulent period. An impassioned debate pitted those who backed a central political role for the UGTT during the transition phase against others who appealed for the union to focus solely on social issues. Various groups mounted attacks on the UGTT after January 14, and some, such as the RCD, went so far as to urge the union to disband. Certain groups even attempted to rewrite the events leading up to the fall of Ben Ali, omitting the role played by the union in the uprising and downplaying the actions of its members as the work of a handful of individuals who acted on their own initiative.

One question continued to crop up during the debates: what is the main goal of the UGTT? To seize power, impose the thinking of far-left groups, or help the economic and political elite stay in power?

In the pages that follow, I will focus on how unionists view the UGTT's role during the transition phase leading up to the elections. I will then turn to the campaigns carried out against the UGTT, which greatly influenced the events that would follow and provide insight into the clashes between various political actors. I will contrast unionists' interpretation of the events with criticisms from various stakeholders. Next I will use the unionists' assessment of the UGTT's actions to shed light on the internal and external challenges the organization faced in restructuring the Tunisian political landscape. Finally, I will explain how the union's unique identity serves as a useful framework for understanding the various strategies adopted.[3]

Image 3.1 Kasbah Sit-in, January 23, 2011.

Image 3.2 El Menzah Sports Palace Sit-in (Kobba), February 28, 2011.

The UGTT: Central Power or Countervailing Power During the Transition Phase?

The shifting political situation in Tunisia in between Ben Ali's departure on January 11, 2011, and the National Constituent Assembly elections on October 23, 2011, can be divided into three phases.

The first phase, which lasted from January 15 to 28, 2011, saw the formation of a "national unity" government led by incumbent prime minister Mohammed Ghannouchi,[4] comprising members of the former Ben Ali cabinet (RCD),[5] members of the "legal" opposition[6]—the Progressive Democratic Party (PDP),[7] the Democratic Forum for Labor and Liberties (FDTL/Ettakatol)[8] and Ettajdid[9]—and union figures with close ties to the UGTT. The government's main responsibility was to prepare for the presidential elections expected to be held within six months.[10] The appointment of RCD ministers to key positions in this initial government was met with public backlash—protesters from inland regions immediately banded together to demand its dissolution. The FDTL and UGTT ministers resigned the day after the government was formed.[11] The UGTT shifted its position at the urging of its base, taking part in setting up a national council tasked with protecting the revolution and backing the public pressure on the government. Following the occupation of Place du Gouvernement (Kasbah I),[12] the square facing the seat of government, the cabinet was reshuffled on January 27, 2011, and the RCD figures were ousted from the central ministries.

During the second phase, which began in mid-February, Place du Gouvernement was occupied for a second time (Kasbah II). On February 25, 2011, a crowd of nearly 100,000 demonstrated in front of the seat of government, brandishing messages that included calls for the Ghannouchi government to resign and for National Constituent Assembly[13] (ANC) elections to be held. This movement led to Mohammed Ghannouchi being replaced by Béji Caïd Essebsi—who had served as minister several times under Bourguiba and as President of the Chamber of Deputies under Ben Ali[14]—as Prime Minister. The 1959 constitution was suspended and constituent assembly elections were scheduled for July 24, 2011. Interim President Fouad Mbazaa and the government ministers pledged not to run for office. The Béji Caïd Essebsi government, which was described as technocratic or skill-based and derived its legitimacy from national unity, as well as in its expertise, led the country during the run-up to the elections on October 11, 2011. The government was supposed to shield itself from the political bickering, managing day-to-day business and preparing for the constituent assembly elections. However, in actuality, positions were given to former Ben Ali and Bourguiba ministers, as well as well-connected elites from both incumbent and opposition circles. A new institution called the High Authority for Realization of the Objectives of the Revolution, Political Reform and Democratic Transition was tasked with overseeing the political transition. Six authority members represented the UGTT out of a total of 155 from various political parties and areas of civil society.[15] The UGTT's purview shifted from providing guidance and protection to the social movement to playing a high-profile role in politics.

> The UGTT decided not to join the government but the most important thing to remember is that the union helped ramp up the pressure—it was clearly a key participant in the Kasbah I and Kasbah II sit-ins. During the *intifada*, the UGTT served as a refuge for the social movements, supporting initiatives led by unionists and political activists from certain regions that had joined the movement. After January 14, the UGTT

assumed leadership of the events and the *intifada*. . . . To understand the UGTT's role in the Kasbah I sit-in, consider the big meeting at the Arab Maghreb Workers' Union headquarters. All the political powers were present, including those that formed part of the government, such as the PDP. . . . Jrad chaired the meeting, which says a lot about the role of the UGTT in the fall of the second government.

(Choukri, journalist)

How do the unionists view the role played by the UGTT in managing the transitional period that transformed the post-January 14 political landscape?

The UGTT assumed a central political role in the country, bolstered by its part in ousting Ben Ali, the weakened position of the RCD and rifts among the opposition. Freed from state control, the union decided to impose its will during the transition:

Beginning on January 18, the UGTT began to show more confidence—you could tell that it had decided to ignore the government's instructions and it began to act more as a partner to the state that could impose its will. From that point onwards, the leadership began to chart a new path and the balance of power shifted in the Executive Board. . . . The UGTT's renewed confidence, which enabled it to break free from certain limitations, can also be explained by the shockwave that hit the interior ministry and its weakened position afterwards. . . . Questions can also be raised about the relationship between the UGTT and the army, which became the country's primary security force. . . . How did relations evolve between the two institutions? These questions are difficult to answer, but one thing is sure: the UGTT played a vital role in transforming the political landscape.

(Tarek, journalist)

Former UGTT Deputy Secretary General Mohamed Trabelsi went so far as to claim that the UGTT could have governed the country and led the transition phase, but was prevented from doing so by the lack of broad political consensus both inside and outside the union:

After Ben Ali fled and the regime had fallen, the two most influential institutions were the army and the UGTT. The army couldn't take power because it wasn't prepared or well versed in exercising power. . . The UGTT couldn't do so because it had not reached the political consensus required to govern during the transition phase. . . . There wasn't a clear vision of how to proceed—everyone was taken aback and there was no consistent take on what to do because there were independent unionists and unionists who showed more loyalty to the leaders of their political party. . . . The UGTT couldn't take power but it could have led the transition; it could have brought everyone together and united the democratic forces in the country to establish the rules of the democratic transition. A number of factors prevented the UGTT from taking the lead during this period: a lack of clarity, a lack of objective perspective on the situation, the diverse make-up of the UGTT leadership, the fact that the UGTT's abilities were underestimated, and a lack of charismatic leaders.

At the same time, the interviewees' accounts highlight how the UGTT, like every other political actor, had to cope with the fluctuations and uncertainty caused by the unstable political situation. The UGTT, like all other political organizations, was pulled in two directions: it was urged both to act as a countervailing power and to negotiate with the government. In the end, the UGTT's self-identified role as a countervailing power led the union to seek to build consensus with the various political and social forces at play. This made the union an adversary to both political camps and a lightning rod for passionate emotions from all sides. In the pages that follow, we will see that the negotiations over the UGTT's role in the transition phase developed from a multi-faceted process characterized by doubts, adjustments and clashes spurred by the advance of the protest movement and quarrels among the political class.

The UGTT Tests the Waters

A rift emerged in the post-January 14 political landscape over how to assess the situation—was it a revolution?—and appropriately manage it, i.e. whether to seek continuity or break with the former regime (International Crisis Group, 2011). The political parties that decided to join the government, such as the PDP and Ettajdid, viewed the situation less as a revolution than a politically rudderless uprising, and thus backed institutional continuity and avoided overly direct opposition to the former regime in order to prevent chaos. The PDP Secretary General explains (quoted in International Crisis Group, *op. cit.*):

> What took place was more than an intifada but less than a revolution; it put us in a delicate intermediary phase in which we were somewhat forced to build on the old. The transition phase has to build on what already exists, which means constitutional continuity with a transition at institutional level. Why? Because while this a popular revolution, it lacks political direction. We have to limit the damage and combine the political rupture with the existing institutions.

This rift also divided public opinion. The close-knit unity of the mythic people that rose up to "drive out the dictator" gave way to political and social disputes (Abdessamad, 2012). The Kobba[16] sit-in held on February 28, 2011, for instance, was organized by middle-class groups—managers, civil

servants and small business owners—who refused to let their Kasbah counterparts speak on behalf of the people. The Kobba group declared themselves the "silent majority," a term echoed in the press the next day. They
supported Prime Minister Mohammed Ghannouchi, rejected the Kasbah II
protestors' push for a radical break and called for people to return to work,
emphasizing the need for economic stability and gradual reforms.[17]

The divide between those who supported institutional continuity and
advocates of a break with the former regime made an impact on the
UGTT, which, as the country's leading political force, was not immune to
the wavering over what position to adopt as the balance of power grew
increasingly unstable. Under pressure from demonstrators calling for the
departure of the RCD brass, the UGTT reversed its decision and removed
its three cabinet appointees on January 18, 2011. The move was met with
fierce criticism, in particular from legal opposition parties such as the PDP
and Ettajdid, which decided to remain in the government. The government
backers accused the union of political opportunism—taking advantage of
the protests on the street to consolidate its own power, against the country's
best interests. The blame was laid on the UGTT Executive Board, which
was said to have exploited the new political situation to divert attention
from its cozy relationship with the Ben Ali regime. Aisha, human rights
activist:

> I think that there is a great deal of political opportunism in the positions
> taken by the UGTT's leaders. These are people who were with Ben Ali;
> they wanted to mark their territory and clear their name. You saw how
> they left the first Ghannouchi government because they thought they
> could get a bigger piece of the pie. . . . The UGTT left the government
> so that it could exert more pressure—it enabled union leaders to take
> things up a notch and act like big shots. . . . The UGTT claims to be the
> country's largest political force. I agree that the UGTT played a vital
> role in the national movement, but I think that they manipulated the
> working class for political reasons that they never revealed. The fight
> on January 26 was between Bourguiba and Achour, but it should have
> been a fight against the high cost of living.

Another human rights activist, Bilel, agrees, asserting that the Executive
Board joined the protest movement to improve its negotiating position in
the new political landscape:

> In my view, you have to make the distinction between the Executive
> Board and the UGTT as an organization. The Executive Board always
> knows how to take advantage of a given situation—it joined the two
> Kasbah sit-ins to display its power, consolidate its political role and gain
> more leverage in the new political landscape.

When questioned about uncertainty within the organization, the unionists interviewed gave a very different account of how the events unfolded. While the interviewees concurred with certain criticisms directed at the Executive Board, they stressed that the UGTT was not a monolithic entity and that the UGTT's leadership faced such intense pressure from the protest movement—and the base and intermediary branches—that it had no choice but to join the Kasbah I sit-in:

> Jrad and the Executive Board can't betray the will of the UGTT's base. The Executive Board monitored the local and regional unions' demands and demonstrations. The decision whether or not to join the government was made at the highest levels of the UGTT, the administrative commissions. We joined the government based on an agreement governing how the portfolios would be allotted, and the government failed to respect that agreement. The first Ghannouchi government had control over the central ministries and left the UGTT with scraps. They gave us the Ministry of Local Development, which handles all the problems. What can you do with that ministry in the midst of a revolution, when you don't have adequate resources? No matter how hard you try, you can't get anything done. . . . Truth be told, they couldn't give a damn about us and that's why the UGTT left the cabinet and decided to join the Kasbah I sit-in.
>
> (Rafika, union activist, Health Care, Tunis)

This same ambivalence is thought to have influenced the central leadership's stances during the second Ghannouchi government. The UGTT is described as having left and returned to the Kasbah II protest movement due to pressure from unionists advocating a radical break with the former regime:

> The UGTT leadership accepted the composition of the second Ghannouchi government. We disagreed with the leadership and asked for the immediate removal of all RCD sympathizers, but the leadership thought that it had to be a gradual process carried out in steps. As usual, the leadership was reluctant but ended up agreeing with us. The Kasbah II sit-in was not rejected by the leadership—they supported it. The UGTT wasn't satisfied with the progress made by the government, which hadn't dissolved the political police, parliament, the Chamber of Councilors or the RCD. Faced with the government's refusal to satisfy the will of the people, it was only logical for the UGTT to reject the government and call for its fall. The UGTT needs to and will remain a force that supervises and exerts pressure, without joining the government.
>
> (Fathi, union activist, Textiles, Tunis)

Viewed from this perspective, this ambivalence appears to reflect the same dynamic within the organization during the period from December 17, 2010 to January 14, 2011. The central leadership was more or less willing to continue to make compromises with the incumbent power, while the intermediary and base branches closer to the thrust of the popular movement demanded a break with the former regime. In the end, while the UGTT was tempted to accede to power or support continuity with the former regime, the union yielded to growing pressure from unionists who backed the uprising. The challenge for the UGTT was to maintain consensus and protect the organization's unity. The union subsequently reprised its traditional role of exerting pressure, hastening the fall of both Ghannouchi governments:

> The UGTT supported the appointment of its allies to cabinet positions, a decision on which union members could not reach a consensus [*ijmâ'*]. There were unionists who rejected the move, saying that the UGTT's primary role was as an opposition force. The UGTT leadership [*markaziya*] said that they had supported close allies' candidacies in order to help the government manage the dialogue between the various partners; and because the government had neglected to consult them on the composition of the cabinet, they asked the candidates they were supporting to step down. That is how the UGTT ended up on the side of the grassroots movement and sit-in participants—it rejected the government and the unionists who said they were with the people. They hastened the fall of both Ghannouchi governments.
>
> (Sghair, union official, Transportation, Gafsa)

> I think that, as an organization, the UGTT has to continue to pressure and rein in the government. It can't join the government and pressure it from the outside.
>
> (Noura, union activist, Primary Education, Tunis)

In addition to political backing, the UGTT also provided financial and logistics support to both Kasbah sit-ins:

> There was public pressure on the UGTT to support the Kasbah I sit-in both politically and materially, which led to the union supplying water, food, etc. And they continued to play that role.
>
> (Karim, union activist, Energy, Tunis)

> The UGTT provided logistics support and donated money, tents and food—all that was from the UGTT, especially the Tunis Regional Union.
>
> (Raoudha, union official, Health Care, Tunis)

This episode was key—it represented the first in a series of events that directly called into question the UGTT's reach and limits. Is the UGTT an insider or an outsider? That is the central question that came up in most discussions involving the trade union confederation. At the urging of the intermediary and base branches, the UGTT quickly relinquished its vague designs on power and served as a somewhat unique countervailing power:

> The UGTT's decision to join the government was conditional and it removed the three candidates it had put forward after discovering that the cabinet was mostly made up of symbols of the regime. At that point, the union feared for its unity; the challenge was to maintain cohesiveness within the union. That decision was obviously made within its organizational bodies and, following several discussions, the UGTT decided to take on a neutral role and not become involved in leading or managing the transition phase with the government. The union preferred to supervise the initiatives established by the various governments.
>
> (Mongi, union official, Higher Education, Tunis)

The UGTT is a countervailing power in the sense that it alternates between strategies for applying pressure and negotiations, enabling the union to maintain both internal unity and political influence. It should be noted that the unionists' preferred term is "counterbalance," which avoids the confrontational aspect of "countervailing power" and highlights the union's consensus-building approach. The UGTT reinstated its past stance of remaining independent from the government—a cornerstone of the union's identity—as its sole guiding principle during the transition phase, to take full advantage of its traditional role as a counterbalance:

> One unique aspect of the UGTT is that it spans the entire political spectrum, because of its history. The reason that the UGTT has been able to maintain cohesiveness (*luhma*) is that it has always defended its independence [*istqlaliya*] by keeping an equal distance from all political parties, especially those in government. . . . You have to remember that the UGTT's central leadership is not the only group with decision-making power; it has to take the base into account. Few union members supported the idea of the UGTT joining the government in order to push its own agenda. Our slogan has always been independence [*istqlaliya*] from power. . . . The UGTT represents labor and has a negotiating role; we can't put forward leading union figures for cabinet positions and continue to negotiate with the government. The UGTT had to remain a negotiating partner that defends workers, with a vision for democracy and the Constitution. . . . The UGTT has always been a counterbalance and must remain so.
>
> (Ridha, union official, Postal Service, Bizerte)

Tensions were running high between the UGTT two political parties, the PDP and Ettajdid, which had joined a government that had obviously made some mistakes. The UGTT's criticism wasn't directed at the PDP or Ettajdid but at the government policies that had failed to live up to expectations. The UGTT's positions were dictated by its role as a counterbalance, a supervisor that oversees the government's actions, despite some viewing it as an adversary.

(Moutaa, union official, Higher Education, Tunis)

Cherif, a teacher and unionist in Sfax, expressed similar views, noting that the UGTT cannot be both judge and jury, and that the pressure from union members serves as a reminder that the union's strength is closely intertwined with its role as a counterbalance:

The UGTT has always been a decisive counterbalance in the Tunisian political sphere. The union, like the two other parties [Ettajdid and the PDP] that joined the government, was seeking an effective means to engage in politics. I think that, in the beginning, the strategy at the UGTT and those two parties was far from political—their focus was on saving the country. But they forgot one important thing: the revolution had radically changed the country's ideas, conscience and political order. The people who actually set the revolution in motion could not hand over power to the old guard; they knew that you can't teach an old dog new tricks. . . . The UGTT stepped down because it listened to the sincere unionists who thought that it couldn't be both judge and jury and that the UGTT's role was to defend the people and not the government. This pressure on the UGTT led to the resignation of its representatives in government and the union became involved in the daily demonstrations and sit-ins.

The two sit-ins differed from a political standpoint. The Kasbah I sit-in saw the arrival of new social and political forces, mainly from inland regions, which spontaneously formed groups representing each region. Political parties such as the Tunisian Workers' Communist Party (PCOT) and Ennahdha and organizations like the UGTT had a higher profile and were more closely involved in the second sit-in, Kasbah II, a departure from the impromptu nature of the first event:

There were more Islamists at Kasbah II; they took part in the coordination and media committees and even did the cooking. PCOT was present but not in the majority. . . . Kasbah I was more impromptu—the atmosphere was completely different [at Kasbah II] without the people from Sidi Bouzid, Gafsa and Metlaoui who had taken part in Kasbah I.

(Noura, union activist, Primary Education, Tunis)

The UGTT played a major role in the second sit-in. The situation had changed: most of the parties had received their authorizations by that time and the January 14 Front had been formed. . . . The Islamists took part in the Kasbah II sit-in in large numbers and had extensive material resources, but the driving force behind the sit-in was the UGTT.

(Fathi, union activist, Textiles, Tunis)

The UGTT thus found itself at the center of an unprecedented set of circumstances: it had to cope with a weakened government with declining legitimacy on the one hand, and political parties unable to keep pace with emerging forms of political and social organization on the other. Faced with this decidedly unstable political situation, the UGTT was compelled to devise new means to exert pressure and fulfill its role as a counterbalance. Next we will look at the strategies adopted by the UGTT to protect its position and influence the course of events.

The UGTT Takes the Lead in the Institutional Experiments During the Transition Period

The UGTT and the National Council for the Protection of the Revolution (CNPR)

The government's lack of democratic legitimacy resulted in the UGTT taking center stage in discussions to establish broad-based mechanisms for managing the transition.[18] The UGTT led efforts to establish the National Council for the Protection of the Revolution (CNPR), which institutionalized and structured discussions between the Ghannouchi II government and the opposition.[19] The council comprises 28 different organizations, including political parties such as the FDTL (Ettakatol), Ennahdha and the January 14 Front,[20] as well as powerful associations like the Tunisian Order of Lawyers and the LTDH:

> The UGTT chose to oversee the various transition governments' actions. The UGTT led efforts to establish the National Council for the Protection of the Revolution and the union further cemented its leadership role by organizing the discussions and hosting various meetings with civil society and political parties. . . . So the UGTT has a clear role as a conduit for official communication with the government.
>
> (Mongi Amami, sociologist and former director of the
UGTT research and documentation department)

Structured around the UGTT, the CNPR has local committees across Tunisia, most of which formed spontaneously at the start of the uprising:

> The CNPR was a reaction to the people's plea for a break with the former regime. Organizations such as the LTDH, the UGTT and other,

primarily left-wing, groups heeded the call and the council was active across the country.

(Salem, union activist, Postal Service, Sidi Bouzid)

While the UGTT and, more broadly, the CNPR are depicted as countervailing powers, the true nature of their role and its limitations remains ambiguous. The CNPR's members considered themselves the custodians of the revolution's legitimacy and, capitalizing on the government's lack of democratic legitimacy, demanded decision-making power rather than an advisory role. One CNPR member:

There is no government opposition with decision-making power because there is no parliament. It's dangerous. It's as if we were living in a country without a legislative branch, where the executive branch handles both executive and legislative duties.

Another added:

We think of the council as the "pilot" of the transition. In practical terms, that means a council with the power to supervise, submit proposals and veto, comprising all areas of civil society and the opposition and sanctioned by an executive order from the President.

(International Crisis Group, op. cit.)

The paradox lies in the fact that the CNPR both contested the democratic legitimacy of the Ghannouchi II government and asked it to officially recognize the committee's decision-making power. The Ghannouchi II government was staunchly opposed to the idea and only willing to allow the CNPR an advisory role:

In addition to playing a central role in organizing both Kasbah sit-ins, the UGTT also worked to devise a framework to protect the revolution, hence the idea for a council for the protection of the revolution, which was backed by the UGTT, the January 14 Front and other political parties. There was also a newcomer on the political scene, Ennahdha, which had considerable financial and human resources and took part in both the regional and Kasbah sit-ins. The CNPR comprised representatives from the UGTT and other trade organizations; the engineers', lawyers' and judges' unions; the LTDH; and most political parties. The council, which was formed to supervise the government, faced fierce opposition from the government and certain political parties, especially because the CNPR was also seeking decision-making power.

(Mourad, union activist, Primary Education, Sfax)

Several movements and organizations inside and outside the council also raised objections.[21] They feared that the UGTT and certain elements on the far left would use the council as an instrument of political power rather than a means to support the democratic transition. Take, for example, Omar Mestiri, a founding member of the National Council for Liberties in Tunisia (CNLT), quoted in the International Crisis Group (*op. cit.*) report:

> At the CNLT, we rejected both the opaque approach proposed by the government and that of the revolution council. We had developed the idea for a council, an authority that would be neither decision-making nor advisory body, but would serve as what we termed an "advisory requirement" for the government. A council that would have a central role in the process, which would define the overarching strategy without serving as a de facto government.
>
> Unionists were present but the UGTT swayed minds when it backed the push for the CNPR. The UGTT wanted to make its presence felt as a countervailing power. In my opinion, the UGTT should have joined the [CNLT's] council, in order to influence the course of events, make changes and exert pressure. When you're a source of pressure and oversight, you can't make decisions—that's the government's job.
>
> (Noura, union activist, Primary Education, Tunis)

The CNPR was also criticized for its limited representativeness and political parties' dominant presence. Some union members believed that the emergent social and political forces that sparked the revolution were not adequately represented, which cast doubt on the revolutionary legitimacy claimed by the council and, in turn, its attempt to gain decision-making power:

> The CNPR members were mainly elites, who are not in touch with the streets or the people. They could have cast a wider net and let everyone participate, instead of a handful of people coming to the UGTT local and declaring themselves the Council for the Protection of the Revolution. What were their working methods? What exactly is the Council for the Protection of the Revolution? How do you protect the revolution with people who didn't take part in it? How do you protect the revolution with people in the council who were against it? How are you going to protect the revolution?
>
> (Adnene Hajji, union leader, Mining, Redeyef)

The CNPR was made up of people from the UGTT, political parties and other organizations who were selected by cooptation—the regions were not very well represented. The political powers in Tunisia need to understand that the revolution gave rise to new political and social forces. There are leaders today who need to understand that they did not take part in the revolution they had been dreaming of for centuries—it was the poor and marginalized who acted on their own to make the revolution happen, it was not led by the political parties.

(Taoufik, union activist, Health Care, Sidi Bouzid)

These criticisms notwithstanding, the clash between the CNPR and the government provided an opportunity to reshape the country's political order. While the "legal" opposition parties such as the PDP and Ettajdid joined the government, other political forces that had been outlawed or repressed—the Islamists and the far left, as well as organizations that had been reined in, such as the UGTT and the Tunisian Order of Lawyers—demonstrated through the CNPR that they were capable of making their voices heard and influencing efforts to overhaul Tunisian politics.

The UGTT and the High Authority

The decision to establish a constituent assembly represented a break with the transition process set in motion by the political elite in the days that followed January 14, 2011, but it only partially met the demands of the protest movement. The debate between the proponents of institutional continuity and those who claimed revolutionary legitimacy was settled by a compromise: the CNPR and the various commissions formed by the Ghannouchi government would be replaced with the High Authority for Realization of the Objectives of the Revolution, Political Reform and Democratic Transition (known under the French acronym ISROR or simply as the High Authority). This new moniker combined "revolution," "reform" and "transition" to merge the revolutionary and legalist approaches in an entirely new way (International Crisis Group, *op. cit.*). The High Authority was established as a means to overcome the deadlock between the National Council for the Protection of the Revolution and the government. An executive order dated February 18, 2011, stipulated that ISROR would serve as an "independent public authority" responsible for "reviewing legislation relating to political organization and proposing reforms capable of meeting the aims of the revolution as regards the democratic process."

Another duty of the authority was to "issue an opinion on government activity, in cooperation with the Prime Minister." The government thus retained all executive and decision-making power, while ISROR took over management of the transition, defining electoral law and organizing the elections. A two-tiered system was established: the Authority Council of Experts, a group of legal specialists who define and implement electoral law; and the High Authority Council, comprising unions, political groups, civil society associations and other respected figures who examine the proposals put forward by the Council of Experts.[22] This system granted ISROR very extensive advisory and proposal-making powers that enabled the authority to influence decisions without having actual decision-making power. This suggests that the clashes between the various political and social forces gave way to an inclusive, consensus-based approach. The role of managing the transition was handed over to a wide-ranging group of institutions, political stakeholders, unions and associations, which were tasked with guiding the country toward a democratic regime. ISROR gave the country the founding documents for this period labeled the "democratic transition."

The UGTT worked within this new configuration to build consensus among the various political and social forces at play. The union helped create an institutional framework for discussion and dialogue that opened the rebuilding of the Tunisian political sphere to new political and social stakeholders. The UGTT's organizational culture closely reflects its diverse make-up, a factor that would enable the union to skillfully manage political disagreements. Interviewees describe the creation of the High Authority as the result of long negotiations between the government and political and social movements in which the UGTT played a key role, culminating in a solution with broad support (Ben Achour, 2011):

> When he took office, Béji Caïd Essebsi stated that he wasn't willing to share power with anyone. That led to the creation of the High Authority for Realization of the Objectives of the Revolution, Political Reform and Democratic Transition. . . . After a long fight, the UGTT accepted an authority with several parties and associations. The UGTT played a decisive role.
>
> (Chedhli, union activist, Secondary Education, Sfax)

> Coordination meetings were often held between the UGTT, lawyers, the League and the Democratic Women, first for the demonstrations and later as part of the High Authority. . . . When the decision was made to expand the High Authority at regional level [March 17, 2011], the UGTT, the League and law firms with regional branches were asked to appoint regional representatives, which led the organizations to further coordinate their efforts.
>
> (Halima, ATFD)

High Authority members also describe the UGTT as playing a mediator role that helped settle thorny issues:

> Through its representatives, the UGTT played a significant role in the High Authority. For example, when they adopted Article 15 barring RCD supporters, it was by unanimity/consensus (*ijmâ'*) or agreement (*wifaq*). The government sought to abandon the article, but the UGTT lobbied, refused and threatened to withdraw from the High Authority. They said, we have made a unanimous decision and it is out of the question to renege on it.
>
> (Cherifa, ATFD)

There was agreement within the High Authority about the importance of preparing for the ANC elections and on reform. They also had to manage the RCD's "leftovers." There were disagreements, especially within the political reform body, and the UGTT acted as a mediator to help people see eye to eye. We needed broad consensus within the authority and with the government.

(Taoufik, LTDH)

However, as with the CNPR, several controversies tainted the legitimacy of ISROR, in particular the process for appointing members, who were co-opted from the well-connected elite. For their part, the most critical unionists accused ISROR of hijacking the revolutionary process by upholding the traditional powers (political parties and organizations) as the sole leaders of the transition, at the expense of the new social forces that emerged during the uprising, which had yet to truly organize. They accused the UGTT, a key stakeholder in the process, of having exacerbated the marginalization of these new forces and blocked the revolutionary process:

The High Authority succeeded in coopting a large section of the political elite, January 14 Front activists, independents, civil society activists and regional activists. You could say that the High Authority succeeded in "clearing out" the political scene. The UGTT could lobbied for more than just an advisory body, a puppet. It could have pushed for more decision-making power for the High Authority. The High Authority dealt a fatal blow to the revolutionary movement.

(Mouloud, regional committee member, Gafsa)

We wanted direct elections that would enable those who took part in the revolution to be represented. The Electoral Code prepared by ISROR hijacked the revolution and advanced the major political parties' representation in the National Constituent Assembly. In my opinion, Ben Achour's authority hijacked the revolution.

(Mohammed, unemployed, Union of Unemployed Graduates, Sidi Bouzid)

The fact is that the popular movement in Tunisia currently has no political representation. The UGTT could have supported the new stakeholders, the young and unemployed people who sparked the revolution, instead of turning to the traditional political powers. The emerging political forces need to be represented; otherwise the revolution set in motion by the Tunisian people will soon be stolen from them.

(Sami, union official, Health Care, Bizerte)

Several interviewees criticized the UGTT's inability to sustain the CNPR, which they thought better represented the revolutionary forces, and lamented the Béji Caïd Essebsi government's stranglehold on the revolutionary process:

> The unionists think that they made a mistake when the UGTT gave up the fight for the CNPR. The UGTT was in a strong position at the time and had the lawyers' and the League's support, at a time when the government was weak. The CNPR could have been powerful, but Béji Caïd Essebsi entered the picture. Béji Caïd Essebsi is shrewd and was able to completely reverse the course of the battle. He successfully co-opted the three organizations [UGTT, LTDH and the Order of Lawyers] by, for example, accepting the demands of the outsourcing sector to mollify the UGTT. He granted the lawyers the new law they were seeking and that hurt the protest movement.
>
> (Raouf, unemployed, Union of Unemployed Graduates, Gafsa)

> In my opinion, the hijacking of the revolutionary process began when ISROR was created. The problem lies in the fact that at the Kasbah II sit-in, slogans like "The people want the fall of the government" and "The people want a National Constituent Assembly" were on display, but no one specified what type of government or ANC should be established. I think that the UGTT was not up to the task during that period. It could have offered alternatives to the Béji Caïd Essebsi government, for example. It could have supported the CNPR and encouraged the local revolutionary committees to unite and form a parliament that represented the revolutionary forces. Everyone—the UGTT, associations and political parties—rushed to join ISROR. They didn't care about supporting the revolutionary process; they were only focused on increasing their individual gains and/or staking out a place alongside those in power. Naturally, the most important issues, like the transitional justice system and the matter of the martyrs of the revolution, fell by the wayside after that point.
>
> (Maher, unemployed, Union of Unemployed Graduates, Sidi Bouzid)

As a result, the UGTT began to be viewed as a central power propping up the political and economic regime rather than a key player in the revolution:

> The UGTT slowed the revolution's momentum. In any case, the three governments [Ghannouchi I and II and Béji Caïd Essebsi] never ventured beyond Ben Ali's talking points (pledges on jobs, correcting laws, etc.). All three were counting on having staying power. When Béji Caïd Essebsi took office, he spoke about the prestige of the government [*haybat addawla*] and announced the return of the Bourguiba regime—or at least its policies. The Béji Caïd Essebsi government kept in place the core decisions made by the previous governments that had resigned due to public

pressure and the Kasbah and regional sit-ins. The UGTT played a decisive role in forming the three governments, nearly joined the first before caving to pressure, and later supported the second government. And the third government wouldn't have existed without the UGTT's blessing.

(Mourad, union activist, Primary Education, Sfax)

Paradoxically, not only did the UGTT disappoint the revolutionaries and advocates of a radical break with the former regime, it was also widely criticized by those who backed institutional continuity. Mining union activist Mohammed holds the UGTT responsible for the fall of two governments and believes the union caused political chaos:

The UGTT was criticized for two reasons. Some people felt that it was most at fault for the fall of the government. They blame the fact that the union joined the government and then withdrew shortly thereafter for the political chaos that ensued. The second reason is that the UGTT, working within the Council for the Protection of the Revolution along with other political parties, had called for the parties close to the former regime to be removed from power. The UGTT was attacked and doubts were raised about its motives for wanting to expel the parties. It's understandable that the UGTT took a stand against the people it considered to have supported the former regime.

Those parties [the PDP and Ettajdid] were initially satisfied with the UGTT's role as a mediator and then threw themselves into the arms of the Ghannouchi government at the first chance they had. They thought that the UGTT had kept them from splitting up the pie with the Ghannouchi government and the holdovers from the RCD. I think that the UGTT did sabotage their move, in a sense. They forgot that when the UGTT is on a good run, it's a force to be reckoned with, and those who stand in its way better watch out.

(Bechir, union activist, Primary Education, Sidi Bouzid)

What is more, while a temporary truce had been reached in the political battle, there was no solution in sight for the country's social problems. The unrest continued in the inland regions, with a rise in strikes and demonstrations that fueled the idea that the UGTT was often responsible for the "social chaos" at hand. The UGTT's position as both a political and social actor resulted in its leaders being targeted by attacks and defamation campaigns. Most of the unionists interviewed believe it was the "counterrevolution" that targeted the UGTT, because it had the greatest ability to mobilize followers and was the only truly organized opponent. Union activist Kamel:

When the UGTT left the first government, the political parties in the cabinet, UTICA [an employers' organization], businessmen and the media all waged a major campaign against the union. This campaign against Jrad was an attempt to turn public opinion against the UGTT. In response, the UGTT supported the activists who had taken to the streets, clarified its positions and pushed on with the fight. That is how the balance of power shifted—the UGTT backed the Kasbah sit-in and brought about the fall of the government.

(Kamel, union activist, Textiles, Tunis)

Former members of the RCD manipulated people and incited them to attack the UGTT offices. They targeted symbols like Jrad and Amara Abbassi in Gafsa, telling them, "get out of here, you symbolize the former regime." Those people thought that the UGTT had played a major role in the fall of the regime, so they had to break up the union, to make it suffer what the regime had suffered.

(Mouloud, regional committee member, Gafsa)

For his part, journalist Imed points out that the methods used are classic techniques used by the former regime in the 1970s and 1980s to neutralize the power of the UGTT:

When the UGTT took the lead in the events after January 14, an offensive was launched by political forces, businessman, the police and all other actors that had start to reorganize after the shock of January 14. Needless to say, they had a clear target: the UGTT. The current anti-UGTT rhetoric reminds me of what was written in the press when the government attacked the UGTT in the 1970s and 1980s. You see the same methods—burning UGTT offices and harassing unionists—ingredients, style and mentality.

This situation drove the UGTT and all the other political and social forces to reshape the power relationships that defined the fast-changing Tunisian political world. The UGTT, which has operated at the crossroads of the workers' movement and national issues since its inception, figured prominently in yet another political crisis. The union's stated goal of helping the country transition to democracy was at odds with its desire to protect its own power in the new political landscape. The UGTT's position as an intermediary between the social movements and the government provided the union with useful negotiating tools. The union's close ties with the social movements enabled it to influence government actions and major political decisions. In return, by winning a few concessions for the protest movement, the UGTT prevented the risk of a direct clash between the old and new political forces. However, the UGTT's critics also believe this approach eliminated the potential for a radical break with the former regime. The UGTT did much to encourage the creation of intermediary institutions—namely the CNPR and ISROR—capable of fostering negotiating and mediation capabilities that extended beyond one-on-one relations with the government. The UGTT has two conflicting aims—to serve as a counter-vailing power and to maintain institutional continuity—and its approach is distinct from that of both a negotiation-based trade union and a political movement seeking to seize power. At times, the UGTT has trouble keeping pace with its own extensive political action, but it is not a political party and has no desire to become one. Proclaiming to be a "counterbalance" enabled the UGTT to avoid being confined to a purely defensive role, but the union didn't lead the political transition all by itself, either. Ironically, this mission to build consensus among the various political forces earned the UGTT opponents on both ends of the political spectrum. The UGTT was targeted by those who held it responsible for the fall of the government and by those who believed it had hijacked the revolutionary process.

Public relations were one of the UGTT's main weaknesses during these attacks, which deepened the lack of understanding between union members and large swathes of the public. In the next section, I will look at two major media storylines that galvanized opinions about the UGTT, both as regards its stature as a union and place in politics: "Jrad Out" and "The UGTT Is to Blame for the Social Anarchy."

The "Jrad Out" Campaign: The Organization Is Mistaken for Its Leader

Following the UGTT's resignation from the Ghannouchi I government on January 18, 2011, a number of media and political storylines appeared regularly which condemned the hand-wringing within the UGTT and raised questions about the power the union was seeking to acquire in the shifting political sphere. Abdessalem Jrad, a member of the UGTT Executive Board since 1983 and Secretary General since 2000, was held responsible for the direct clash between the UGTT and the three transition governments, Ghannouchi I and II and Béji Caïd Essebsi. He became the target of all accusations. Some called Jrad out for supporting the deposed president, citing as evidence his meeting with Ben Ali on January 12, 2011, hostile statements regarding the popular uprisings and a praise-filled letter addressed to Ben Ali (Guerfali, 2011). Others accused the union leader of corruption, pointing to documents pertaining to plots of land that he is said to have acquired with help from the government. Journalist Amine expressed outrage at the situation:

> Just as life was starting getting back to normal in Tunisia, the UGTT refused to end the dispute and sought to plunge the country into an unprecedented crisis. As crazy as it seems, given how it's common knowledge that the UGTT Central Committee [sic] was a government insider and took advantage of the system for 23 years. The brunt of the blame lies with Mr. Secretary General, who felt it appropriate to secure

high-level positions for three of his sons at Tunisair [an airline]; to sign a call for Ben Ali to run for office in 2014, on behalf of the union; and, worse, to be the first person to meet with the ex-president.

The UGTT's Secretary General and Executive Board are suspected of opportunism—joining the revolution movement and aiding in the fall of two transition governments solely to revamp their image and avoid being judged for their ties with the former regime. "How on earth did the UGTT, Jrad and the others become the leaders of a revolution that they ignored during the first two weeks and then joined at the last minute, when the die had been cast?" fumed the journalist Ridha Kefi on the website Kapitalis. The "Ben Ali Out" slogan was replaced by "Jrad Out" and criticism piled up both in the media and on social networks.

Tens of thousands of people liked Facebook pages with names like "Get Rid of Abdessalem Jrad," "Get Abdessalem Jrad out of the UGTT" and "Abdessalem Jrad Must Leave the UGTT and Let Tunisia Move Forward." Some even compared the UGTT to the RCD and called not only for Jrad to step down but also for an end to the organization as a whole, using the slogan "Jrad Out, UGTT Out." This campaign peaked when Jrad criticized Béji Caïd Essebsi's appointment as prime minister, on February 28, 2011. The Kobba movement or "silent majority" and others held a demonstration demanding Jrad's resignation in front of the UGTT headquarters on March 5, 2011 (Mouterde, 2011).

In addition to the accusations against the Secretary General, a number of concerns ware raised about the UGTT's role in the new political landscape. Walid, a member of the "Jrad Out, UGTT Out" Facebook page, believed that the UGTT had to carry out its own revolution by removing Jrad and focusing on its role as a union:

> Abdessalem Jrad, you joined the UGTT Executive Board as Deputy Secretary General in 1983 and have been a member ever since—longer than Ben Ali was in power! It is true that you have made sacrifices for the union's cause in your time there, but now it's time for you to step down. You're not being asked to leave because you normalized relations with the Ben Ali regime in recent years, but because it is time to turn the page. Arguments like "I have to see us through this tricky phase" or "there is no one to replace me" should not dare rear their ugly head. Mohammed Ghannouchi, whom many people had a favorable opinion of but nonetheless wanted to see leave as a symbol of change, had the political courage to bow to the will of the people, good or bad as it may have been. Tunisia needs new leadership from a new generation, to turn the page. The UGTT should carry out its own revolution, refocusing on its role as a union rather than as a political blackmail artist, and Abdessalem Jrad needs to go!

Another member of the same page explained that, as a union, the UGTT should not interfere with the government and the prime minister's decisions:

> Mr. Jrad, must I remind you that the UGTT isn't a political party and should not have a say in choosing the prime minister or the cabinet? In no way is that the union's role or one of its prerogatives. I don't think that Tunisians rose up against the tyranny of Ben Ali's political dictatorship to fall into the hands of Jrad's union dictatorship. Mr. Jrad, let me ask you one simple question: who stands to gain from the chaos you have wrought by stirring up trouble and inciting discord?

Past actions by the UGTT Executive Board, which was accused of abetting the government during the Ben Ali era, were often put forward as reasons to deny the union the role it intended to play in the new political arena:

> There is a gigantic gulf between Hached's UGTT and Jrad's UGTT. The UGTT will always have its past and played a major role in Tunisian history, but it has become a central part of the establishment—they were the quickest to support Ben Ali at every step of the way. I don't know if there was a real debate within the union. But I see the outcome—they are always present, supporting him during the 2009 elections to justify a whole raft of measures or to distance themselves from any initiative put forward by the PDP or Ettajdid. At the same time, there were key moments like the Maya Jribi and Nejib Chebbi hunger strikes, a lot of moments when the UGTT could have taken action but didn't.
>
> (Ahmad, journalist)

The Executive Board and Secretary General were very quick to react. Abdessalem Jrad denied all the accusations entirely, stating that he had been "the first to declare his assets" and urging anyone who uncovered a secret bank account in his name to report it to the union. Other Executive Board members gave Jrad their full support. Houcine Abbassi, then Deputy Secretary General for Legislation, explains his perspective (Mouterde, *op. cit.*):

> Those who criticized the UGTT are ex-RCD members and enemies of the revolution. My supporters are united and ready to act. Abdessalem Jrad was never close with Zine el-Abidine Ben Ali and all the documents making the rounds are false. . . . We are going to fix our internal issues, but that's secondary. It's the country that is in danger, not the organization.

In a televised interview, UGTT spokesman Abid Briki described the trade union confederation as a "big machine" that was rock-solid and could turn the political tide at will, especially if it felt threatened.[23] He also noted that all previous attempts to destabilize the union had failed. While the Executive

Board is obviously expected to support the Secretary General, some wondered what had prevented dissenting union members at loggerheads with the committee from taking advantage of the campaign against the union to "cleanse" the organization of everyone who had cooperated with Ben Ali. Others were surprised by the strength of the organization, which succeeded not only in maintaining unity and protecting its leaders, but also continuing to bring all its weight to bear in Tunisian politics, despite the firestorm of reprisals targeting all the country's institutions:

> The winds of the Tunisian revolution rattled nearly every institution in the country. Only one has managed to keep its apparatus intact: the UGTT. It's rather surprising to see a union plagued by long years of cronyism and corruption at the highest levels escape unscathed from the political earthquake that just hit Tunisia. In addition to its leading figures remaining in place, the UGTT, or at least some of its officials, have had the luxury of being able to confidently assume a central role in the talks held in recent weeks. It is no secret that the old union again has its sights on bringing its full weight to bear in the shaky world of Tunisian politics. It is an opportune time to take a look at this fortress of a union's supernatural resistance to the storm of score-settling that followed the fall of the former regime.
>
> (Ben Othman, 2011)

How did the UGTT manage to overcome the risk of a split within the organization in the face of such extensive defamation campaigns? How did the UGTT succeed in holding on to its power in Tunisian politics? To attempt to answer these questions, I will look at union members' interpretation of the "Jrad Out" campaign and how they reacted to these attacks.

The UGTT Is More Than Jrad Alone

There was unanimous agreement among the unionists interviewed that the campaign against Jrad aimed to capitalize on internal divisions that had emerged between the Executive Board and the base and intermediary branches during the uprising, in order to weaken the union and neutralize its political influence during the transition period:

> The UGTT is the only organized force in the country, which is why they wanted to disrupt it and push it from an offensive to a defensive stance. . . . The UGTT's weakness was clearly the leadership's position during the uprising, which destabilized the union. As a result, the UGTT, which had been an integral part of the revolution, became afraid of it. The anti-UGTT campaign didn't let up; it continued during the Béji Caïd Essebsi government.
>
> (Ahmad, former senior UGTT official, Sfax)

It's easy to attack a political organization by focusing on one person. The personalization of all types of causes is a major problem in Tunisia. It is not something that can be fixed overnight. The roots of the problem lie in the colonial era. There was Monsieur le Prince—"Sidi el Bey"— and then we had the "great" Bourguiba—the "Supreme Fighter"—a reputation that Ben Ali tried to claim for his own. . . . This personalization problem has always been present. It's something that has been used against the unions: the UGTT was attacked because its leader Abdessalem Jrad was completely corrupt. You can attack one person to target an entire movement.

(Chaïfa and Hamdi, 2012, 94)

Union members' main argument in defense of the UGTT was to stress the importance of separating Jrad from the union as a whole and distinguishing between the organizations within the union and their members:

The UGTT is not Jrad. The UGTT has organizations, regional unions, general unions, base unions, etc. You can't reduce the UGTT to Jrad as an individual. That doesn't mean that Jrad isn't an activist—Jrad went to prison and suffered under the Bourguiba and Ben Ali regimes.

(Najoua, union official, Health Care, Tunis)

The interviewees often emphasized that, unlike in other organizations, where the officials appointed by the president make all decisions, the UGTT has well-established decision-making mechanisms for electing leaders, placing limits on their power and curtailing interference from the regime. The union members were adamant that Jrad could not override the will of the decision-making bodies, which alone held the power to decide his fate. Noura explains:

I'm not for or against Jrad because I don't believe in the cult of personality [*za'amatiya*]. Jrad cannot defy the organization's will. He could not delay the general strike, even if the government asked him to. People say a lot of things, like that there was an agreement between Jrad and Ben Ali on January 13 that included a payment. If people have evidence, they should come forward. People wonder why union members don't want to "get rid" of Jrad. We can't remove someone who was elected.

(Noura, union activist, Primary Education, Tunis)

The union members interviewed do not interpret Jrad's meeting with Ben Ali solely as a "compromise of principles." While they recognized the close ties between the Executive Board and the regime, many pointed to the UGTT's central role as a negotiating partner, which required the union to maintain open lines of communication with the government to manage the country's affairs.

Jrad is being blamed because he paid a visit to Ben Ali on January 13. What is our defense? Our defense is the government—we can't have a communications blackout with the government because they have to be a partner in the dialogue, we have to negotiate with them, and most importantly, no one knew at the time that Ben Ali would step down.

(Najoua, union official, Health Care, Tunis)

As far as the relationship between the Secretary General and Ben Ali is concerned, you can't criticize him for meeting with the President because that is part of his job, to help find solutions to problems by negotiating with the government.

(Fathi, union activist, Textiles, Tunis)

These different viewpoints reveal how the lack of consensus over the meaning of Jrad's meeting with Ben Ali is a product of the UGTT's unique role as both a negotiating partner that helps the government function and as a pressure group. This made any attempt to break with the regime problematic for the union.

Here again one finds signs of the UGTT's unique political culture, which often paired pressure and negotiations that regulated the union's relationship with the government. It would have been all the much harder to cut off relations with the government given that, at the time, no one could have predicted the fall of Ben Ali:

As I said earlier, the media depict the Secretary General as being complicit with the government because he couldn't let the relationship appear damaged or openly break with the government. As a voice for employees, you have to maintain a relationship with the government. Otherwise you can't operate, especially because the government is one of your negotiating partners. So whom do you to negotiate with? With the other partners, including the government. This aspect of the situation is delicate—even if you don't agree with certain things, you can't take a totally hostile stance. You can disagree but you can't be hostile and cause the relationship to break down. Yet the public views the Secretary General's relationship as the key element, as a form of abetting the government, especially during the most crucial moments. . . . He is not the only one responsible for his endorsement of the President's campaign—the Administrative Commission issued a decision in favor of the endorsement. So he's not the only one responsible, there was a body that made the decisions. There were obviously discussions that took place and votes were held, but the majority had also been a bit manipulated—Ben Ali did everything in his power to make sure that the vote turned out in his favor; he influenced the Administrative Commission's decision.

(Hichem, union official, Higher Education, Tunis)

Corruption, Mismanagement or Quid Pro Quo?

Corruption allegations against Jrad were the second argument widely used to discredit the UGTT. Some unionists condemned the role played by the RCD and other parties like the PDP and Ettajdid in the defamation campaign while also calling for an independent investigation to establish the facts and judge those responsible fairly:

> I was in prison on January 13 and heard Ben Ali's last speech. I saw how the leaders of the legal opposition were happy with Ben Ali's speech. It was understandable—Ben Ali's speech surpassed everything that they had hoped for, it topped their strategic plans. They accepted to join the government. The UGTT was against the second government, which is why the parties in that government waged the defamation campaign against the UGTT. It's a classic: each time the UGTT sides with the people, they prepare the corruption allegations.
>
> (Amar, human rights activist, Gafsa)

> Jrad and the Executive Board accepted the investigation into the corruption allegations; they cannot be asked to step down without evidence. The PDP and Ettajdid started the campaign as a reaction to the UGTT criticizing them and opposing the government. But the UGTT maturely chose not to react because, in spite of our differences, Ettajdid and PDP members remained comrades who were like us before January 14—they have a brilliant history as activists and were persecuted by the regime. So the UGTT took action against the RCD but didn't retaliate against the PDP and Ettajdid. We even called for everyone to calm down because clashing with them would not have served the country's interests.
>
> (Kamel, union activist, Textiles, Tunis)

When asked about the corruption allegations, some interviewees gave the more or less rote reply that the situation had to be put into perspective—mismanagement is different from corruption and it is more appropriate to focus on the errors made in allocating the UGTT's resources:

> You have to distinguish between the valid criticism of the UGTT's mismanagement and the hostility toward the organization that emerged in the campaign against Jrad. . . . Following the law was important with that whole issue. When you are aware of major corruption scandals and known crimes that don't have anything to do with Jrad, but no one talks about them—people shot to death, people who have pillaged the country—when you see that the focus is on Jrad, you can only guess that the primary goal is to damage and weaken the organization. They [those who back the government] want to neutralize his role in the movement underway in the country.
>
> (Mounir, union official, Textiles, Ben Arous)

The UGTT has a few companies, like Hotel Amilcar, whose management has not been able to keep up with the competition. It has insurance schemes, which directors stole from in collusion with the regime. It also collects dues from members, builds facilities, pays its employees and oversees management of day-to-day operations. The UGTT does not manage huge budgets or major economic projects. From what I have observed, there may be finance officers who might have cheated by spending a bit extra, unionists who leave on assignment and take 2,000 dinars instead of 1,000. I don't see that as corruption—that's not what I call corruption, it's just mismanagement.

(Belgacem, Regional Committee member, Gafsa)

Box 4 The Thin Line Between Compromise and Compromised Principles

When people heard about the meeting between Jrad and Ben Ali, they couldn't understand it. Most people thought that because the UGTT was negotiating with the government, it meant that the UGTT supported the government. In reality, the UGTT has to negotiate with the government in order to win concessions for workers. The UGTT is required to negotiate with the government, no matter whether it is good or corrupt. . . .

No political party can compare with the UGTT, which stood up to the regime in spite of everything! We clashed with the police, our comrades were beaten, demonstrations for Gaza and Iraq were repressed. . . .

There have always been clashes with the regime and it's not fair to say that the UGTT has been subservient to the regime. It's true that the UGTT negotiated with the regime but the union doesn't support the regime as a principle. If you look at all the UGTT statements and press releases, you'll see that there has always been opposition to the regime. At the same time, the UGTT has to thank Ben Ali when he accepts concessions for workers. . . . It's all a matter of tactics. . . .

The UGTT was the last organization to endorse Ben Ali's presidential campaign, because it didn't have a choice—it couldn't risk the concessions for workers and wanted to prevent UTICA from coming out on top in the negotiations. The UGTT made compromises [*tuhâdin*] with the government to improve its negotiating position with employers and win concessions for workers.

The UGTT does not support the government out of love for the regime or a sense of justice; it does so because it has no choice.

Mouloud, Regional Committee member, Gafsa

Others criticized the media coverage of UGTT corruption media for focusing solely on Jrad, sparing officials from political parties and national organizations who had also benefitted from the ousted president's "generosity." Corruption reached the highest echelons of power and became systemic, a common way of doing business in Tunisia. This corruption was closely intertwined with cronyism, which was fueled by the centralization of power and the fact that decision-making responsibilities were in the hands of individuals. At the same time, the interviewees stressed that the embezzlement was not solely a matter of corrupt individuals, pointing to the organic relationship between the UGTT and the party-state as a key to understanding the overlapping individual and corporatist interests vital to the survival of the authoritarian system. The government's attempts to exert control over the union apparatus greatly impacted how the UGTT operated. The regime maintained a sophisticated system of privileges designed to forge relationships based on quid pro quos, which, in turn, created allegiances difficult from which to extricate oneself:

> All organizations were affected by corruption. Why? The entire system acquiesced in the corruption, not just individuals. There was a time when the political powers that be lacked legitimacy, because we didn't have democratic elections. Without legitimacy, the political powers had to form allegiances, to gain the allegiance of all organizations, in order to assert their hegemony and dominance. In return, they had to grant privileges. That was the system, how they operated. And the UGTT was not the only one to take part in the system. All organizations and associations—aside from a few associations that valued their independence, such as the LTDH, CNLT and ATFD— were subject to this social system. It's not surprising that privileges were granted, because that was part of how the system worked, and all UGTT officials were exposed to it. Apart from two or three people who were "clean," everyone in the Executive Board enjoyed privileges of some sort.
>
> (Brahim, union activist, Textiles, Sfax)

> The unionists who reached the Executive Board generally were given a salary three times higher than their initial wages. In practice, the government manages to turn the Executive Board members into civil servants dependent on its financial support. They entered into a relationship based on quid pro quos that few were able to escape from.
>
> (Mahmoud, union activist, Textiles, Tunis)

> Union officials already have a lot of advantages. They travel, leave on assignment and have a lot of advantages. Their children receive scholarships and are given opportunities. They stay in the same position for years; corruption becomes a career that is difficult to leave behind.
>
> (Sofiane, union activist, Energy, Sfax)

The allegiances and forms of dependence that bound the UGTT Executive Board to the government were also replicated in certain companies, in particular state-run corporations. These ties structured the relations between company executives and union officials, helping to pacify employer-employee relations and cementing the government's control over the UGTT:

> The corruption at the UGTT has greatly benefitted from the civil service and public companies. There is an implicit confluence of interests between union officials and the heads of certain companies, even if they appear to be opposed to one another. . . . I'll talk about the sector I know best, a sector with a lot of money and a lot of corruption. In my sector, the UGTT has a say in the appointment of certain executives. Do you think that it is appropriate for the UGTT to appoint the CEOs of public companies? That explains their involvement in hiding certain cases of corruption. In my company, the union official goes into the CEO's office whenever he pleases and gives him the names of people to hire or fire—he is very powerful.
>
> (Souheil, manager at a state-run company, Energy, Tunis)

> From 1987 to 2011, the politicians' strategy was to achieve peaceful employer-employee relations by any means necessary. Strikes were unacceptable. . . . Executives at state-run companies had to achieve a peaceful solution by any means necessary and avoid making waves. The cost of this artificial peace is certainly greater than that of normal employer-employee relations, in which conflicts that cannot be resolved sometimes result in strikes. So we had to avoid strikes at all costs and we paid for it. It wasn't the higher-ups that paid for it, it was our companies and our country's economy. This commitment to smooth relations resulted in systematic concessions for the unions, increasing the wage bill, from modest employees and all the way up the ladder. . . . In a way we sacrificed the company.
>
> (Mahfoudh, former senior executive at a
> state-run company, Transportation)

Anyone who voiced discontent with this sophisticated system of quid pro quos was stripped of their duties:

> Jrad has been a UGTT activist for a long time. First as a base-union activist at the national transportation company, where he forged his career at a union transformed into a bureaucratic apparatus by the Ben Ali regime. At the UGTT, putting pressure on management or the government to gain a few benefits for employees and a lot of benefits for oneself had become a habit. . . . That's what explains the cozy situation of career unionists like Jrad and his son, who led the union at Tunisair [an airline].
>
> They had such a cozy situation that Jrad and certain members of the Executive Board launched the "*Tajrid*"[24] campaign in 2007, which

aimed to help them remain in power at the UGTT and to strip dissenting voices of their union duties. But then the revolution came and Jrad
and unionists of his ilk, opportunistic as ever, changed their tune.

(Afef, journalist)

Afef's remarks reveal how the authoritarian system meddled with the
UGTT. They show that corruption was no trivial matter; it was extensive
and criticized, but often considered a by-product of the authoritarian system. The lack of clear rules at the highest levels of government blurred the
lines between corruption, mismanagement and simply trading small privileges. Government could manipulate these rules based on the circumstances
to tighten its control over various institutions. The power struggle between
Jrad and Béji Caïd Essebsi is an excellent illustration of the UGTT Executive Board's relationship of dependence with the administration, which was
maintained by using cases of corruption as leverage. Jrad and UGTT spokesman Abid Briki openly criticized Béji Caïd Essebsi succeeding Mohammed
Ghannouchi as prime minister (Ghaith, 2011). Béji Caïd Essebsi and Jrad
met following the latter's remarks and the UGTT Executive Board subsequently decided to tone down its grievances. Radhi Ben Hassine, a union
official in Tunis, believes that the UGTT leadership made the decision after
Prime Minister Béji Caïd Essebsi threatened to take legal action against Jrad:

> There is no official proof but people say that Béji Caïd Essebsi threat-
> ened Jrad: if the UGTT continued to disturb the government's actions
> he would go public with corruption scandals. He is also said to have
> threatened to support other unions if the UGTT continued to disturb
> the government's actions. The UGTT leadership is said to have agreed
> to support the Essebsi government and stop causing a flap and, in
> return, the interim Essebsi government agreed not to forge ties with
> other unions.

Journalist Ahmad expresses anger at the UGTT Executive Board's political about-face and decries the lack of freedom within the union, which he
says is beholden to the former regime due to its relationship of dependence.

> When Béji Caïd Essebsi replaced Ghannouchi, there was a succession
> of crises between the government and the UGTT. The UGTT lead-
> ership wondered why they hadn't been consulted and were abso-
> lutely livid. You've seen the first UGTT statement and how searing it
> was. . . . Jrad and Briki went on television to ask why Beji had been
> appointed prime minister without their knowledge. It wasn't until a
> day or two later that Béji Caïd Essebsi reached out to Jrad personally
> and showed him his file and said, "If you want me to release it now, I
> will," and that's when Jrad calmed down. A lot of people interpreted
> that as Jrad being in collusion with the new government, but behind

the scenes it actually was a personal matter. They were going to air all his dirty laundry; there had already been a few leaks but they all had been controlled. The common people are thrown a bone here and there so that we can have a bit of fun—it's a way of feeling that we are keeping up with what's going on, a bit like *Le Canard enchaîné* [a French satirical newspaper].

(Ahmad, journalist)

Gafsa-based unionist Ammar views the situation along the same lines. He believes that the defamation campaign against Jrad achieved its goal of persuading the Executive Bureau not to support the protest movement:

The first phase of the revolution ended with the exit of Ben Ali—the dictator left and the revolution continued. The UGTT goes whichever the way the wind blows, as the song goes [*tmih ma'a lariyah*]. The UGTT has kept its trap shut ever since Beji arrived! Every time the UGTT sides with the people, the media machine starts bringing up corruption at the UGTT and they get scared and quiet down.

How, then, did dissenting unionists—who had always criticized the UGTT Executive Board's "collusion" with the government—react to this controversy?

Box 5 "The Regime Had a Corrupting Influence"

The regime was able to expand over the course of more than 20 years—leading to the blockage and resulting explosion that you're aware of—because the UGTT, as a mass organization, played the regime's game. . . . During the Ben Ali era, the UGTT would receive instructions, apply them and take a stance that defended everything that was decided at the political level.

This whole crooked system developed gradually, especially from 1990 onwards, and the UGTT played an active role in it. . . . Proof of this can be seen in how the moment that doubts arouse about UGTT Secretary General Ismaïl Sahbani's intentions and aims, a corruption scandal broke which surely hadn't been prepared over the previous 24 hours. I can't comment on the details of the allegations because I don't know them, but whatever the case may be, this is clearly standard practice. . . . And if they released this information, there is some truth to it.

The regime had a corrupting influence and Jrad was under its thumb. They knew how to choose corruptible people—people who are given duties and the first day they even slightly veer off course, they face legal repercussions. . . .

Having seen up close what's happened in the transportation sector from the early 1970s up until now, I can confirm that the union officials who played an important role in the sector—gaining the legitimacy to play a role on the national stage—are generally unsavory characters, both in terms of their personal morals and their approach to union work. They care little about what could be termed the "common good," the interests of the company, which is state-run, or even the interests of the workers they are supposed to defend. And they sort of had their heyday when the regime was in place, from 1987 to 2011, because the regime understood their true motives. . . . There was an alliance at the top which meant that, whatever happened, they would be loyal to the regime, to which they had given assurances. But they needed legitimacy, so they were automatically condemned to double talk: one message for the regime—those with decision-making powers at the highest level—and another for their members, designed to foster legitimacy and credibility.

What surely happened is that they would get caught between these two messages and be asked, "What do you really want?" And they would reply that they needed solutions and measures that cemented their credibility with their members: "So give us something! And while you're at it, give us something for ourselves and for our friends and families!" And that's how it would work. When there was a sticking point they'd receive a call: "What do you want?" "Hire my son! Hire so-and-so! Give me the other plot of land! Give my children a scholarship to study abroad! Give me this benefit, that special privilege. . . ." And it worked well. Miraculously, the strike notices would be canceled and everything would end up running smoothly. Everyone was happy: the politicians and the administration were happy because they had avoided a crisis or resolved a crisis situation, and they [the union leaders] were happy because they had given their members something to chew on and because they had gotten something for themselves.

That is how a lot of union leaders became rich, built beautiful villas, had their children educated in the USA and elsewhere, and got their children into branches closed off to the common people. . . . It's all very shady, but unfortunately, that's the way things worked for many years.

Mahfoudh, former senior executive in a
state-run company, Transportation

Crisis Management: A Mix of "Tribal Instincts" and Legalistic Rhetoric

Both the dissenting unionists and partisans of "union bureaucracy" viewed the "Jrad Out" campaign as an attack on the entire organization. They reacted swiftly, setting aside their internal disputes to join forces and protect the organization's unity.

I think that the people behind the anti-Jrad campaign are mainly targeting the organization. . . . That's why we protected Jrad and the outgoing members of the UGTT Executive Board. One of the rules we abide by within the organization is that the UGTT doesn't abandon its children. . . . The unionists will continue to defend the organization and even the outgoing leaders.

(Karim, union official, Energy, Tunis)

Initiatives were organized to say, "We got rid of Ben Ali, now it's Jrad's turn," but most union members refused to join in that refrain. They said, "We're going to hold off on that front." They said, "Now isn't the right time, there are other wars to fight. . . ." I don't know if they were right or wrong. The anti-UGTT campaign started with the primary teachers' strike. Jrad was in the crosshairs and documents about land he had purchased started to make the rounds, as well as videos with him and the President and of his May 1 speech. I think that people were fed up; it was difficult for union members to pick a side. . . . What could they have done? Join everyone in insulting Jrad? The problem is that the UGTT isn't Jrad alone and they had to protect the organization.

(Romdhane, union activist, Mining, Redeyef)

Even opponents within the UGTT who had been isolated by the Executive Board during the Ben Ali era joined this solidarity movement to protect the unity of the organization, setting aside their vendettas to focus on the crisis at hand:

The union's opposition does not coexist with the UGTT—we disagree but we belong to the UGTT and we had to protect the UGTT's unity, especially in that time of crisis.

(Radhi Ben Hassine, union official, Energy, Tunis)

Some ventured to describe the unionists' attitude during the campaign as a "tribal instinct," a spirit of solidarity that grew organically in order to protect the organization's survival. Interviewees said that this tribal instinct was rooted in the methods developed by the organization, which had experienced crises and attempts to undermine its solidity throughout its history. It is public knowledge that the different schools of thought within the UGTT band together when the union or one of its leaders is attacked, says Moncef:

There was an anti-UGTT campaign after January 14, you know. People who have never belonged to a union cannot understand the organization's culture. The UGTT operates like a tribe. It has endured several crises and paid dearly.

The Campaign to Blame the UGTT for "Social Anarchy"

A series of different initiatives emerged in the aftermath of January 14, 2011: strikes in various industries, demonstrations organized by the unemployed, and a movement to "get rid of" ex-RCD figures in various private and state-run companies. In response to these voices calling for a radical break with the former regime, the three transition governments argued that the immediate priority was political stability, without which there was little chance of an economic recovery taking hold. They appealed for calm and condemned the social activism erupting across Tunisia. The UGTT was accused of stoking what several figures called the "anarchy" breaking out in the country, as a means of capitalizing on the demonstrators' demands to achieve political prominence. This campaign was exemplified by the charges of an UGTT "dictatorship" during the Kobba sit-in; critics accused the union of attempting to behave "like a political party" (Thedrel, 2011). Censure of the social movements was widespread both in the media and statements by the political class, which refused to accept the UGTT's role in the new political landscape:

> It's strange to see people [from opposition parties] attack the UGTT and social movements despite having built the legitimacy of their own message on condemnation of repression and the denial of freedoms. Let's suppose that the UGTT is behind the social movements. That means that the union is supporting an expression of the people's will. They should have negotiated with the UGTT instead of attacking it.
>
> (Mohamed Trabelsi, former UGTT Deputy Secretary General)

> The workers made legitimate social demands that should have been viewed in their proper context. The former regime should have been targeted, instead of the demands being exaggerated or used to attack the UGTT. It is important to remember that the former regime deprived people of their political, social and economic rights. The regime oppressed the people and didn't let them express themselves. When the government lost its grip on power, people started to express themselves and society began to defy the state, as in all revolutions. The same thing happened in the UGTT, where the base rose to prominence, as well as in UTICA and with the farmers—it was a completely natural turn of events.
>
> (Mohsen, union activist, Postal Service, Sfax)

The public was particularly critical of corporatist demands, arguing that unemployment should be the top priority in light of the country's difficult economic situation. This view held that people with a job should not have the right to strike or petition for a raise:

> The revolution occurred because there is too much unemployment in the country; this revolution emerged to condemn injustices and corruption. You could have joined the movement and said, "As employees, we are relatively privileged, now it's time to focus on the people don't have a job or resources." Instead, you asked for yet another raise! And your movement continues to this day and is even more harmful to the country's economy and the public interest. That's something that needs to be called out, it's a situation that does not compute, that isn't at

all acceptable—you were the first to declare yourselves revolutionaries and, as such, to defend the unemployed, yet you take maximum advantage of the situation to benefit those who already have jobs and are relatively privileged. I have to react when I hear people speaking on behalf of the UGTT trying to put themselves in the shoes of those who speak on behalf of the country's true interests. They have no right to speak, act or behave in that way; they have no authority to convey that message after the wrongs they've done to the country in the past.

> (Mahfoudh, former senior executive at a
> state-run company, Transportation)

The protesters were even labeled as criminals and the union leaders as manipulators. Romdhane explains:

We started hearing people accuse the sit-in participants of being crooks and thieves. Some people think that all political and union work is a crime. There is a way of thinking that maintains that if you start to organize, the leaders will manipulate and exploit you. People will understand over time that when you stand up for your rights, you can't bypass organizations.

> (Romdhane, union activist, Mining, Redeyef)

How, then, did the unionists view this campaign? Union members' initial reaction was to draw a distinction between the demonstrations organized by the UGTT and those that emerged spontaneously or were even spurred on by the former regime to discredit the UGTT. A member of the union opposition (*al-liqâ' an-naqâbî*) gives her perspective:

Honestly, I don't think that the UGTT called the sit-ins. Perhaps in the beginning, and then realized that people were against that sort of demonstration. Then came the campaign against the UGTT. You have to remember that there are demonstrations and strikes everywhere, even in non-unionized companies. . . . Personally, I'm against sit-ins whose sole aim is to get rid of those who symbolize the RCD, and now is not the time for sit-ins to demand pay raises. . . . I don't think the UGTT is behind the sit-ins, because that wouldn't have been in their interests. At one point, I found myself defending the UGTT from those were saying that the UGTT was giving money to people to cause chaos and bring the country to a standstill. It's not true that the UGTT wants to "push the country to the brink." Even though I'm part of the opposition within the union and want to fire all the leaders, I can't objectively say that the UGTT is behind all these demonstrations, because it has no reason to do so.

> (Faten, union activist, Textiles, Tunis)

Several interviewees noted that the revolution stemmed from socioeconomic demands and strikes are a classic component of revolutions. Béchir believes that the misbehavior occurred in the most unstable sectors, which are not always organized by the UGTT:

> Who is taking part in the sit-ins? Those who aren't affiliated with any specific organization. Those who know the UGTT are well aware that its most active sectors are in education, where, as you can see, there are no strikes. . . . The calls for sit-ins are coming from unstable sectors without ties to the UGTT, which is creating a sort of social anarchy [*infilât ijtimâ'i*]. Clearly, social anarchy and a lack of security are two classic phenomena that have occurred during the major revolutions in world history. . . . That said, I fear that the revolution, which was partly social in nature, will be co-opted for political gain, leading to the worst possible outcome for the country if its social problems are not addressed.
>
> (Béchir, union official, Primary Education, Sidi Bouzid)

Meanwhile, as the impromptu strikes were taking place, some unionists accused ex-RCD networks of instigating the chaotic sit-ins:

> I think that political parties like the RCD are behind the sit-ins, because UGTT strikes are regulated. Take the private sector, for example. It's one of the toughest areas but we decided to hold off on our demands during the difficult transition period. A lot of initiatives have been postponed to pacify the situation. . . . We are not bound to follow the government's orders; we're an independent organization with our own rules that govern our actions. The UGTT has been blamed for a lot of things that aren't its fault.
>
> (Farah, union activist, Textiles, Bizerte)

> Most of the sit-ins were organized by RCD members as part of a campaign against the UGTT. Their goal is to say, "Look at the UGTT and what it's up to—it wants to ruin the country." But the major unions affiliated with the UGTT, such as Education, haven't gone on strike. The teachers finished the school year despite being provoked and some subjected to violence; their instructions were "no strikes."
>
> (Najoua, union official, Healthcare, Tunis)

Other union members explained that some bosses had taken advantage of the campaign against the UGTT to carry out redundancy plans without having to face pressure from the unions or politicians:

> The union initiatives continue in this type of situation. For instance, there may be a general strike in Sousse. The owner of a furniture

company released a press release accusing the UGTT of trying to drive the country to bankruptcy and overthrow the government. In truth, he's the one who caused the situation by laying off 300 employees, which led the UGTT to mobilize and prepare for a regional general strike. It could happen any day now if they are unable to negotiate the re-hiring of all those employees, at the very least.

(Jemli, 2012, 65)

It is also worth adding that certain union branches had ties with the former ruling power that made it even more difficult to distinguish between the demonstrations held by the UGTT and those co-opted by the deposed regime. Salah explains:

Most of the chaotic sit-ins were in non-union sectors. That type of disturbance can also happen in corrupt unions that have had a falling out with the union bureaucracy. Those are often unions have been linked to the RCD in the past.

(Salah, union activist, Mining, Redeyef)

A manager at a major state-run company shares his experience:

Here's what happened. The corrupt people at the RCD formed an alliance with the corrupt people at the UGTT. That's what happened in our company. We wanted to get rid of the VP and CEO and open an investigation into acts of corruption with billions at stake. The UGTT cooperated with us normally early on and all the staff were on our side. We issued two joint press releases and then the UGTT refused to sign the third, on the grounds that "We don't want to fire the CEO." I think that there were secret negotiations. . . . The UGTT issued a press release insulting us: "These people are wrongly accusing management and we are against them." The next day the police called us in for questioning, my phone line was cut off and the punishment began.

(Souheil, manager at a state-run company, Energy, Tunis)

In another incident, several unionists recalled the violent clashes between rival factions in the mining town of Metlaoui, which left 11 people dead and more than 100 injured over the course of three days in June 2011 (slateafrique.com, 2011). Violence flared after rumors circulated that Gafsa Phosphate Company (CPG) planned to hire members of certain clans and not others. The union members accused RCD sympathizers of deliberately sparking a violent conflict while security forces turned a blind eye. Romdhane looks back on the events:

Unlike in Redeyef, there was no organization backing the protests in Oum Larayes and Metlaoui, which was a problem for both CPG and

the Béji Caïd Essebsi government. As soon as there was an agreement
with one group of unemployed workers, another group would ask for
the same thing. The situation became absurd. They needed a radical
solution and there was the incident where members of the two clans
killed each other because of fake hiring lists. They killed each other
under the "watchful eye" of the police. The Ministry of the Interior, led
by Habid Essid, was involved. . . . The government needed people to
kill each other to get its way. There haven't been any sit-ins in Metlaoui
since that incident.

(Romdhane, union activist, Mining, Redeyef)

The counterrevolution in Gafsa was embodied by the forces of the
past: the RCD and businessmen close to the Trabelsis [the family of
the deposed president's wife]. They were the ones who were behind the
chaotic sit-ins, roadblocks and tribal conflicts. . . . Exploiting tribalism [*urûchiya*] is a classic technique that France used when coloniz-
ing in order to break the resistance. Bourguiba also used it and Ben
Ali took it a step further. When you have unions set up on a tribal
basis and work is split up in the same way, it's easy to manipulate
people—employed and unemployed alike—which is what happened
in Metlaoui. Exploiting tribalism is one of the tactics used by the
counterrevolution.

(Ammar, union activist, Secondary Education, Gafsa)

In the demonstrations organized by the UGTT, the breakdown in centralized decision-making at the union also spurred an eruption of industry-
specific and corporatist demands. The UGTT, like all other organizations in
the country, underwent a crisis of authority and was overwhelmed by the
various initiatives formed in the base and intermediary unions, which didn't
always confer with the central leadership before taking action:

The UGTT played a very important role in the Kasbah sit-ins, but
there was a wave of union-backed trade sit-ins held without centralized
decision-making. There were strikes in several sectors. The unionists,
who most often instinctively defer to instructions from the base and
general unions, started to hold strikes and sit-ins in their companies,
without conferring with the decision-making bodies, regional union or
general union. The new state of affairs in the country had left the government in disarray and the UGTT, which had experience managing
and controlling strikes, had lost its handle on the situation. . . . After
January 14 the union members had more leeway to make decisions,
whereas before, a base union couldn't announce a sit-in or strike without consulting the central leadership. They don't fear the central leadership like they used to.

(Anouar, journalist)

Union work is based on negotiations that are viewed as a means of influencing the power relationships determined by the UGTT's ability to mobilize its forces, based on a combination of industry-specific considerations, regional issues and personal interests. The UGTT uses those elements to carry out negotiations. Holding a strike used to require a meeting of the Administrative Commission for the sector with an Executive Board member present—you couldn't strike without the Executive Board member signing off on it and you had to give ten days' notice. Now you can just send a letter the day of the strike, because the UGTT is completely overwhelmed and it is difficult to negotiate with a government that doesn't have any authority. . . . Meanwhile, you have a lot of one-upmanship and some former militias and employee trade groups have joined other unions like the CGTT and the UTT, further upping the ante.

(Moutaa, union official, Higher Education, Tunis)

While the UGTT was fending off various attacks after the fall of the regime, Mohammed Ghannouchi's interim government unilaterally authorized the formation of two new trade union confederations. Each was established by a former UGTT member: the General Tunisian Labor Confederation (Confédération Générale Tunisienne du Travail, or CGTT) by Habib Guiza and the Union of Tunisian Workers (Union des Travailleurs de Tunisie, or UTT) by Ismaïl Sahbani,[25] a highly controversial figure. The people I spoke with saw the introduction of trade union pluralism in this highly unstable situation as additional evidence of efforts to distort the UGTT's image and divide the union movement:

In my opinion, trade union unity is the best option because you have the upper hand in negotiations with employers. When there are several unions, management and the government play on that plurality in an attempt to divide the union representation. At the same time, I support people's right to establish the political parties and organizations they wish. Union pluralism in Tunisia is a natural development, but it is not an absolute necessity. . . . Unfortunately, the counterrevolutionary forces are exploiting union pluralism to break up the UGTT. It is very difficult to imagine Sahbani—a corrupt member of the old guard who established a total dictatorship at the UGTT—taking charge of a new union.

(Ridha, union official, Postal Service, Bizerte)

What stance did the UGTT adopt as the number of strikes continued to grow? While the UGTT did not initiate all the strikes, most unionists believed that the union's identity as a voice for employees prevented it from stopping or condemning the strikers:

The impromptu sit-ins were organized by workers who had suffered repression. When they gained their freedom, they also wanted to regain their dignity. The UGTT had nothing to do with the chaotic sit-ins. The UGTT didn't call the sit-ins, only strikes with specific advance notice. The UGTT couldn't ban the sit-ins, either, so it tried to supervise them. But there were also strikes organized by the UGTT, like the local authority strike held when the government failed to implement the agreement securing employees' status and pay raises. Subcontracting was also an issue. . . . All those strikes were legitimate given the workers' difficult situation.

(Kamel, union activist, Textiles, Tunis)

You have to look at the specifics. The UGTT leadership didn't call the sit-ins but it didn't have the resources or will to stop them. Let me make myself clear: the UGTT didn't call the sit-ins. The UGTT only backs organized initiatives, organized strikes. That said, the UGTT leadership can't condemn the sit-ins and it's not in their interest to back them, either.

(Omar, union activist, Energy, Tunis)

The UGTT was quick to take an official position on the matter. Various Executive Board members stressed that while the UGTT did not back these chaotic strikes, it absolutely did consider them a legitimate form of protest at a time when freedom of speech was returning after years of dictatorship and injustice. They also criticized the government's repressive policy with regard to the protesters:

Abdessalem Jrad assures that the UGTT rejects these unauthorized, chaotic strikes, but we also refuse to make them a punishable offense. We want to call attention to how severely the protestors have been threatened and terrorized. We have to respond with a dialogue-based approach, to find practical solutions. We condemn the chaotic strikes and sit-ins that aren't authorized but we won't punish them. We caution that it is dangerous to adopt a repressive, violent policy in response to these strikes and we encourage the use of dialogue as means to find realistic solutions that address these problems.

(Ridha Bouzriba, UGTT Deputy Secretary General in charge of health care coverage and workplace safety, Al-Maghreb, December 27, 2011)

As a result of the situation described above, the forces that the unionists labeled as "counterrevolutionaries"—ex-RCD members, bosses and businessmen—are said to have supported the chaotic strikes in order to discredit the UGTT and deny the union its rightful place as a key player in the transformation of Tunisian politics. Instead, interviewees say, these individuals sought to keep power in the hands of the same economic and political elite. The UGTT was targeted by the attacks because, despite its complex positioning and diverse make-up, it seemed to be among the rare organizations capable of resisting attempts to restore the status quo ante, through its ability to drum up support:

> Béji Caïd Essebsi and the previous governments wanted to marginalize the UGTT. They wanted to push the UGTT out of Tunisian politics. There were calls for the UGTT to focus solely on issues related to economic demands. To that end, political parties, former RCD members and people with ties to the current government planned a campaign against the UGTT. Sit-ins were one of the main aspects of the campaign. In my honest opinion, the UGTT took a clear, patriotic stance; it was against the chaotic sit-ins, supported all legal forms of activism, backed down on a lot of material demands in specific sectors, and showed a predisposition to postpone negotiations and pay raises. The UGTT even intervened to fix problems caused by the sit-ins organized outside its control. . . . There are political parties and bosses that I count among the counterrevolutionary forces which organized sit-ins by greasing people's palms. . . . Their aim was to get people to miss the old regime and think that citizens are incapable of governing themselves. It's a political game whose goal is to lay the blame for the chaos on the UGTT, in order to marginalize the union.
>
> (Nejib, union activist, Primary Education, Sfax)

> The Ghannouchi government's lack of popular legitimacy is what enabled the emergence of the movements, which formed as a consequence of the former regime. For example, people working in the country's poorer regions and living hand to mouth, or people working as subcontractors who didn't have an actual employer. They didn't have the right to organize, they didn't have the right to protection and they didn't have organizations to represent them. In light of that, it is quite understandable that they are expressing themselves, and doing so in a very impromptu, sometimes violent manner. . . . There are the people who enjoyed the UGTT's protection and those who were marginalized. The UGTT supported the marginalized and defended their right to organize and gain union representation. . . . If you look closely, you'll see that the people who crafted the campaign against the UGTT are from service-sector companies that subcontract. It's a known fact that the service sector has traditionally been unstable . . . and service-sector companies suffered from the revolution, which worked against their interests. . . . The companies and forces that took advantage of instability and fragility in the workforce were key players in the campaign targeting the UGTT. They include businessmen, former Destour officials and members of industry groups. After the RCD disbanded, its members

held the UGTT responsible because it had not opposed the decision to disband the party.

(Rami, union activist, Textiles, Ben Arous)

The UGTT withstood both campaigns and successfully maintained its cohesiveness, but an unresolved issue continued to dominate discussions regarding the union: why wouldn't the UGTT settle for a role purely focused on union issues that would spare it from these heated controversies?

Can the UGTT Focus Solely on Union Issues?

The controversy over the role the UGTT should play during the position period—countervailing power, government partner, joint decision-maker or government watchdog—re-opened the debate regarding the UGTT's identity. Passions flared over the union's position as a key stakeholder in transforming Tunisian politics. Those who viewed the UGTT primarily as a union movement were wary of its political moves and several figures called for an urgent return to the traditional union role of defending workers. On the other side, there were those who wanted the UGTT to foster the re-emergence of political freedoms, with some calling for the union to take on an exclusively political role. The UGTT did more than merely regulate politics during the transition period. It also took action to defend its position and power in a political landscape undergoing sea change, which further fueled tensions:

> The UGTT wants to protect its political position and advantages, to remain a powerful, leading organization capable of whipping up support from the "streets." That's why they don't want to settle for a role only as a union, defending workers.
>
> (Aisha, journalist and human rights activist)

When questioned about their idea of the UGTT's role, the unionists interviewed noted that the UGTT has traditionally been situated at the crossroads of two movements: social activism and national liberation. This history has made the UGTT a nexus for union, political and social initiatives that has always played a prominent role in the national political scene:

> There is a conflict between the people who want the UGTT to return to a role focused purely on union issues in specific industries and those who want the UGTT to continue to play a political role. Under the dictatorship, the UGTT had a political role and wasn't a trade union organization in the classic sense—it has always combined labor, political and social initiatives, all the way up until the revolution. What's more, it has been the source of alternative culture, taking part in the Human

Rights League's first steering committee meeting and providing a space
for the first Tahar Haddad feminist activists at the UGTT research office.
The UGTT established a theater troupe, music groups and sports clubs.
The union was aware of the importance building a civil society capable
of defending social rights and community networks. It was a way of
helping people channel their efforts against colonization, injustice and
the dictatorship.

(Mohamed Trabelsi, former UGTT Deputy Secretary General)

In the pages that follow, I will delve into three aspects of how the UGTT's
union and political roles intertwine: the UGTT's status as a structural component of Tunisian politics, the political dimension of union work, and the
union's relationship with political parties.

First, the UGTT's history, which has made the union a central stakeholder
in Tunisian politics. The UGTT has taken part in all the political battles,
from the national struggle for independence to the development of the Tunisian state and the revolution:

The UGTT has been criticized for supporting the Kasbah I and Kasbah II sit-ins. Several political factions do not appreciate the UGTT's
actions, because they wanted to have free rein. The UGTT has secured
a place in history through its role in all the battles against colonization
and its representation in the first constituent assembly. As the country's
first working-class organization, it cannot abstain. . . . Yes, the UGTT
plays a role in worker's issues, but it can only be effective in that regard
in the right political landscape.

(Najoua, union official, Healthcare, Tunis)

Furthermore, union work is political by definition because it is inherently
tied to economic and political choices:

The line between unionism and politics is so thin that you can't see it
with your bare eyes. There is no union work as such. We push back
against the line of thinking at the UGTT according to which union work
and politics don't mix, and have done so since the 1970s. You can't
form a union and say that you aren't interested in politics. You can't
form a union and call yourself a unionist if you don't think politically
or ideologically, it's just not possible. When you talk about the public's
purchasing power you're talking politics, you're at the very heart of it.
Who affects purchasing power? There is a direct connection with policy
choices and programs. When you talk about social justice and fair distribution of wealth, you're talking politics.

(Adnene Hajji, union leader, Mining, Redeyef)

Where the interviewees do make a distinction is between the political dimension of union work and the political parties' cooptation of the UGTT. The UGTT was the only outlet for political dissidents to express themselves during the dictatorship, a fact that is reflected in the remarks of the unionists, whose disdain for political parties was a constant in the interviews. Union members often suspected the parties of seeking to co-opt the UGTT to advance their own partisan agenda:

> The union clearly has to handle problems in specific industries, a role that the political parties cannot fill. Take the example of Redeyef, where everyone attacked the UGTT and wanted to break it up. . . . The political parties are incapable of fulfilling their political role; they come to the UGTT and want to peddle their political propaganda even though they have their own offices. They can assemble a crowd and give speeches whenever they like, but the political parties are incapable of even holding a public meeting. They can't even hold a conference, roundtable or even a discussion.
>
> (Omar, unemployed, Redeyef)

The UGTT's longstanding disdain for the PSD/RCD single-party system is often projected onto the other parties—even those in the opposition. The UGTT's much-vaunted independence from the regime is instituted as a practical philosophy that structures the union's relations with the other political parties. In the unionists' view, the UGTT has to base its political positions on what is best for the union movement. In times of crisis, UGTT membership often trumps political affiliations:

> I'll give you my honest opinion of it all. As you are aware, I was a member of parliament. I was one of the five people who represented the UGTT and I was a member of the RCD. Understandably, I was under a lot of pressure when the uprising took place, but, when it comes down to it, first and foremost I'm a unionist. I resigned from parliament on January 18, 2011, and my resignation was published in the newspaper *Ach-Cha'b*. . . . The UGTT is a mosaic of all political leanings. And members are judged based on their contribution to the union, irrespectively of their ideas or political party, and first and foremost I'm a unionist.
>
> (Mondher, regional committee member, Sidi Bouzid)

The interviewees often remarked that, while the various political parties attempted to influence the UGTT's policy positions in one way or another, the UGTT's unique origins and development prevented it from being a puppet to the parties. The UGTT's political role, traditionally structured based on a dependence/independence relationship with the ruling power, bestows an exclusive status on the union: a counterbalance in the political arena that is not required to become a political party as such:

> A subtle approach is always required to understand the UGTT. The UGTT cannot be separated from politics, just as the UGTT cannot take political positions. . . . The UGTT has to refrain from entering into the political battles waged by politicians because there are people of all political stripes in the union and that could be dangerous. So the UGTT has to take a stance on major political decisions because that's the country's history, but it can't get mixed up in political battles. If the UGTT were to enter into the political war, people could say it was playing the direct political role of a political party. The UGTT serves to balance out power in the country.
>
> (Radhi Ben Hassine, union official, Energy, Tunis)

> The UGTT has always forbid itself from seeking political power. But it has also always refused to confine itself to representing workers' demands. It has always believed that social problems often stem from policy directions and economic choices, and therefore takes a keen interest in politics and economics. The UGTT serves social and human causes in this way, ensuring that partisan or clan politics and individual material gain do not eclipse social considerations. That is why the UGTT prides itself on its role as a proactive stakeholder and counterforce. The UGTT is actually a counterbalance.
>
> (Mongi Amami, sociologist and former director of the UGTT research and documentation department)

According to the interviewees, this means that even the political parties led by union figures who claim to have close ties with the UGTT cannot, under any circumstances, be considered "UGTT parties":

> The Tunisian Labor Party[26] considers itself the party of the UGTT. The FDTL also considers itself the party of the UGTT because its founders are UGTT activists. But the UGTT represents several different political leanings, so no party can be called the party of the UGTT.
>
> (Sami, union official, Health Care, Bizerte)

> As an experiment, the Tunisian Labor Party could be an interesting experiment that boosts pluralism. Union figures belong to the party, which could become an ally of the UGTT and gain unionists' support. It could also become one of a number of parties whose work focuses on social issues. It could be useful as an experiment but you can't say it's the party of the UGTT.
>
> (Mouloud, regional committee member, Gafsa)

The UGTT has to perform a balancing act—influencing major policy directions and protecting its political power while keeping all the parties at arm's length—that causes misunderstandings with regard to its role:

> There are three or four parties whose name contains "labor": the Communist Workers' Party, the National Democratic Labor Party, the FDTL and the Tunisian Labor Party. All these parties—their officials, members, visions and organizations—originate from the UGTT [*sic*] and have a union background. In my opinion, the UGTT still represents a safeguard for the country, because there is still a long fight ahead and the UGTT's role is to defend Tunisia. Hached said, "I love you, my people," not "I love you, worker. . . ." The UGTT needs to remain political without becoming a political party or being exploited by political parties.
>
> (Nejib, union activist, Primary Education, Sfax)

The UGTT's efforts to foster a balance of power earned the union attacks from each of the transition governments:

> The anti-UGTT campaign started with the announcement of an open-ended strike in primary education. It's hard to stomach seeing political leaders like Chebbi or Bharim—who sided with the UGTT in the fight against Ben Ali—publicly attack the UGTT. They say that the UGTT has entered into politics, that there are known political blocs manipulating the UGTT.
>
> (Romdhane, union activist, Mining, Redeyef)

> The PDP and Ettajdid felt betrayed by the UGTT when they all joined the Ghannouchi government. They did it together with the UGTT, but when the UGTT decided to withdraw at the same time as the FDTL, they felt betrayed and wouldn't forgive the UGTT leadership. In addition, they thought that the UGTT could take part in politics, albeit timidly, because we were under a dictatorship. But now we have a democracy and everyone has to assume their proper position. The UGTT can't take the political parties' role. That's why they had that reaction to the UGTT.
>
> (Omar, union activist, Energy, Tunis)

Any act that wrested control from the hands of the regime immediately took on a political meaning during this period, when the goal was to throw off the yoke of the single-party system. One the UGTT's founding acts, which established its identity as a union, was to declare itself self-sufficient and independent from regime oversight. While this made the UGTT a prominent political stakeholder, the union is not a political party, as its members never cease to point out. The UGTT was nevertheless required to continually maintain the political conditions that enabled the union to operate within an authoritarian system. That held true throughout the Bourguiba and Ben Ali regime and the UGTT continued to pursue that approach during the transition period, because a stable balance of power had yet to be established. The UGTT sought to expand the scope of its political action in order to resist the campaigns attempting to weaken its unity, thus ensuring its survival. The UGTT's role and identity had been closely intertwined with the single-party system, but the new political landscape enabled all political parties to circumvent the union. Several interviewees thought that this shift would have an impact on the UGTT's political stances and its internal organization. Abdeljelil Bedoui, a UGTT economist, expert and advisor, explained that this new relationship with the government could do away with certain forms of alliance and would surely affect how the UGTT operates internally:

> The relationship will change from this point forward. The next government won't need to form an alliance to establish a certain level of legitimacy. Its legitimacy will come from the elections, which I hope will be democratic. As a result, even the organization [the UGTT] will have to undergo a transition. It can no longer count on the state for privileges or political support. They have to count on their base and gain its backing and consent. . . . It's inevitable, because the parties are now able to exist and work outside and independently of the union's reach. In theory, they no longer need the union to exist; they can now exist freely in compliance with the law. I hope that the organization will devote more time and effort to its traditional role of representing workers and serving as a countervailing power. Because others in political parties can assume the role of the opposition. The UGTT cannot join the government because it no longer has the allegiance that made it feel close to or part of the system. If anything, I think that the situation will become healthier and clearer, and that the organization will inevitably be required to strengthen its democratic practices and ensure good governance. Logically and objectively, the process is moving in that direction. It certainly won't happen overnight, because it's a matter of mentalities and attitudes; it will certainly take some time but that is where they are headed.

For her part, Hèdia believes that the overhaul of Tunisian politics may lead the UGTT to focus on its union and social duties:

> I don't belong to any political party or movement. I wear a veil and I mix with everyone—the PCOT, the Arab nationalists, the Democratic Modernist Pole—they're all my friends within the union and we agree

on quite a few points. If you want my personal opinion, I don't like the political parties exploiting the UGTT. Thank God that after the revolution, the political parties were legalized and everything is going well for them. We don't fear for them anymore. In all honesty, it's better for people to keep their political work within their political parties and let the UGTT perform its union and social role.

(Hèdia, union activist, Textiles, Bizerte)

The interviewees' remarks reflect the fact that the UGTT's identity as an organization is deeply rooted in its unique political history. The transformation of the union clearly cannot be dictated from above and will depend both on the political sphere and on economic and social relationships.

In Conclusion

Like all political and social actors in Tunisia, the UGTT suddenly found itself facing the challenges of a tense, unstable political climate. The UGTT took center stage in discussions to establish consensus-based mechanisms for managing the political transition, due to the government's lack of democratic legitimacy and the weak position of the opposition parties. The UGTT grew in prominence through its contributions to the various institutional experiments conducted to structure the dialogue between the political and social forces present in Tunisia and govern the country together. The UGTT owes its high-profile position in the political transition to the fact that it was the only collective platform for action that had remained shielded from total single-party dominance, which enabled it to retain an ability to rally support. Not only did the UGTT unite unionists in defense of their professional interests, it yet again served as the staging point for much broader political initiatives related to managing the political transition and protecting its own power amidst far-reaching political restructuring.

More than a traditional trade union and different from a political party, the UGTT became a key stakeholder in the political transition through its ability to forge compromises between those who backed a radical break with the former regime and those who favored institutional continuity. The UGTT used its ability to drum up support and its position as an intermediary between the social movements and the government to secure the significant political and organizational resources required to make an impact in the political battle through pressure and negotiations. The union's close ties with the social movements enabled it to influence government policy and the major political decisions related to managing the transition period. What is more, the UGTT's work to obtain a few concessions from the ruling class for the protest movement eliminated the risk of a direct clash between the old and new political forces. The UGTT's harshest critics, however, believe that this also eliminated the possibility of a radical break with the former regime.

Meanwhile, the union's positioning as a counterbalance, as the unionists like to describe it, enabled it to maintain its power and take part in leading the political transition, but also made it a target for various political players. The UGTT was taken to task both by those who held it most responsible for the fall of the two transition governments and by those who accused it of co-opting the revolutionary process. In the short term, the unstable political situation and rising political, social and economic challenges threw the UGTT's unity into doubt. Once again torn between plans to take part in the political transition and the need to side with the workers' movement, how would the UGTT leadership react to these attacks and prevent a rift from emerging?

On October 23, 2011, the Islamist party Ennahdha won the National Constituent Assembly elections with 41.47% of the votes, securing 89 of the 217 seats. Ennahdha, lacking an absolute majority, formed a coalition government with two left-wing parties, the Congress for the Republic[27] (CPR; 13.82% and 30 seats) and the center-left Democratic Forum for Labor and Liberties (FDTL/Ettakatol; 9.68% and 21 seats).

Béji Caïd Essebsi was replaced by former Ennahdha Secretary General (1981 to 1984) Hamadi Jebali as Prime Minister; CPR Chairman Moncef Marzouki was appointed President of the Republic and FDTL Chairman Mustapha Ben Jaafar was appointed President of the National Constituent Assembly. The elections thus ushered in new political leaders that had belonged to the opposition to Ben Ali, marking a shift away from the political class that had governed the country for more than 50 years. Tunisia transitioned from a government of experts hailing from the Destour lineage to a government of democratically elected politicians, most of whom from the opposition. The 22nd UGTT Congress was held two months later, on December 22, 2011.

In the next chapter, I will focus on the impact of this new political configuration on the UGTT Congress proceedings, during which the union selected new members for its ruling bodies and set its political and social policy directions. What new forms of legitimacy and what place would the UGTT be able to claim in the political and social sphere, during this period of profound change?

Notes

1. The term "democratic transition," a common phrase in everyday language and political science at the end of the 1980s, quickly rose to prominence in the political debate, rivaling "revolution" and "revolutionary process." The use of the term is indicative of the tensions that existed from the outset between the various actors with regard to the direction that the political transformation should take. Both domestic actors, such as representatives from political parties and civil society, and outside actors such as financial backers (e.g. the European Union, UN and World Bank) spoke of the democratic transition, mainly

in reference to holding free, open elections; guaranteeing the fundamentals of political competition; and protecting civil liberties.

2. "Key" is the adjective often used by the unionists to assert the strength of their organization.

3. The quotes in this chapter are excerpts from interviews primarily conducted between February and June 2011. They offer a window into the internal divisions within the UGTT over what position to adopt in the new political landscape and the differences of opinion with regard to the attitude taken toward outside attacks.

4. Ghannouchi served as prime minister from November 17, 1999 to February 27, 2011.

5. The National Defense, Interior and Finance ministers from the Ben Ali government kept their positions until the reshuffle on January 27, 2011.

6. The term "legal opposition" refers to the Tunisian political parties that had received legal authorization from the Ben Ali regime to engage in political activity.

7. The Progressive Democratic Party, or PDP, is a Tunisian social democratic party founded on December 13, 1983. The PDP was granted legal authorization on September 12, 1983, and merged with other parties to form the Republican Party, Al-Joumhouri, on April 9, 2012.

8. The Democratic Forum for Labor and Liberties (FDTL or Ettakatol) was founded in April 1994. It is affiliated with the Socialist International (IS).

9. Ettajdid (Renewal) is a center-left political party founded on April 23, 1993.

10. The Ghannouchi government set up three commissions in mid-January to oversee the democratic transition: the High Commission for Political Reform, chaired by Yadh Ben Achour, a legal specialist who had resigned from the Constitutional Council in 1992; the National Fact-Finding Commission on Abuses Committed during Recent Events, led by former Tunisian Human Rights League (LTDH) President Taoufik Bouderbala; and the National Commission for the Investigation of Cases of Corruption and Embezzlement, chaired by Abdelfattah Amor. The commissions were proclaimed to be open to civil society and staffed solely by apolitical experts.

11. The three ministers put forward by the Tunisian General Labor Union (UGTT)—Houcine Dimassi, Abdjelil Bedoui and Anouar Ben Gueddour—resigned on January 18, 2011.

12. The term "Kasbah" is derived from the Arabic word *qasabah*, meaning "fortress" or "reed." As Kasbah Square in Tunis is located in front of the Prime Minister's Office, the location is used as shorthand for the ministry. The square is recognized as one of the urban symbols of the Tunisian revolution, along with Avenue Habib Bourguiba. The Kasbah I movement began on January 23 2011, when Tunisians from inland regions occupied Kasbah Square, under the Prime Minister's windows, to demand that the Ghannouchi I government step down.

13. This demonstration led to riots on Avenue Bourguiba that were violently repressed (five deaths) but ultimately led to the resignation of Prime Minister Mohamed Ghannouchi.

14. President of the Chamber of Deputies from March 14, 1990 to October 9, 1991.

15. Commonly known as the High Authority, this body comprises 155 members representing 12 political parties, 19 associations and trade unions, and 11 out of the 24 governorates, as well as 62 lawyers, legal specialists and other "national figures."

16. The name of the square near El Menzah Sports Palace where the demonstrators met.

17. Cf. the March 2, 2011 edition of Swiss daily *Le Temps*.

18. Sana and Rafâa Ben Achour (2012) identify three phases in Tunisia's transition: a constitutional transition period that began on January 14, 2011, a broad-based transition period and a democratic transition period initiated by the creation of the National Constituent Assembly (ANC).

19. Twenty-eight organizations met at the Tunisian Order of Lawyers head office in Tunis on February 11 to sign a communiqué establishing the National Council for the Protection of the Revolution and calling for the President to recognize the revolution by executive order. They sought decision-making power in addition to an advisory role.

20. Formed on January 20, 2011, the January 14 Front lies squarely on the left of the political spectrum. The Front is dominated by the PCOT and the Democratic Patriots' Movement, and also includes several left-wing and Arab nationalist organizations, backed by a close-knit group of UGTT activists. The Front called for the dissolution of institutions inherited from the former regime, such as the Chamber of Deputies, Senate and Supreme Judicial Council, as well as for constituent assembly elections to be held within a year.

21. These include the National Council for Liberties in Tunisia (CNLT), the Tunisian Association of Democratic Women (ATFD), the National Union of Tunisian Journalists (SNJT) and the Tunisian Human Rights League (LTDH), which all withdrew from the project at the outset.

22. The proposals that the High Authority Council accepted and approved by a majority vote were submitted to the Council of Ministers and the President's Office for approval by executive order.

23. Nessma TV, November 16, 2011.

24. The discipline commission, chaired by a member of the Executive Board, intervenes when a unionist is accused of breaking union regulations. Many union members have been stripped of their responsibilities within the organization via the commission after having objected to Executive Board decisions or questioned the authority of the Secretary General.

25. Sahbani served as UGTT Secretary General from 1989 to 2000.

26. Founded by Abdeljelil Bedoui, a UGTT economist, expert and advisor, on April 28, 2011.

27. The Congress for the Republic (*al-Mu'tamar min-ajl al-Jumhûriya*) was established in 2001 by activists from left-wing, Arab nationalist and political Islam movements.

4 The Tabarka Congress

Revolutionary Zeal Tests the UGTT's Unity

In times of crisis, unionists always say that it is important to protect the *chqaf*, imagery used by sailors in reference to the ship [*flouka*]. Farhat Hached and Habib Achour hail from Kerkennah,[1] an area that lives off the sea, so it's understandable that their proverbs are related to that environment. Protecting the *chqaf* from storms means that you have to throw things overboard to protect the boat, you have to lighten the load on the boat. Farhat Hached was the first to use the term and Achour also used it several times, mainly in moments of crisis. He says that we have to save the boat—the UGTT—because it's our boat and it has to reach terra firma [*bar al-amân*].

Mohamed Trabelsi, former UGTT Deputy Secretary General

The theme of the 22nd Tunisian General Labor Union Congress, held in Tabarka from December 25 to 28, 2011, was "I love you, O People," a posthumous homage to martyr leader Farhat Hached, who founded the union confederation in 1946. The congress was held at a crucial moment in Tunisian history, after the uprising on December 17, 2010, and the National Constituent Assembly elections on October 23, 2011. The 22nd UGTT Congress should therefore be regarded not only as an important event in the UGTT's history, but also as a milestone in Tunisian history. The congress is where the UGTT makes its most critical decisions, from electing new leadership to setting policy directions for union and political initiatives. Publicly, the UGTT continued to express confidence and highlight its role in the revolution and democratic transition. In reality, however, the 22nd Congress was held amid an extraordinary political climate and the union's unity and place in Tunisia's fast-moving social and political landscape was at stake. Tensions began to rise inside and outside the organization over the UGTT's role as a political actor and its duties as a union. Not only did the union have to overcome the defamation campaigns waged after Ben Ali's departure, it also had to contend with changes to the traditional model of trade unionism, namely the arrival of two new unions: the General Tunisian Labor Confederation (Confédération Générale Tunisienne du Travail, or CGTT) and the Union of Tunisian Workers (Union des Travailleurs de Tunisie, or UTT). In addition

Images 4.1–4.3 Scenes from the Tabarka Congress in December 2011: The Conference Room, the Podium and the Handover of Power from Abdessalem Jrad (Left) to Houcine Abbassi (Right).

Source: © Montassar Akremi, UGTT.

to those pressures, a number of important issues were on the agenda at the congress, including plans to restructure the union, efforts to draft a new Tunisian constitution, and the platform for economic and social action that was to be proposed to the government. The time had come for the UGTT to iron out the details of its role in the new political sphere. Some 500 delegates attended and a plethora of Executive Board candidates—50, including 7 women—campaigned, demonstrating the high stakes of the congress.

The new UGTT Executive Board elected at the Tabarka Congress in December 2011 represented a victory for the "left-wing consensus" list and Houcine Abbassi, who was appointed Secretary General. To what extent did the 22nd Congress enable the UGTT to break with past practices, rise to the main challenges facing national trade unionism and keep pace with the transformation of Tunisian politics? How did the UGTT prevent internal and external tensions from bubbling over?

To answer these questions, I will first present the challenges described by my interviewees. Then I will hone in on the issues that influenced the delegates' voting decisions.[2] Finally, I will review the outcome of the congress in terms of the areas in which the UGTT broke with the past or maintained continuity in the new political and social landscape.[3]

Organizational Challenges and Political Hurdles

The congress provides an opportunity for the UGTT to set forth its goals as a trade union, as well as for democracy and the country as a whole. The 22nd Congress in Tabarka was held during a particularly tense period. In addition to the usual organizational challenges, the UGTT had to make vital political decisions in order to chart a path that would maintain unity within the organization. The delegates interviewed expressed two major concerns: the role that the UGTT would have in the political transition and its place in the post-election political and trade-union landscape. Would the UGTT succeed in adapting its bodies, organization and traditional lobbying methods to reflect the country's new economic situation and support the democratic process?

Organizational Challenges

The interviewees were unanimous in naming what they called "the challenge of restructuring the union bodies" as the top priority for the UGTT. One core aspect of this restructuring was to decentralize decision-making—a key issue for unionists—in order to better adapt to economic and political changes and, above all, free union members from the hegemonic power of the Executive Board. The traditional, hierarchical, centralist structure was roundly criticized for impeding the emergence of democratic movements within the UGTT. For many years, this structure had concentrated power in the hands of the union bureaucracy and allowed the political regime to interfere with union affairs. The relative power of the secretary general rivaled that of Tunisia's president. The UGTT's centralized decision-making processes and certain internal regulations enabled the secretary general to control how the union operated. A former Executive Board member described the situation:

> Organizations like the UGTT are influenced by the structure of the government, namely the centralization of administrative, financial and decision-making processes in the hands of Ben Ali. The UGTT was influenced by this system and, much in the same way, had centralized power within the organization. However, the growth of the private sector and economic liberalization forced the UGTT to revise its methods. Once the country opened up politically, this completely centralized power ceased to exist and the UGTT had to rethink its own exaggerated centralism.
>
> (Mohamed, former union leader, Sfax)

One of the centralized provisions widely criticized by the interviewees was the ten-day strike notice. This provision required prior approval from the extended Executive Board for strikes sanctioned by base-union authorities. The Executive Board would often use this provision as a means to maintain its dominance over the unions and curb their zeal, or to sign agreements against activists' will:

> The fact that we need the signature of the central office [*markaziya naqâbiya*] and ten days' notice to strike is not right, not acceptable and even breaches international conventions. The UGTT's structure gives a lot of power to the Executive Board with regard to managing and implementing policy.
>
> (Sami, union official, Health Care, Bizerte)

> The goal is to free ourselves of centralized decision-making. It's important to have a governing body, but they shouldn't control my every move and act. I feel hemmed in by the current system for every type of action. Take a strike notice, for example. You have to go back to the regional union, which can turn you down and tell you that the situation described does not merit a strike. We don't have any independence and it's a problem.
>
> (Fatma, union activist, Textiles, Bizerte)

Moreover, the centralization that bolstered the Executive Board and Secretary General's power was underpinned by a skillfully developed system of privileges. The power structure within the union's chain of command remained in place through alliances formed with the regime and privileges granted. This cronyism was also prevalent in the union's internal affairs, structured relations between different levels of the hierarchy and sustained the Executive Board's dominance. Gaining access to privileges and cementing one's power within the organization became contingent on allegiance to the union's bureaucracy. The granting of job transfers is a mechanism that provides a perfect illustration of how this system of privileges worked. Union officials transferred to the central office were no longer bound to certain duties and enjoyed a higher social status that earned them recognition. However, they then had to do what the Executive Board expected of them. Union practices dictated that the transfer could be terminated early if the official disappointed or clashed with the leadership (Hamzaoui, *op. cit.*).

> The Executive Board's strategy for domination is as follows: if the Executive Board members are unable to enforce their decision, they are capable of buying people off with money or exploiting the transfer privilege. For our part, as the opposition, we had a lot of work but they never transfer us. When you give a unionist a transfer, he gets up when he wants, he goes to the UGTT when he wants, he goes on trips, he gets bonuses, and he distances himself from the opposition. When corruption doesn't work, they use force. They pressure people to tamper with the delegations. We've seen everything under the sun. In the beginning, you don't understand and over time, you find out everything—people who suddenly pay off all their debts or find a job for their children. They have the money and the network to attract people. If they can't find a weakness in their opponent, they bring him before the internal discipline commission.
>
> (Raoudha, union activist, Primary Education, Tunis)

> It's time to end privileges like transfers, which can be used to opportunistic ends. If you're a union official and have privileges . . . at any given time I can tell you to sign a statement, and if you don't, I'll take away everything. How can you defend workers if you receive privileges? I don't understand this system!
>
> (Sofiane, union activist, Energy, Sfax)

> Unionists have always had privileges. Ben Ali granted them privileges. For example, unionists' children are never unemployed—they all have privileges. They were given promotions at work. So and so would start as a teacher, be appointed director, get transferred and retire with a director's salary. People are only transferred with the government's blessing. A transfer is a promotion for union members—especially in education—and has been since the Ben Ali era.
>
> (Khaled, union official, Health Care, Tunis)

More repressive measures are also known to have been used. The discipline commission could strip unionists who opposed the central office of their union responsibilities:

They decided to dispose of us. They started inventing financial claims against us. They said that we had overspent but never provided us with the documents to prove it. We sent a bailiff to obtain evidence from them, but they couldn't accept that we would lodge a complaint against them. It was unheard of for a unionist to file a lawsuit. We asked for public meetings to be held with the unions to defend us, because the UGTT's machine had started working against us and Abdessalem Jrad used the media to discredit us and accuse us of theft. They prevented us from holding our meeting. . . . They threatened us and locked the room where we were going to meet. One of my friends was "frozen" [*mujammad*] for seven years and they "froze" me for two years.

> (Karima, union activist, Health Care, Tunis)

Democracy was a key principle at the UGTT: taking to the voting booth and complying with the UGTT's regulations, motions and rules. But it was a point of contention between us and the union leadership, who wanted to muzzle the democratic voice of the left-wing opposition. Several unionists were stripped [*tajrîd*] of their union responsibilities over several different periods. In addition to cancelling the May 1 [Labor Day] commemoration, some union leaders forbade sit-ins at UGTT offices and asked union bodies and regional unions to follow suit.

> (Fahmi, union official, Primary Education, Sidi Bouzid)

Escaping from the union bureaucracy's grasp thus depended on unionists' ability to end this system of privileges. Some proposed changes to the union's structure as a means of promoting democratic practices:

The Executive Board is elected by the Congress and if one of its members is found to be corrupt, he would go before the discipline commission, but there are no clear mechanisms for establishing a verdict. I think that we have to devise a structure that develops democratic practices within the UGTT, which reshapes how the various levels of the organization interact with each other and reworks the union's decision-making process.

> (Taoufik, union activist, Health Care, Sidi Bouzid)

I think that the UGTT definitely has to carry out a radical restructuring during the next phase, with changes to the statutes [*qânûn assassî*] and rules. It also has to rethink the make-up of organizations within the union, because the current structure cannot accommodate the growing number of members. For example, certain sectors are not under the aegis of a single general federation; it is important to separate the sectors in the new structure so that each sector is better organized for campaigning and assuming its responsibilities, with decision-making powers. Decision-making absolutely must be decentralized.

> (Omar, union activist, Energy, Tunis)

While Article 10 resolved the issue of term limits, questions remained regarding certain sectors and regions' participation in the decision-making process. Mohamed proposed extending the term-limit rule in Article 10 to the intermediate branches:

> We resisted the Executive Board's attempt to amend Article 10 during the Monastir Congress [December 2006] and we limited appointments to two terms but, as part of restructuring the UGTT, we need to expand this restructuring to the intermediate branches to ensure that power changes hands within the union. It is not right that certain regional union and general union members serve more than two terms.
>
> (Mohamed, union activist, Postal Service, Sfax)

More broadly, transparency was a ubiquitous goal among my interviewees, who saw it as a means of curtailing cronyism:

> There is a lot of corruption in the phosphate and oil sector. The problem with union work in the sector is that employers pay union officials three times the average salary. It's a real problem. Where we are, at the oil union, the system is crooked. There are completely unskilled people with union responsibilities; the union here is a gang that is sometimes more dangerous than the RCD. We won't be able to talk about transparency until the day the UGTT issues policy and financial reports at regional level. Transparency has to be everywhere. . . . The mafia and the Trabelsi family are firmly entrenched in the oil sector, which is very corrupt. There has always been collusion between the UGTT Executive Board and the RCD. . . . Is that how the UGTT serves as a counterbalance? I'm not so certain. For the UGTT to truly become a counterbalance, it has to amend the conditions for eligibility in the union and all its organizations, and update its rules. There should be one set of rules that apply to everyone; we need controls on how membership cards are issued, the financial reports need to be released, and we need to encourage transparency.
>
> (Kais, union activist, Energy, Sfax)

The events of the revolution led some regional unions and federations to make decisions unilaterally, without waiting for approval from the Executive Board. This set an interesting precedent that heralded new relations between the intermediate organizations and the central leadership and represented an opportunity to put an end to the Executive Board's hegemonic excesses. But this was clearly easier said than done. The UGTT had long operated based on the single-party system and a regime that used both repressive measures and a network of allegiances to subdue the UGTT Executive Board (c.f. Chapter 3). As a result, structural changes alone would not suffice to overhaul the UGTT. A new organizational structure would not immediately erase the system of social relationships that had governed the UGTT and the Tunisian political sphere for decades. As much as there was a need for restructuring, in truth, the overhaul of the UGTT was contingent on political developments and the social pact negotiated by the various components of Tunisian society.

Moreover, the UGTT has traditionally had a more robust presence in the public sector. As the economy liberalized, the structure of the employment market shifted dramatically and the expanding private sector and declining job security increasingly weighed on workplace relations. The UGTT was faced with a pressing need to adapt its structure and its traditional forms of action and dialogue with employers to reflect the new face of the job market. The need to restructure was made all the more urgent by the increase in UGTT membership after the revolution began, the vulnerable legal status of private-sector employees, and the lack of regulatory framework:

> The union's battleground will be the private sector. The private sector is a real priority. I work in the public sector and government bodies do a good job of regulating the civil service. But the private sector is marginalized and oppressed—that's where there is a lot of oppression. . . . There is a low rate of union membership in the private sector because workers are afraid of getting fired. Training unions in the private sector is a major challenge and the situation has deteriorated due to economic liberalization.
>
> (Sami, union official, Healthcare, Tunis)

Another unionist shares her perspective:

> The private sector is one of the hardest areas for union work. Company owners threaten to fire people who establish unions. Some Labor Code statutes governing the private sector haven't been changed for years. Leaders come and go but the laws are still the same. The minimum wage is 295 dinars; you can't live on 295 dinars, especially with how the cost of living has risen since the revolution. The private sector faces huge difficulties; its collective agreement is a disaster. Why? Because the people who wrote it just followed the regime's orders—the agreement wasn't drafted independently. We need an independent UGTT to revise the Labor Code. We have made gains with the revolution, especially with regards to securing a recognized status for certain employees.
>
> (Farah, union activist, Textiles, Bizerte)

Union leader Mohamed adds:

> You can imagine. The UGTT's structure and regulations are the same, even though the sociology of the working class defended by the UGTT has changed. For example, only two of the eighty Administrative

Commission members are private-sector representatives, despite the growing number of workers in the private sector. It's a sad reality.

(Mohamed, former union leader, Education, Sfax)

The interviewees cited the appointment of women to decision-making bodies as one of the UGTT's major organizational challenges. According to UGTT statutes and regulations, each regional union must have a commission for working women, and women are well represented—47%—in the base unions and union campaigns. Yet they remain absent from leadership roles. This is partly due to the fact that eligibility to serve on the UGTT Executive Board is limited by requirements pertaining to previous offices held at various levels (local, regional and federal) of the organization. These requirements reduce the number of women eligible and prevent them from rising to the central leadership.

The UGTT needs to overhaul its structure, management methods and the role of women—all those are major problems. Women represent 50% of members in the base unions but when you go a step higher, to the general unions and federations, women only represent 5%. If you go a step further up in the hierarchy, to the regional unions, there are only 2 women out of 216 members. . . . What is the explanation? Firstly, men dominate the union environment, and secondly, they don't always take women into consideration. In addition, you have to hold office twice in order to be eligible for a general union—the eligibility requirements are strict. For example, you have to serve two three-year terms in a base union to be eligible for an intermediate union, and then you need two four-year terms to be eligible for the Executive Board, so it takes at least fourteen years to gain a place on the Executive Board. How are women supposed to get an opportunity to become a candidate? We have established a women's committee and we're running a campaign for the inclusion of women in the Executive Board. Post-January 14, it's time for things to change. Pre-January 14, we were lobbying for a quota, but that's a thing of the past—now we want equal representation.

(Souad, union activist, Healthcare, Tunis)

Another unionist condemned the discrimination against women and dissident women unionists, in particular:

People want women to take part in meetings, strikes and sit-ins, but when they want to take on responsibilities, they're attacked from all sides. In my case, I'm part of the union opposition [al-liqâ'an-naqâbî dimoqratî] and have been accused of adultery. In some cases they call the husband to prevent his wife from running for office; they'll do anything to pressure and attack people. They buy people off, they harm women's reputation.

(Raoudha, union activist, Primary Education, Tunis)

Opinions are divided, however, with regard to the solution. Some believe that a quota system is the only solution capable of ensuring women gain access to positions of responsibility. Others are critical of that solution and believe those positions should only be granted based on merit. One union member shared her view:

> I am not for a quota system. I want women unionists to assert themselves and seize opportunities and I would like to see men support them. I view merit as the only valid criterion.
>
> (Faiza, union activist, Banking, Tunis)

The solution would then be to amend the eligibility requirements:

> Encouraging the presence of women in decision-making bodies is vital, but I'm against a quota system. I think that politics has to be opened up to women, so that they can take part in all decisions. That said, we have to be careful not to get caught up in the political scheming Ben Ali used in the past. Ben Ali has already used quota systems. I think that approach is insulting to women. I do my part by opening up the union to women and helping them. Women have to convey their ability to seize their rightful place. All the same, we need to change the eligibility requirements for the Executive Board. As things stand, you have to be of a certain age to become an Executive Board member.
>
> (Karim, union official, Energy, Tunis)

The same problem exists for young people, who are affected by job insecurity more than any other category of workers. Young people have low union membership rates and are unable to gain access to positions of power. Unionists are also divided on this issue. Some believed that experience is needed to take on that type of assignment:

> Young people are not very well represented in decision-making bodies because the young generation is afraid—the union scares them—because, whether we like it or not, the government targets the UGTT. We tend to protect the young people; we don't want them to be on the frontline. We prefer to enlist people of a certain age who have some experience to lead the fight against the government.
>
> (Mounira, union activist, Textiles, Ben Arous)

Others believed that young people have their rightful place in decision-making bodies:

> It is impossible for young people under 35 to be elected to the board under the regulations [*qânûn assassî*] currently in effect. Suppose that a unionist begins work at 23 or 24 years old. He has no easy path to the Executive Board. Imagine that he has served two successful terms in an

intermediate branch [a prerequisite for an Executive Board campaign].
He still can't gain a place on the Executive Board until he is 40 years
old—after the internationally recognized youth cut-off age of 35.

(Salah, union official, Higher Education, Sfax)

The UGTT clearly needed to restructure its organization in order to adjust
to the new economic environment and developments among the working
class, while also instituting the democratic processes key to supporting the
political changes underway. It remained to be seen, however, whether a new
organization could emerge from the overlapping sector, regional and political interests that had come to shape union practices.

Political Hurdles

All the interviewees agreed that the main challenge of the 22nd UGTT Congress was to reach a consensus regarding a policy approach to the political
and social changes underway in Tunisia. Banker and unionist Hassanine
summed up the issues at stake: "The advent of the revolution left the UGTT
at a crossroads. It had to deal with trade-union pluralism. When a country
accepts political pluralism, it also has to accept media pluralism and union
pluralism." During the single-party era, the UGTT was the only forum for
different political viewpoints, and the UGTT congress was often a political
competition to make inroads within the union. How would the arrival of
political and union pluralism impact the organization?

Political Pluralism

There was total agreement among the unionists interviewed that the congress
should serve as an opportunity for the UGTT to assert its independence and
self-reliance—the only means of staying above the fray. The unionists would
often recite the same phrase: "although our aims are equal parts political
and social, we have to keep the political parties at an equal distance." The
question, then, was not whether the UGTT had a political role to play, but
rather how to define the nature and limits of this role:

> The key is for the UGTT is to retain its independence from the govern-
> ment and political parties. The UGTT must remain independent and
> free of any ties with the government. It would be good to reach a con-
> sensus on how to organize things and cooperate, but the UGTT has to
> remain self-reliant.
>
> (Fatma, union activist, Textiles, Bizerte)

Maher, member of the Union of Unemployed Graduates (UDC):

> Ennahdha is going to mount an offensive against the UGTT. Ennahdha
> is going to try to subdue the UGTT through the congress and it's a real

problem. I don't have any problem with unionists' political affiliation—
everyone is free to choose a political party and I also defended that
freedom for the UDC, but I refuse to let the organization be exploited
for partisan ends. . . . When I say that Ennahdha wants to exploit the
UGTT, that doesn't mean that the left is not doing the same; all the
political parties use the same techniques.

Citing these concerns, several unionists emphasize the importance of
electing a new Executive Board capable of protecting the organization from
political clashes and abolishing old practices:

I hope that there will be a good Executive Board. Emotional or partisan thinking shouldn't play a part in the selection of the new Executive Board members. We need real activists who care about union work
because this is a difficult period and the leaders who take the reins have
to be capable of protecting the organization. This is the most critical
period, so we absolutely must support the real activists, no matter what
part of the organization they belong to.

(Fadwa, union activist, Health Care, Sfax)

We have to assert our independence; for a long time the Executive Board
had to bow to the government. Mark my words: if the real activists fail to
form a united front, the union bureaucracy will renew their terms at the
congress in December 2011, which would be a disaster. (Adel, union official,
Secondary Education, Redeyef)

Along similar lines, human rights activist Nouri laments the exploitation
of the UGTT for political ends and hopes that the end of the dictatorship
will represent a fresh start for the union:

Has the left not replaced its partisan, political battle with the union
battle by making inroads at the UGTT? In so doing, it has hurt the
organization a lot. Has the left focused on the goals of union work,
namely guaranteeing social equality? After all, the purpose of a union
is to combat exploitation, is it not? Haven't the goals of union initiatives been sacrificed for partisan considerations? Several workers
believe that the political activists who joined the UGTT have worked
against its interests, because political parties' interests often take precedence over labor issues. That's some apolitical unionists' main criticism
of certain politicized unions like Health Care and the Postal Service.
The UGTT establishment often uses these politicized unions for political aims, preventing effective negotiations with employers that win
concessions for employees. We can only hope that the political parties'
newfound liberty will help the UGTT to adapt and focus on its role as
a union.

The political parties remained weak, however, leading most unionists to continue to view the UGTT as the only bulwark against the

hegemonic excesses of the ruling power. They sought to protect the UGTT's independence, but also saw the union as the sole guardian of the "modernist" gains Tunisia had made. Moreover, the various left-wing factions that had suffered a bruising defeat during the ANC elections were particularly active within the UGTT. For unionists belonging to these political groups, the congress represented a substantial opportunity to close ranks and join forces to achieve the same political goals by setting aside internal disputes and parochial rivalries. This caused the political battle to take precedence over union and social concerns, with resistance to Ennahdha becoming the leitmotiv of the campaign.

The problem is that the political parties are weak and will keep up the strategy they used under Bourguiba and Ben Ali: entryism and taking over organizations. I think that the political parties that took refuge in the UGTT pre-January 14 will continue their efforts to coopt the union. . . . The political parties' fight over the constituent assembly is set to continue, with repercussions for the UGTT. And the alliances formed at the UGTT congress will mirror those established within the ANC.

(Adel, union official, Secondary Education, Redeyef)

Mounir, a textile union official based in Ben Arous, added:

I think that the religious parties' message is double talk that lacks honesty and clarity. One can attempt to be modernist and have different practices. The Islamists clearly have to be given a chance—they have a right to take part in the elections—but it would be dangerous to let them dominate the political arena and the UGTT's role is to work to achieve the modernist project.

Other unionists downplayed the risk of Islamists taking over the UGTT and considered the real challenge to be removing the RCD members, who were well represented in the union's various bodies. They also regretted that political considerations had overshadowed issues related to restructuring the organization.

There have always been Islamists with ties to Ennahdha in the UGTT, but they don't have a strong political presence. The RCD is well represented via the secretaries general of certain federations and regional unions. There were a few attempts to oust them but they were very limited. The unionists are focusing on national politics rather than the internal structure of the UGTT; political problems are overshadowing union issues.

(Akremi, union official, Primary Education, Sidi Bouzid)

Box 6 Independence: An Important Issue for All Unions

The issues of trade unions' independence from the parties arose as soon as Bourguiba took power. If you weren't a member of the PSD [Socialist Destourian Party], you couldn't take part in Tunisian politics. Everyone whose party was refused legal authorization took up union work, even certain people who are now members of Ennahdha. . . . Most members of [the students' union] UGET, for example, had a political affiliation other than the RCD. Almost all of the core founders of the UDC had been UGET members. . . . The issue came up at the UDC as soon as we received our permit, but things were different for us because we had established a basis for action: defending employment law. It was more difficult to attack us in that area. The only way to attack us was to accuse us of having a political agenda—it was easier to say, "He belongs to such and such political movement" and then to link the UDC to that party. But it was still a real problem, and it began to hurt us. . . .

Another problem was union education. We still have yet to make the distinction between union work and politics. It's hard to get the point across that you can belong to a union without having any political affiliation, that you can be independent. Union independence is a major challenge. You can't prevent someone from adhering to an ideology or being a card-holding party member, but it is their responsibility to refrain from imposing their ideology and methods on the union. Members of the UDC central, regional and local offices should not hold responsibilities at political parties. In order to protect the organization's independence. The UDC's principles are sufficient for establishing a policy direction. We don't want to get caught up in an ideological conflict. We went through that conflict at the UGET, I experienced it firsthand and saw what an enormous waste it was. We can't repeat that mistake, especially given all the former UGET members who are now at the UDC. Union independence is a vital principle and a lesson we can't forget.

Excerpt from an interview with Maher Hamdi
(Chaïfa and Hamdi, *op. cit.*, 93).

Union Pluralism

Union pluralism was the second topic addressed at length by the interviewees. There was general agreement that while union pluralism has its rightful place, in Tunisia it was primarily implemented as a means to undermine the UGTT. Many pointed a finger at the "counterrevolutionary forces" from the former regime, who they say attacked the UGTT in order to stymie its political efforts.

> The creation of new union confederations raises a lot of questions, especially because they haven't brought anything new to the table in terms of ideology. The UGTT was already open to all employees, regardless of

status, gender or political opinion. The decision to allow union pluralism reflects a confluence of several different aims. Firstly, it is a punishment for the UGTT for the role it played in the revolution and the
general strikes in January. It was also an opportunity for employers
to divide the union's united front. Many companies didn't hesitate to
provide support to the new organizations, in order to establish "home-
bred unions" that were more conciliatory. Finally, these federations
were a godsend for former RCD "trade branches" seeking a fresh start
after the dissolution of their parent organization. When you talk about
union pluralism, you have to talk about it both in theory and in practice. Negotiations with employers are often dictated by the balance of
power. When a union is united it has the upper hand; when there are
several unions, employers and the government will capitalize on that
in an attempt to divide employee representatives. From a democratic
standpoint, people are obviously free to choose whatever political parties and organizations they wish. There is no reason to deny them that.
Unfortunately, however, counterrevolutionary forces have close ties
with the unions, like Sahbani's UTT, which is exploiting the revolution
to steal workers' money. He served as UGTT Secretary General for a
long time under Ben Ali and did a lot of harm to the UGTT by making
corruption widespread. Now he wants to be a trade union player, which
is unacceptable, especially because he is strongly suspected of stealing
money from the UGTT.

(Radhi Ben Hassine, union official, Energy, Tunis)

One of the newly formed unions, the UTT, was led by former UGTT Secretary General (1989–1999) and Ben Ali ally Ismaïl Sahbani, raising further
doubts about the intentions behind union pluralism. Sahbani had worked
to muzzle the UGTT, stifle the protest movements and bend the UGTT to
the will of the regime and employers. He was forced to resign in September
2000 and later charged and convicted of corruption and embezzlement in
October 2001. Sahbani's ignominious past fueled skepticism among UGTT
members about the true aims of union pluralism:

The goal of union pluralism is to break up the UGTT. Former UGTT
leader Sahbani is notoriously corrupt. He's been to prison and his followers must have a dark past like him. The two unions that were created
cannot compete with the UGTT's history and fighting spirit; they can't
attract the sort of high-quality union officials there are at the UGTT.

(Adnene Hajji, union leader, Redeyef)

Union pluralism is a good idea in theory but when I see people like
Sahbani—who is corrupt, went to prison and now presents himself as
an activist heading a union—I think to myself that there is a problem.

Union pluralism has become a venue for increasingly ambitious efforts to weaken the UGTT.

(Aisha, human rights activist, Tunis)

Other unionists questioned who was funding the creation of the new unions. They believed that companies were seeking to undermine the working class and advance the free-market economic model predominant in Tunisia:

> The Tunisian dictatorship enjoyed broad support from the Europeans and Americans and, right after January 14, the European Union decided to fund and support union pluralism in Tunisia, with the knowledge that it had failed in several countries. The idea is to advance free-market economic principles. It is obvious to me that the goal is to break up the UGTT, the only organization capable of uniting Tunisian workers and defending their rights.
>
> (Sami, union official, Health Care, Tunis)

> I'm ok with union pluralism when the people in charge are honest. What strikes me as odd at the moment is the massive influx of funding for these new unions. I wonder where this money is coming from. The government isn't saying anything but it certainly can't be from membership dues. It's true that the UGTT helped bring down the Ben Ali regime, which altered where a lot of people's interests lie. As a consequence, it could be a strategic move by some people to break up the UGTT by encouraging others to form unions.
>
> (Souad, union official, Health Care, Tunis)

For his part, nurse and unionist Khaled noted that the new union confederations were not backed by their own alternative vision as a union and did not necessarily offer benefits for workers. He also criticized their one-upmanship, which he viewed as evidence of their leaders' opportunism:

> Promoting union pluralism is adding fuel to the fire in a time of social turbulence, exaggerated salary demands, one-upmanship, misconduct and illegal strikes. We're dealing with a union organization that is far and away the country's most popular—quasi-hegemonic—and two union confederations formed without any real planning or local roots, which don't add anything. Even their logos and letterhead copy the UGTT; they offer nothing new. All they want their piece of the pie! They started by raising the stakes. The textile company in Ras Jebel closed because of rising union demands. The UGTT had reached an agreement on pay raises, the textile company was in trouble, and then the UTT members arrived to say that the raise wasn't large enough. There was a

mass strike and the management closed up shop and left! They were left unemployed, with nothing in return!

Other unionists' revealed that in their eyes, the ultimate goal of union pluralism was to fracture workers' unity, especially given the fact that the decision was made during the rather unstable political transition:

> As regards union pluralism, I think that it wasn't wise to authorize pluralism during the transition period because it could undermine a union organization that had a very important role in the revolution and afterwards and helps achieve the goals of the revolution. When you look at the current consequences of union pluralism—what's happening on the street, the sit-ins and the rising number of strikes—you see how the new unions have upped the ante.
>
> (Karim, union official, Energy, Tunis)

> In my opinion, as things stand today, any attempt to form a union in the name of pluralism is designed to disrupt union work in a very unstable political environment. There is always the risk of businessmen buying off people in the government to maintain the old laws and break down unionists' unity. I don't think the situation can withstand union pluralism.
>
> (Samira, journalist)

> Union pluralism is different from political pluralism. Union pluralism is rooted in economic issues and demands specific to sectors. If we establish union pluralism, there will be competition between the unions, which will fracture workers' unity. It's a real problem. We've seen it in Morocco and Algeria and it failed.
>
> (Sghair, union official, Transportation, Gafsa)

In the same vein, UDC member Sabra saw a connection between union pluralism and efforts to weaken the UGTT, and explained that other organizations like the UDC had been affected by the same phenomenon:

> With all due respect to the party activists, the UGTT was the only place where one could exercise one's rights in Tunisia. The union had existed since the colonial period and despite all the challenges it faced, it was the only refuge in Tunisia—a sort of stronghold. There is no way that our interests will clash with theirs. What's more, the new unions that were recently established [the CGTT and UTT] are staffed by corrupt former UGTT officials who were able to obtain permits. The truth of the matter is that the goal isn't pluralism, but to weaken the UGTT, the only national organization capable of uniting everyone regardless of political differences. Meanwhile, there are also efforts to divide the

UDC. With more than 10,000 members, we now have a certain amount of power. We were elected to the constituent assembly in Jendouba and have regional offices and a base of 30,000 supporters. A parallel association, the Tunisian Association for the Defense of Graduates and Employment [ATDDE], was founded at the trade union center on February 25. Ennahdha has also created a league of unemployed graduates. We think that former RCD members are behind the ATDDE.

(Chaïfa, Hamdi, *op. cit.*)

One of the purposes of the congress was therefore to shore up the union's unity and cohesiveness. One of the interviewees explained:

Union plurality is now lawful, but we prefer union unity. The congress has to enable us to shore up the organization's unity. Union pluralism is a real challenge and we need to revamp the structure of the UGTT, update its organization and close ranks to rise to that challenge.

(Anis, union activist, Mining, Redeyef)

Some of the unionists made a point of mentioning the various attempts at union pluralism that had ended in failure. They expressed confidence in the UGTT's heritage and staying power, while also belittling the new unions' leaders as "orphans" of the UGTT:

I'm not afraid of union pluralism—we're sure of ourselves. There have already been attempts to create new unions, in 1946 and 1978, and it didn't work. The two new unions were established by "children" of the UGTT. I don't understand why they did it, normally there's no reason to stray from the UGTT. Union pluralism isn't an issue for me.

(Fatma, union activist, Textiles, Bizerte)

I think it's shameful that former UGTT members founded the new unions. I don't understand these people who belonged to the UGTT and had the privilege of being involved with the UGTT and Hached's heritage and history. I don't understand how these people made the decision to leave the UGTT for opportunistic reasons or for vote-getting. I think that people who leave the organization become orphans without an identity. Your identity is your UGTT membership, your identity is the heritage of Hached and his successors. I don't understand how people can leave the organization. I can withstand repression, marginalization and exclusion within the organization. . . . It is my duty to remain loyal to the organization because I can't let my conflicts with unionists push me to leave the organization. The people behind past attempts to create parallel unions have paid dearly. That sort of act is unforgiveable; history won't forgive them.

(Ridha, union official, Postal Service, Bizerte)

Other unionists thought that union pluralism could nonetheless provide an opportunity to restructure the UGTT more swiftly:

> The UGTT has never been a revolutionary union. Don't forget that the UGTT lent political support to Ben Ali. Don't forget that before the revolution, the UGTT didn't touch major issues like pensions or the social security fund. I think that if union pluralism is instated, the UGTT will have to carry out reforms. If the UGTT comes up against union pluralism, it will have to become more democratic. It will have to become more effective to attract more members and unionists and prevent people from joining the new unions. . . . I think that union pluralism is positive because people will be free to choose the organization that suits them best and I think that will curb cronyism at the UGTT.
>
> (Raoudha, union activist, Primary Education, Tunis)

Finally, various interviewees stated that the goals of the revolution had not yet been achieved. In their view, the challenge for the UGTT was to propose a viable social and economic program capable of steering Tunisia away from the free-market model and providing solutions to the socioeconomic issues raised by the revolution. For instance, UGTT spokesman Abid Briki said during his speech at the congress: "The UGTT rejects the government's decision to meet Tunisia's prior commitments to the European Union and the USA. These commitments have only hurt Tunisia and its workers, in particular." Another unionist struck a similar tone:

> There is a lot of talk about democratic challenges and the UGTT's political role in leading the democratic transition, but it's important to remember that it was the economic and social demands of the country's marginalized that sparked the revolution. The UGTT needs to stop acquiescing in the government's free-market policies and offer a real economic and political alternative.
>
> (Adel, union official, Secondary Education, Redeyef)

In sum, the interviewees' remarks reveal two schools of thought that coexist and sometimes clash at the congress. Most unionists viewed political action as the top priority, in particular maintaining the unity required to establish an even balance of power with the new government. Another group with fairly strong representation in the base and intermediate branches favored socioeconomic issues as the priority for action, while also calling for more democracy and decentralized decision-making within the union. The challenge at the congress was to address these conflicting pressures from each side while maintaining unity and the power to take action.

Box 7 Union Pluralism Puts the UGTT to the Test

The UGTT is now the only organization of its type in modern Tunisia to have persevered for six decades. But each time there was problem between the union leadership and the government, the latter would hatch a rival union to weaken the UGTT and make it step back into line. This phenomenon occurred in 1956, in the early 1960s and in 1984, under Ben Ali's rule. The remnants of the former regime, business owners and groups representing interim job companies subjected the UGTT to deadly attacks between February and April 2011. We realized that this phenomenon resulted from certain errors and gambles made by union leadership, which has to take total responsibility for the harm this has done to members' confidence in how our union's decision-makers handle issues related to workers. During the Tabarka Congress, we took a critical look at ourselves and recognized the errors we have made along the way. This state of affairs led several members to seek out protection for their rights at other organizations, but many are now coming back into the fold. What worked against us is the fact that the structure of the UGTT has remained static since it was founded, preventing the union from adjusting to new developments in the job market. The UGTT needs to be restructured.

Sami Tahri, Deputy Secretary in charge of Information
(*Le courrier Tunisie*, May 29, 2012)

Consensus: The Watchword of the Tabarka Congress

The 22nd UGTT Congress began proceedings on December 25, 2011 in Tabarka, with 581 delegates in attendance. Working under the helm of Abdessalem Jrad, who was elected Congress Chairman, the delegates addressed burning questions regarding the future of the central leadership, base branches and regional and sector organizations. The congress would quickly—and spectacularly—lay bare the political tensions affecting the union and the looming risk of implosion. The delegates' speeches during the plenary sessions focused on the challenges described above, punctuated by impassioned debate over two major concerns: the Executive Board's close ties with the former regime and the Executive Board members' ambiguous positions between December 17, 2010 and January 14, 2011. Remember that several regional and general unions actively supported the protests against the Ben Ali regime without first consulting with the union leadership. Understandably, there were calls for the Executive Board to answer for its actions during the Ben Ali years. Abdessalem Jrad's responded to these appeals by noting that no one is perfect: "Criticize the leadership. Everyone makes mistakes. But don't jeopardize the organization's unity." The Executive Board used the last day of the congress as an opportunity for a *mea culpa*, with all members recognizing their error in backing the deposed president's candidacy in 2004 and 2009. Jrad ended the proceedings by admitting for the first time, "Yes, we made a mistake by voting for Ben Ali." Executive Board spokesman Abid Briki attributes the leadership's past support to the circumstances of the era, when "all forms of power were concentrated in the hands of a single person."

The crisis situation at the UGTT led the various factions within the union to close ranks and prevent infighting between unionists close to the former regime—in particular members of the outgoing leadership—and those who backed a radical stance. The second major concern that dominated discussions was the importance of defending the organization against the attacks it was suffering. Secondary education unionist Naceur Zeribi: "The unionists have to set aside their differences to fight the smear campaigns designed to undermine their organization." According to the unionists interviewed, the main challenge was to maintain unity. The new majority—Ennahdha and the CPR, in particular—had scant union representation and picked up where their predecessors had left off with hostile statements toward the UGTT, making unity of even greater importance to the delegates. In unison, the delegates rejected the six-month moratorium on strikes and political truce requested by President Moncef Marzouki on December 16, 2011. Alongside applause for the rousing speeches underlining the importance of independence from the government, the congress saw the union move in a decidedly political direction.

On the economic and labor front, the delegates reacted to accusations blaming the UGTT for the rise in strikes and social tensions. Various speeches rejected responsibility for the chaotic strikes held without consent from the central office, while also emphasizing that it was important not to punish those accountable. The unionists asserted that the only valid explanation for the social upheaval was the years of despotism and injustice suffered by the Tunisian people. In their remarks, they claimed that the legal and constitutional vacuum created by the first transition government and the torpid response to social demands had stoked social tensions across the country. They also condemned the repressive approach taken with protestors and called for a dialogue aimed at finding tangible solutions. The resolutions at the congress represented a clear rebuke of the predominant economic model in Tunisia, a critique of the "the failure of the free-market model based on speculation, the free movement of capital, privatization and stimulation of exports at the expense of domestic demand." Several unionists called for amendments to the Association Agreement established between Tunisia and the European Union and to agreements with the United States signed by the previous government. Finally, the UGTT announced a platform for economic and social action detailing the main lines of the initiatives that would be carried out during the subsequent phase.

The delegates argued that the UGTT needed to maintain its political role without neglecting its union duties, while also asserting their independence from political parties and the government. "What Tunisia needs today is a strong union organization that is independent from the government," declared Mongi Ben M'barek, Secretary General of the Postal and Tele-communications Federation. "Our organization now must play the role of participant, guardian and guide in the democratic process underway." The delegates portrayed the UGTT as the custodian of Tunisia's "modernist" gains and underlined their intention to make their voices heard and play a full-fledged role in the political transition.

The delegates also adopted a draft constitution that the incoming leaders were tasked with defending at the National Constituent Assembly. The general directive was to seek consensus and protect the general interests of the organization, which, according to the unionists, was morally obligated to help bring democracy to Tunisia and address workers' concerns.

To what extent, then, did the delegates' voting behavior reflect these organizational and political challenges?

The System of Allegiance and Efforts to Retain Power Shape the Democratic Process With the Union

When questioned about how elections are held at the UGTT Congress, most of the interviewees confirmed that—aside from the Sahbani era when the UGTT was ruled with an iron fist—the voting process was often transparent and compliant with union rules. Lazhar, a teacher and union official in Tunisia, said on the topic:

> If your question pertains to the procedures that govern elections, the elections at the UGTT have always followed the rules established by the delegates. The one exception is the Sahbani period, when we witnessed obvious vote-rigging; that's the dark period in the UGTT and Tunisia's history.

With regard to the controversies surrounding Jrad's corruption, Redeyef-based unionist Adel pointed out that that the proper procedures were also followed at the previous congress in Monastir:

> Jrad was elected leader of the organization—you can't just go and tell him to get lost after January 14! What right would you have to do that? We told Ben Ali to get lost because the elections were a mockery, but the procedures are often respected at the UGTT Congress.

Others remarked that while the voting procedures had been followed, the voting was guided by political horse-trading and alliances rather than the candidates' platforms. The results of the elections were often decided in advance:

> One of the major challenges the UGTT faces is the challenge of democracy. It is true that the election procedures are followed, but voting is

rarely done based on a platform. The culture at the UGTT is based on bureaucracy and alliances that we commonly refer to as "skullduggery" [*tkanbîn*]. But I hope that things will change, I hope that the delegates will vote for platforms instead of people.

(Lazhar, union official, Primary Education, Tunis)

Analyses of the UGTT delegates' voting behavior reveal the importance of the history of the Tunisian workers' movement—the UGTT, in particular—which shaped the organization's identity and continues to influence unionists' voting decisions. One aspect of this history is regional loyalties, which are considered a structural component of voting patterns (Amami, *op. cit.*). Historically, regional loyalties have had a major impact on the make-up of the union leadership and the UGTT has always operated via an unorthodox combination of regional segmentation and hierarchical bureaucratic procedure. Salah Hamzaoui explains that this phenomenon has endured due to political and economic disparities between regions. Hamzaoui asserts that

the effective division of the country into regions with their own set of values increases the use of regional belonging as an instrument for defense or domination, which, in turn, revives and strengthens inter- and intra-regional loyalties. One only has to look, to give an example at the UGTT, to the polarized relations at the union between the two major union regions, Gafsa and Sfax.

(Hamzaoui, *op. cit.* 21–77)

He notes that the Sahel region is in the minority within the union, but dominant economically and politically, theorizing that at the top echelons of the union, political and economic power is governed by regional divisions.

One illustration of this can be seen in Mongi Amami's analysis of voting behavior at the Monastir Congress in 2006, where the candidates were clustered around two main hubs: Sfax/Gafsa, the "traditional" hub that sought to retain its hegemony over the union by claiming "historical legitimacy," and the northwest/southeast, termed the "hub of insubordination" (Amami, *op. cit.*). The shifting composition of the Tunisian working class has brought additional factors to the fore that accentuate the effect of regional alliances on voting behavior, namely the fact that more workers belong to specific sectors and/or have a political affiliation. Voting alliances determine the electoral clout of sectors such as education and far-left political groups like the Tunisian Workers' Communist Party (PCOT), the Democratic Patriots' Movement and the Arab nationalists. As such, the Executive Board members' ability to retain or gain power within the union—and privileges for their communities of alliances—is dependent on their control over the various networks within the union. This results in often-delicate compromises involving the various regional, sector and political factors at play.

> What we call the "union bureaucracy" [*birûqrâtiya naqâbiya*] plays a vital role in determining the composition of the Executive Board. The bureaucracy spans all sectors, because the various figures in the Executive Board have networks in every sector. The Executive Board has a leading role in establishing [electoral] lists with broad support, based on three criteria: a division of seats (*mûhâssassa*) based on political affiliations, regional factors and the sway of each sector. Each sector has a delegation quota; there are sectors with 29 delegations and others with 60. But you have to account for the fact that delegations from a single sector don't necessarily follow the same directives due to the wide range of political leanings among their ranks. The elections are democratic and transparent—the decisions are made at the ballot box—but there are political alliances that are managed by the Executive Board. Everything is planned out at the Executive Board, which oversees the balance between the various regional, sector and political factors.
>
> (Ridha, union official, Postal Service, Bizerte)

In the electoral races, the voting procedures are followed meticulously, but victory is achieved by any means necessary, from coopting delegates in return for privileges to manipulating memberships to gain power:

> The union bureaucracy functions as follows: it asks if such-and-such union section is loyal to it or not. If the section is loyal, everything is ok, but if not they do whatever they can to bribe it. They will help the secretary general find a job for his son or loan him money. They may also pay people to vote for them or create fake memberships. They take advantage of people's weak spots to stomp out any type of opposition.
>
> (Bilel, union official, Postal Service, Sfax)

These arrangements are made possible by the union's well-oiled bureaucracy. The people who control what the unionists often call the "bureaucratic machine"—and union regulations, in particular—have the ability to influence voting via how they distribute delegations for the elections or grant memberships:

> Jrad handled the union regulations. The person who handles the regulations holds the power because he controls the *tkanbîn*, the political trickery and the underhanded moves like coopting people or marginalizing them. He also controls the leadership of the congresses at the base unions and general unions. That means that the person who handles the regulations has a great deal of power within the UGTT. I hope that at

the next congress, the distribution of delegations won't be rigged. You work and you slog away to win over base unions and then you find yourself confronted with the rigging problem.

(Thamer, journalist)

The oil sector is a sector with a lot of money and people have a lot of privileges. . . . The unionists in that sector always have a lot of a lot of privileges. They don't steal, but they get promoted. Recently an oil company hired 50 cleaning women who were co-opted to win the union elections. They were hired on temporary contracts and were promised permanent employment if they voted for the right list.

(Souheil, manager at a state-run company, Energy, Tunis)

The controversy surrounding Article 10 is indicative of the importance attributed to formal rules in the battle to retain power in the union bureaucracy. Radhi Ben Hassine notes that the central leadership attempted, not unlike Ben Ai, to change the rules in order to remain in power. Just as with the regime, dissenting voices could be reduced to silence through repressive measures:

Article 10 limits Executive Board members to two terms, a decision made at the Djerba Congress in 2002. At the Monastir Congress in 2007, the Executive Board sought to overturn Article 10 so that it could remain in power, just as Ben Ali did. We opposed their attempt and there was a fight to leave the article untouched. Everyone who opposed the will of the Executive Board was subjected to punishments like the cancellation of job transfers and smear campaigns.

(Radhi Ben Hassine, union official, Energy, Tunis)

Judging from the commentary above, the election campaigns appear to be determined by a subtle combination of regional issues, sector-based interests and political considerations.[4] The ability to retain power within the union is intertwined with the Executive Board candidates' success in achieving compromises between the various networks. The hierarchy and formal rules governing the voting process are scrupulously observed, but also used to maintain the network of allegiances and the systems of privileges required to keep the union bureaucracy in power. At the same time, the congress is structured in a way that prevents any infringement of the union's democratic procedures from occurring. This formal, stringent form of democracy guarantees legitimacy and renders the decisions made at the congress indisputable. It also lends a certain amount of credibility to the Executive Board that is elected, which is desirable for the political party in power because the government doesn't necessarily want a toothless union. In addition to enshrining the power of the Executive Board in an institutional framework, these formal rules prevent potential overreach in the privilege-based system. In this way, the formal rules do not conflict with the allegiance-based governance, but serve as a check that strikes a balance between criminal inclinations and democratic zeal. The organization has also established additional safeguards such as the Administrative Commission, which makes decisions based on the proportional representation of groups within the union, enabling left-wing activists to offset the Executive Board's designs on hegemony.

While some have put forward the argument that this system prevents unionists from overcoming their regional loyalties (Hamzaoui, *op. cit.* and Amami, *op. cit.*), it actually reflects an approach to social relations specific to the union. These formal, impersonal rules were intended to ensure transparency but the social relationships within the UGTT proved too deeply ingrained. As a result, the rules were read, interpreted and adapted to the web of relationships connecting the various components of the union. However, as this "game" to retain power was closely intertwined with the single-party system, the outbreak of the revolution inspired hope in unionists like Sghair that the Tabarka Congress would represent a break with old practices and usher in a new era of democracy:

> One thing is certain: there will be a new leadership team, because Article 10 in the UGTT regulations limits officials to two terms, so we will definitely have new leadership. I hope that there will be good union activists in the new leadership, people who are in step with the revolutionary process and who support the democratic process. I hope that there will be a fresh approach at the central leadership as well as in the intermediate leadership teams. There has to be a new spirit and attitude at the UGTT, because we cannot protect the revolution with old mentalities.
>
> (Sghair, union official, Transportation, Gafsa)

For her part, Fadwa, a nurse and union activist in Sfax, hoped that the rigged delegations would be put to an end:

> I hope that at the next congress, the distribution of delegations won't be rigged. You work and you slog away to win over base unions and then you find yourself confronted with the rigging problem. . . . The main challenge is to change the Executive Board and prevent holdovers because, generally speaking, the Executive Board looks out for its children and grandchildren and there are always loyalty-based holdovers from one committee to the next. . . . There are several outgoing Executive Board members who will leave behind their followers—there will surely be continuity between the two committees, because they don't want the Executive Board to escape from their grasp.

To what extent did the onset of the revolutionary process reshape voting practices at the Tabarka Congress? How did the 22nd UGTT Congress manage to maintain the organization's unity and avoid a split?

Box 8 The UGTT Machine

The Achourists[5] and the *gfâsa* [in reference to the Gafsa region] are the ones who played a central role in the cronyism at the UGTT and represent the two dominant factions at the union. Regionalism is a sociological reality at the UGTT. Whether you like it or not, objectively it exists and the Achourists and the *gfâsa* are the two factions that have played a significant role in the Executive Board. They can't be ignored and don't have any particular political ideology—they have always remained close to the government without becoming completely subjugated. Their power is built on corrupt relationships and their top concern is always to keep their place within the sphere of power at the union. They were willing to do whatever it took to maintain their position at the union. So they developed networks with a wide range of unions in areas like administration, security, government, and with various political parties. They capitalized on all those networks to protect their position.

I think that the Achourists and the *gfâsa* are professional unionists—together they form what we call the union bureaucracy. The union bureaucracy is an important syntagma, a tool for analysis. The unionists who transformed into administrators within the union represent power. They represent power regardless of the elections and regardless of shifts in political power. These are people who will stay at the UGTT and they are the ones who command the machine described by UGTT spokesman Abid Briki. And they'll continue to play a role in spite of the changes.

Tarek, journalist

The Union's Hallowed Unity Determines Voting Behavior

All the unionists cited protecting the organization's unity from the continued attacks during the political and social crisis as the main challenge during that period. The importance of this goal is reflected in the unionist's bellicose metaphors: battle, resisting, attacking and defending. To what extent and how did this pressing need for unity influence voting behavior?

Fifty unionist candidates—seven of whom women—ran for the 13 elected positions in the UGTT Executive Board. Twenty-five of the candidates later withdrew their candidacy, leaving 38 candidates to compete for the seats on the committee. For the first time in the history of the union, the sitting secretary general did not stand for re-election, and seven other Executive Board members were also ineligible to run for office. The amendment adopted at the Djerba Congress—Article 10 in the UGTT regulations—limits Executive

Board members to two consecutive terms, meaning that only four of the outgoing members could run: Houcine Abbassi, Mouldi Jendoubi, Belgacem Ayari and Moncef Ezzahi.

The candidates ran under three electoral lists. The first was the so-called "consensus" list, which represented a coalition of 17 regions and nearly 15 sectors. The list featured three outgoing committee members: Houcine Abbassi, Mouldi Jendoubi and Belgacem Ayari. The second, the "list for the defense and independence of the UGTT," ran under the aegis of outgoing committee member and Achourist Ali Ben Romdhane's[6] network. It appealed for an end to the bad practices of the former regime, putting forward independent candidates and unionists that had been marginalized by the Executive Board, such as Abdelmajid Sahraoui. The third list, the "fighting list for the unification of the UGTT," portrayed itself as a coalition of all the opposition groups within the union, including the Union Democratic Alliance and the Working Women's' Commission. The list featured figures from the far left, such as Jilani Hammami, and nationalists like Hassen Ouederni. Other candidates ran independently, without the support of any groups.

As expected, the political machine at the UGTT carefully crafted a compromise over the course of several months, enabling the consensus list to win 13 seats on the Executive Board and appoint Houcine Abbassi as Secretary General. The consensus list was successful because it drew support from a broad coalition of different regions and sectors, including the Tunis, Sfax and Ben Arous regions and the education (primary, secondary, higher and supervisory staff), tourism and health care sectors. A great deal of work had been required to reach the consensus, which struck a delicate balance between the wants of the different sectors, regions and political affiliations. At a time when Article 10 of the UGTT regulations had ended the re-election hopes of eight outgoing Executive Board members, there was a need for a list that could restore the UGTT's image and meet the aspirations of the base branches, while maintaining unity among the central leadership amidst the challenges of union pluralism and the shifting political and social landscape. Constructing a list backed by the leading names in the UGTT's old guard required long discussions and bargaining before and during the congress. The election campaign saw a series of secret negotiations and unforeseen developments. Certain delegates running for office were removed from the list at the last minute, while others pulled out of their own accord, in a moment of fear or clarity. Others ran low-key campaigns and established lists in completely unorthodox ways.

Three events had a major impact on the election race. The first was the controversy surrounding the removal from the consensus list of Jilani Hammami, representative of the Tunisian Communist Workers' Party (PCOT) and former secretary general of the Postal Service and Telecommunications Federation. The party's leadership had supported Hammami's candidacy, but the general unions demanded Hfaiedh Hfaiedh, a former leader of the primary education union and a fellow PCOT member. Hammami's detractors justified the move by pointing to his extremism and unwillingness to compromise. The PCOT leadership was quick to react, issuing a press release decrying a putsch and noting that a preliminary agreement had been reached with the chief candidate on the consensus list, Houcine Abbassi, for the party to be represented by Hammami. The press release warned the delegates of the repercussions of this U-turn in the democratic process at the central office. It also alleged that the arguments used to discredit their candidate—his extremism and inflexibility—revealed a desire among the new leadership to carry on managing the central office with the same bureaucratic culture and opportunistic maneuvering. Sami, a delegate who supported Hfaiedh Hfaiedh's candidacy, gave his view of the situation:

> PCOT is one of the influential movements at the UGTT and has to be taken into consideration, but the Executive Board has never been revolutionary in nature. The UGTT's culture and make-up require people with broad support in leadership roles—it was important to prevent the risk of conflict at the highest level of the union. Jilani Hammami is clearly a great union activist, but his radical views are not shared by everyone.

This incident serves as both an example of how the political parties interfere with the electoral process and the import of broad-based consensus when assembling a list. No risks could be taken that could undermine the organization.

The second major event was the intense negotiations behind closed doors concerning the candidacy of Abdelmajid Sahraoui, Deputy Secretary General of the Arab Maghreb Workers' Union. Sahraoui's candidacy was rejected by the consensus list, despite having the backing of the Sahel-based delegates and Ali Romdhane, an Executive Board member and loyal heir to the Achourist legacy. This led to the emergence of the second list, "list for the defense and the independence of the UGTT," which Ali Romdhane established to support the return of Abdelmajid Sahraoui and foster what was termed a "balance between the regions." While the list included popular figures such as Kamel Saad, the presence of individuals closely associated with Ennahdha, like Taher Barbari, acted as a barrier to gaining wide support among the base and competing with the first list. Mohamed Trabelsi explains:

> The Ennahdha delegates are present in the congress and all the parties have their delegates, but we don't attempt to identify the delegates' political affiliations and history has taught us that all sorts of political alliances are possible. The unity forged by the union struggle and the unionists' deep affection for the organization is what brings Ennahdha

MPs together with the other parties. The Ennahdha delegates made their presence known on the first day of the congress by opening their speeches with the *takbîr*.[7] The Islamists appeared on Ali Romdhane's list and acted like a political group like any other, whereas before, during the Ben Ali era, they would work in secrecy. Their attempt failed because they are poorly represented in the union's bodies. But it is clear that the UGTT is a real priority for the Islamists, because the UGTT is deeply rooted in Tunisia's social fabric and all the political factions want to have a presence in the organization.

Unionist and journalist Sadrdi added:

> Some people say that Ali Romdhane's list was an attempt to support Sahraoui. I think that the list also sought to help the Islamists join the leadership. But what ended up being decisive is the fact that most of the delegates were aware of the importance of forming a united front against the government, which is why the second list failed.

The failure of the second list again underscored the delegates' insistence on forming a united front against the Troika government and preserving the union's independence—two key campaign strategy issues.

The final event was the heated debate surrounding the women running for the Executive Board. Despite the solemn statements of principle emphasizing the importance of ensuring a woman was among the 13 members of the UGTT leadership, five women out of the 17 in the running pursued their candidacy through to the elections and none was elected. The consensus list did not contain any women. The excuse given was that the discussions had been very tense and they were been unable to reach an agreement on a woman for one of the 13 spots. Some delegates attributed this failure to the lack of unity among the women, who, they said, were unable to secure a place for a female candidate in negotiations with the regions and sectors. Others like Noura pegged the failure to the left-wing's inability to force through a woman candidate:

> The problem left unresolved was women's representation; no agreement was reached on that issue. There were plans to place a woman on the left-wing consensus list, which won, but it never happened—they "refrained" to prevent the risk of losing votes. The importance of maintaining unity dominated the proceedings at the congress and, as a result, narrow-minded, regionalist thinking masked the real issues, including women's representation.

These three issues demonstrate how the political imperative for unity—rooted in a fear that the organization would split at the seams during this highly volatile political phase—overrode the union's stated organizational goals. However, while the resounding victory of the consensus list showed the organization's ability to maintain unity, one question remained unanswered: to what extent did the congress mark an end to the old voting practices?

The Outcome of the Congress: Continuity or a Fresh Start?

If there was truly a break with the practices of previous congresses, what changed was the reasoning that underpinned the list creation process. In the past, regionalism and cronyism had often overshadowed other factors. The Tabarka Congress marked a shift toward a more central role for political issues in the electoral process, changing how alliances were formed. The political imperative for unity was omnipresent in negotiations to establish the lists, which lessened the influence of the traditional Gafsa/Sfax axis. Sfax-based teacher and union activist Nejib offered his perspective:

> There is a major new development at the Tabarka Congress. Executive Board elections used to be governed by a system of negotiations and sharing [*mûhassassa*] that focused on sector, regional and political issues. For example, regional considerations were the decisive factor in the Monastir Congress. But I've noticed that political and ideological considerations have become more prominent than regional issues in election strategies at Tabarka. There are new regions represented and the traditional Gafsa/Sfax axis no longer has the same pull in the election scheming. The nature of alliances has changed.

Ali, a union activist and teacher in Kef, believes that the Tabarka Congress placed power in the hands of the main public-sector unions, in particular in education and healthcare:

> It's fair to say that political issues dominated the Tabarka Congress, but you'll also find that sectors like primary and secondary education and health care are very well represented on the Executive Board. There are five or six members from education and two from health care—the public-sector unions are dominant.

However, the new alliance structure did not fundamentally change the UGTT apparatus. Several unionists believed that while Article 10 had resolved the issue of ensuring leadership changes, the Executive Board's dominance over the electoral machine nonetheless remained intact. Adel, for example, asserted that certain Executive Board members who were not able to run again were still able to throw all their weight behind loyal candidates who would pick up where they left off:

If the revolution hadn't taken place, the main issue at the congress would have been amending Article 10 of the UGTT statutes. I think that the UGTT succeeded in breaking with the past on several accounts, such as resolving the issue of leadership changes. The plan to amend Article 10 was a source of conflict and political bickering that threatened the UGTT's unity at one point. . . . Jrad didn't run again but the people who had controlled the UGTT for years—like Jrad and Ali Romdhane—weren't going to give up so easily. They were able to support candidates who were loyal to them.

Those who were more critical saw no difference between the 22nd Congress and previous years: there was the essentially the same rush to form coalitions and elect the new leadership. They criticized the use of the same methods and tricks to retain power and ensure continuity between the incoming and outgoing leadership:

> The UGTT continues to operate as if there hadn't been a revolution. They continue to use the same approach—seizing power and jobs—and not to uphold the union's principles or serve workers' interests. Jrad and company continued to use the same methods for doing away with others. They marginalized people who didn't support them. During the congress, there were the same tricks and low blows, and let me tell you, the UGTT will continue to operate the same way at the next congress, with alliances based on sharing [*mûhassassa*] rather than principles. They droned on in their speeches but their acts didn't match up. There is a new political reality and the UGTT can't continue with its old mentality if it wants to keep up.
>
> (Omar, union activist, Energy, Tunis)

Another unionist, Brahim, noted that there could be a break with the old modus operandi so long as the rules governing the UGTT were the same and power was still concentrated in the Executive Board. He regretted the fact that the delegates were unable to move beyond opportunistic scheming to change the face of the Executive Board by voting for more radical unionists who had closer ties with the social movements:

> I don't think that the congress has broken with the past. If the outcome of the congress can be predicted in advance, calculated in advance [*mahsûb bilwarqa wa stylo*], that means that the congress hasn't broken with the past. I also followed the Primary Education Congress. There were delegates there who didn't know what was going on, who followed like sheep. You tell them "here's the list," you mark 13 names and then you leave. They don't even bother to ask, "Who are these people?" or "Why should I mark them?" We won't be able to say we've broken with the past so long as we still have delegates who lack the political awareness

required to defend their ideas, so long as we have delegates who cave to pressure from opportunistic scheming instead of following the political line. Among those elected to the new Executive Board are known figures such as Belgacem Ayari and Kacem Afiya, who will carry over the practices of the old committee. The UGTT regulations are what enable this continuity. We were hoping for the Executive Board to be made up of unionists who had played an important role in the social movements, but that's not the case. . . . Nothing has changed, except the names—power remains concentrated in the hands of the Executive Board. The sector unions can't fight their battles without the Executive Board's approval and blessing.

(Brahim, union activist, Postal Service, Jendouba)

What is more, the Tabarka Congress repeated the same process of excluding women—none of the five women candidates was elected—despite the statements of principle to the contrary. Meanwhile, the matter of including intermediate organizations and marginalized sectors in the decision-making process remained unresolved. Ahmad believed that, notwithstanding small improvements such as Article 10, the Tabarka Congress maintained the same union culture, slowing efforts to adapt to the economic situation and resulting changes in workers' sociology and sectors of membership:

The public sector has traditionally dominated, but we have an increasing number of members from the private sector—in subcontracting, for example—areas that remain marginalized with regard to decision-making, which is something we have to remedy. It's true that Article 10 solved the problem of replacing Executive Board members, but nothing of the sort has been done for the intermediate organizations. There has simultaneously been a break and continuity.

(Ahmad, union activist, Postal Service, Tunis)

In addition, certain delegates on the far left pointed out that although the 22nd UGTT Congress saw through a transition at the top of the union, there was no telling whether the new leadership team would be able to manage the social and economic demands of the popular uprising. They criticized the continued focus on political issues at the expense of social and economic priorities, which were put on the back burner. They also questioned the rules governing the composition of the congress, ruling bodies and voting system:

We spent all our time at the UGTT Congress managing political issues and didn't have time to discuss the UGTT's economic and social program. . . . We were surprised by the emergence of several electoral lists that were presented without an election platform or any predefined plans. . . . The congress is organized in such a way that political scheming overshadows discussions on economic and social issues, which is why we have to overhaul the composition of the congress and ruling bodies.

The list-based voting system has to change and we have to take another look at how to restructure the UGTT.

(Mohamed Trabelsi, former UGTT Deputy Secretary General)

Mourad, a doctor, politically independent delegate and unelected candidate, agreed that placing unity above all other priorities tipped the scales in favor of political considerations, at the expense of organizational and/or socioeconomic challenges:

The voting was not based on platforms or causes, but on forming a common front to protect the union's unity. The overarching theme was to unite the progressive forces and establish an anti-Ennahdha front, which I think was a fatal error. For our part, we are joining together to offer an alternative plan and a new development model, to uphold freedom and democracy. That is why the independents with a plan to restructure the UGTT had no chance of gaining a seat on the Executive Board.

Thus, the UGTT's conservative tendencies triumphed once again over the push for a total break with old union practices, despite the official support for democracy and the changes to the rules of politics in Tunisia.

The UGTT seems to be torn between two directions, one conservative and the other progressive. The UGTT has a conservative culture—it's a conservative organization even if it thinks itself to be revolutionary. It's true that there has always been a revolutionary undercurrent at the UGTT, but the revolutionaries still have the same revolutionary thinking as they did in the 1960s. The UGTT established its structure, regulations and statutes in the 1960s. Truth be told, this conservative streak has endured at the union, which it now needs to do away with and replace with a rotating-leadership system that covers a wide range of base members in all sectors and regions.

(Slim, union official, Health Care, Tunis)

The 22nd UGTT Congress, which was supposed to usher in a new era for this institution at a crossroads and represent a break with old methods, failed in some respects due to the consensus on the need for unity above all else. The central focus of the election campaign during the congress strayed from the organizational overhaul required to defend workers and fulfill the social and economic demands of the revolution. The election ended up becoming a competition to retain power within union and maintain the UGTT's cohesiveness in the midst of a major crisis.

The congress perpetuated the existing political culture at the UGTT, notwithstanding a few changes like term limits at the Executive Board and an increased focus on political positioning in the election campaign. The use of the same bureaucratic rules and the continued posturing in support of resistance to the powers that be largely dictated proceedings at the congress. When queried on the topic, most of the unionists believed that the UGTT would have to overcome its conservative instincts and update its processes in the future, because the revolutionary process had permanently freed the intermediate unions and unionists from the clutches of the Executive Board. Change was unavoidable.

Teacher and delegate Mounira:

> The union bureaucracy essentially has control over the UGTT apparatus; the Executive Board members are professional politicians who know how to do break down the structure of the election and reshape it to their liking. During the election, they were able to secure victories for their allies, despite a few surprises along the way. That said, they are powerful but never able to fully control how the UGTT operates. The revolutionary process freed the unionists, who are no longer subjected to centralized power and will continue to do as they wish in their own union bodies.

Mohamed Trabelsi agreed, stating that the effects of the revolutionary process were irreversible but the transition from an authoritarian culture to a democratic culture required time:

> We must not forget . . . that we are still experiencing the revolutionary phase. And it's completely natural for all countries that have experienced social upheaval and political crises such as those in Tunisia to go through a transition phase so that things settle down. . . . After all forms of democratic change born on the ruins of despotism and totalitarianism, it takes time for everyone to claim their rightful place. The same goes for the UGTT, which has to stake out a position in this new pluralistic environment in order to regain legitimacy and confidence.
>
> (Ferchichi, 2012)

While the new incarnation of the UGTT Executive Board succeeded in maintaining its unity, the UGTT would find itself faced with a new set of political challenges as a union. The first question that arose was whether the UGTT, whose strength lay in its ability to maintain unity among its multifarious components, would be able to resist opposing forces in the new political playing field.

> The UGTT will remain a target for political jabs as it has been in the past, because it's a very influential player in terms of the balance of power. This means that each political party will attempt to use this

political power for its own gain. The Destourians did it, the left did it and the Islamists will try to do the same.

But the UGTT's genius lies in its ability to maintain unity amid difference, governing a highly diversified organization in terms of social make-up and political expression. They wisdom resides in their ability to settle conflicts while also protecting the organization's unity.

(Mounir, union official, Textiles, Ben Arous)

The second point in question was whether the UGTT would be able to play its traditional role as a union while keeping a watchful eye on national politics, in the midst of an economic and political crisis.

Box 9 A Nexus for Union, Political and Social Issues

History has made the UGTT a nexus for union, political and social issues. When Ben Ali pressured civil-society organizations—in particular human-rights organizations—everyone turned to the UGTT: people who had a legal problem, who wanted to have their son transferred from the prison in Kasserine to another closer to home, etc.

Everyone turns to the UGTT, which means that the union has very heavy responsibilities. Not only does it handle labor demands, it also supports victims of injustice and all those who feel wronged. Plus there are the political parties. If a party wants to organize a daylong event on Saddam Hussein, it turns to the UGTT. If another wants to organize a flotilla in support of Gaza, it turns to the UGTT, because you can't get anything done outside the UGTT. The UGTT was able to strike a balance with the government, negotiate with the government and require it to free a political activist or reach other compromises. . . .

The transformation of the Tunisian political landscape means that the UGTT will have to adapt, the political parties will have to assume their responsibilities, and the associations and civil society will have to fulfill their traditional duties. The UGTT specifically will have to maintain its role as a countervailing power by instituting economic and social checks.

Fostering social dialogue is vital—the UGTT will have to oversee the economic and social model. Democracy cannot exist without social dialogue—it's vital.

Mohamed Trabelsi, former UGTT Deputy Secretary General

In Conclusion

One might have thought that the first UGTT Congress organized after the outbreak of the revolution—under the slogan "I love you, O People"—would have assembled the resources required for a radical break with old practices and the overhaul required to place socioeconomic demands on the leadership's agenda. However, the political crisis and the various campaigns targeting the UGTT reinforced the union's most defensive instincts, preserving the organization at the expense of the pressing need to restructure and socioeconomic challenges. The congress revealed the extent to which the real focus for the UGTT was to fight for the political conditions required for its survival and expansion in the emerging political environment.

As a result of the situation, the camp within the UGTT pushing for a radical break from the union's traditional top-down structure and more revolutionary economic and social positions was undercut by the reformist camp calling for unity and closer ranks. The UGTT was able to manage these two camps, which sometimes clash, throughout the congress to suppress internal conflicts. The union elected an Executive Board that, for better or worse, embodied both the social and political elements of the union, combining a desire to launch a counteroffensive and seek institutional solutions through ongoing negotiations. Criticism of and opposition to the attitude of the Executive Board never caused a permanent split during the Ben Ali regime. These divisions would die down amid efforts to find political middle ground and systemic affirmation of the importance of forming a united front against the Troika government. Meanwhile, the continued portrayal of the government as the ultimate adversary to resist gave a significant boost to the victory of a consensus-based approach to politics at the union.

The sweeping changes in Tunisia did not erase the UGTT's core identity as an organization at the nexus of union, political and social issues. This unique identity was further cemented by the series of political crises that took place after December 17, 2010. Political challenges took pride of place at the congress, but the proceedings nonetheless highlighted the extent to which the delegates' voting behavior is determined by regional and sector considerations, which cannot be changed by a simple statement of intent. As strong as the will for reform may have been, reshaping the organization was contingent on developments in the political and social sphere. What is more, the country was weathering an economic crisis that risked escalating tensions between the desire to play a political role rooted in pressure on and negotiations with the government to protect the union's place in the political landscape on the one hand, and practices to break with the past that could be imposed or expanded by the economic and social crisis. How would the UGTT address these conflicting pressures? How would the union protect its political role and what strategy would it adopt with the political elite to avoid upsetting the delicate balance that enabled it to survive these various crises?

Notes

1. Kerkennah is a Tunisian archipelago in the Mediterranean Sea, 20 kilometers off the coast of Sfax.

2. The members of the UGTT General Congress:

   - The members of the national Executive Board
   - The delegates representing the base unions, selected according to a formula devised by the UGTT's National Administrative Commissions to determine the number of delegates by region and sector
   - The secretaries general of the regional unions with representation for their regions
   - The secretaries general of the federations and national unions with representation for their sectors
   - The non-delegate members of the National Administrative Commission (no voting rights)
   - The members of the National Commission on Union Regulations (no voting rights)
   - The members of the National Financial Control Commission (no voting rights)
   - The coordinator of the National Women's Commission (no voting rights)
   - The coordinator of the National Youth Commission (no voting rights)
   - A representative of the National Commission for Former Union Officials (no voting rights)
   - A representative for migrant workers (no voting rights)

3. The quotes in this chapter are excerpted from delegates' speeches, one-on-one interviews and discussions that took place in December 2011. Additional interviews pertaining to the outcomes of the congress were conducted in January and February 2012. The quotes presented here convey both the internal divisions that arose during the three-day congress and the agreements reached to preserve the organization's stability.

4. In Alia Gana's geographic and sociological study (2012) of the elections held on October 23, 2011, it is interesting to note the significant regionalism in voting behavior. This phenomenon is not solely attributable to the objective sociodemographic characteristics of each region; it also stems from sociohistorical and cultural aspects specific to individual regions and reflects the extensive range of networks—family, tribe, associations and cronyism—to which individuals and groups belong.

5. The Achourists comprise the traditional hegemonic faction within the UGTT. The Achourists consider themselves the heirs to Habib Achour, a partner to Hached, and defend a political line that somewhat mirrors Achour's journey: supporting political authority but resisting when workers' interests are greatly endangered. The leaders of this movement are generally from the Sfax region and Kerkennah—the birthplace of Achour and Hached—in particular. Changes in the sociological and political make-up of the UGTT have rendered the Achourists a largely vestigial power.

6. Ali Ben Romdhane is the person who most embodies the legacy of Achourism and, as such, is considered a powerful symbol of the movement's lasting relevance.

7. *Takbîr*, from *Allahu akbar*, is an Arabic expression that means "God is greater."

5   The UGTT as a Counterbalance

I'm always amazed by the fact that, despite all the crises, the UGTT never imploded. When the pressure is at its peak and implosion is imminent, a solution miraculously appears. That's what happened several times with the national dialogue when Tunisia was on the brink of civil war—every time, the country narrowly escaped at the last minute.

Romdhane, union activist, Mining, Redeyef

The UGTT is all that remains when everything else crumbles.

Houcine Abbassi, January 26, 2012

The first major uprising led by the union movement against Bourguiba's authoritarian regime occurred on January 26, 1978, a day known as "Black Thursday."[1] The UGTT called its first post-independence general strike, which degenerated into a bloody clash with the police. On January 26, 2014, Tunisia adopted its first democratic constitution, overcoming several crises and two political assassinations.[2] The adoption of the constitution was a highly symbolic moment in Tunisian history that marked the culmination of several generations' struggle for individual and collective liberties and economic and social rights. It was achieved through a long, arduous negotiation process at the National Constituent Assembly, with the support of a national dialogue coalition comprising the UGTT, the employers' organization UTICA, the Tunisian Order of Lawyers and the Tunisian Human Rights League (UGTT, 2013). The national dialogue began on October 25, 2013, with the aim of defusing a three-month-old political crisis sparked by the assassination of a member of parliament, Mohamed Brahmi, on July 25, 2013. As part of the process, the Islamist-majority Ali Larayadedh[3] government was replaced by a new "technocratic" government whose main duty was to keep clear of the political infighting and organize the upcoming elections.

The UGTT's role as the leader of the National Dialogue Quartet was mired in controversy, with further accusations of political parties using the union to their own ends. Throughout the national dialogue process, Islamists suspected the UGTT of harboring a desire to defy democratic legitimacy and prepare a coup d'état in which the opposition would take power. Unable to reach a consensus on whom to replace Ali Larayedh as prime minister, the Quartet decided to put the matter to a vote as a last resort. Mehdi Jomaa, formerly Minister of Industry in the Larayedh government, won the vote and was named Prime Minister on January 10, 2014. Ironically, the opposition then charged that Ennahdha had manipulated the UGTT.

The national dialogue and the vital mediation by the UGTT proved to be a crucial moment in the transition, raising a number of interconnected questions. What role did the UGTT play in the National Dialogue Quartet? Was the UGTT able to pair political and national aims with a viable economic and social plan? What challenges does the UGTT face in the future? To answer these questions, I will address the impact that the transformation of the Tunisian political landscape had on the position of UGTT. I will then analyze how social movements formed part of this position. Finally, I will focus on the role of the UGTT as an architect of the national dialogue.[4]

Image 5.1 Activists from the Leagues for the Protection of the Revolution Square Off with UGTT Activists.

© Thierry Brésillon.

Image 5.2 Houcine Abbassi (Left) and Rached Ghannouchi (Right) in March 2012.
Source: www.medinapart.com.

Image 5.3 From Left to Right: Mohammed Fadhel Mahfoudh, Mustapha Ben Jaafar,
Widad Bouchamaoui, Moncef Marzouki, Houcine Abbassi, Ali Laraeyedh
and Abdessatar Ben Moussa.
Source: directinfo.webmanagercenter.com.

UGTT and Ennahdha Clash During the Turbulent Political Transition

The country was troubled by disputes over social issues of all kinds after the fall of Ben Ali, which continued after the Constituent Assembly elections. General strikes were held in the inland regions that had sparked the revolution, such as Sidi Bouzid and Makthar, as well as in large cities like Sfax and Tunis. The UDC, various local coordination groups, the UGTT and spontaneous movements formed by young people from the suburbs of major cities were the main actors behind the demonstrations. Ten months after Ennahdha took power, Sidi Bouzid, the city where the "revolution for dignity" began, again became the backdrop for protest movements led by farmers, construction workers and the unemployed. The UGTT supported the initiatives and called a general strike in Sidi Bouzid on August 14, 2012, to demand regional development measures and the release of young unemployed people arrested during demonstrations that had been put down violently by the police. The local Ennahdha office reacted by calling on the UGTT's base and organizations to refrain from taking any political stances and to maintain its independence. The confrontation between Ennahdha and the UGTT began on February 25, 2012, when 5,000 people heeded the union's call and demonstrated in Tunis. The demonstrators protested the alleged dumping of trash by Ennahdha activists in front of several union offices following a strike by municipal employees, one of the poorest-paid groups in the country (Yousfi, 2012).

> They want to silence us so that they can decide our fate by themselves. They want to strike fear into our hearts to keep us from defending our cause and our rights, but we will not give up and we will not back down,

proclaimed UGTT Secretary General Houcine Abbassi. Meanwhile, Noureddine Arbaoui, a member of the Ennahdha Executive Board, asserted that the UGTT was being manipulated by elements from the former regime who were determined to impede the government's actions.

Unionists' emotions were running particularly high because they viewed the square in front of the UGTT as a hallowed place. "The UGTT's square is sacred and the UGTT is sacred, because its symbols—Farhat Hached, Ahmed Tlili and Mohamed Ali Hammi—represent our national identity," said one doctor and UGTT member. A teacher who belongs to the union added: "Attacking the UGTT incites people to take more radical positions, as those who ordered the attacks are well aware. It is the government and the UGTT representatives' duty to conduct the investigations required to find the people behind the attacks." The clash came to a head on December 4, 2012, during the celebrations for the anniversary of the assassination of Farhat Hached. The UGTT threatened to use its ultimate weapon, a general strike, after counterdemonstrations by the Leagues for the Protection of the Revolution[5] ended in violence (Brésillon, 2012).

This type of skirmish had already occurred in the past, notes Sami Souihli, Secretary General of the Union of Doctors and Pharmacists:

> The campaign against the UGTT didn't start with Ennahdha. The transition governments following the fall of [President Zine El-Abidine Ben Ali] targeted the organization, which has systematically been blamed for the economic crisis and chaos affecting the country. People want to shut the UGTT down because it's the only organized counterbalance.

A conflict emerged between Ennahdha—the majority party in the Troika government—and the UGTT over the status attributed to employees, which went well beyond a difference of opinion over labor issues. The disagreement set the stage for a political battle in an increasingly polarized political landscape. Centrist and economically liberal parties formed the opposition: the Republican Party,[6] Social Democratic Path (al-Massar)[7] and Nidaa Tounes.[8] Despite having accused the UGTT of "stirring up trouble" in 2011, the opposition worked alongside far-left parties such as Watad (Movement of Socialist Democrats) and the Tunisian Communist Workers' Party (PCOT; later renamed the Workers' Party) to support the trade union. Rafik, a teacher and unionist in Gafsa:

> The balcony of the UGTT is very important symbolically. The Secretary General gives his speeches from the balcony. During the municipal employees' strike we noticed that [UGTT Secretary General] Houcine Abbassi was surrounded by politicians who had repeatedly criticized the Executive Board during the Béji Caïd Essebsi government. It was really ironic to see people who had criticized the UGTT for supporting Kasbah I and II, like Nejib Chebbi and Béji Caïd Essebsi, now taking refuge at the UGTT. They wanted to use UGTT to their own ends. They wanted to use people, but what transpired shows that they failed— exploiting an institution and then demanding its protection can only be interpreted as a failure.

The opposition, weakened by its poor performance in the elections held on October 23, 2011, began accusing Ennahdha of attempting to establish a religious dictatorship. The political conflict was further exacerbated by searing debates over the inclusion of Sharia law into the constitution, continued violations of individual liberties and "Salafist" groups' threats against the opposition. Kacem Afaya (2012), a member of the UGTT Executive Board, summed up the arguments put forward by the union in the battle:

> There is a major risk that Ennahdha becomes the new RCD in religious clothing. I think that Ennahdha will aim to remain in power at all costs. The party is dominant at the Constituent Assembly and is seeking to establish a parliamentary system, which would give it total power. Ennahdha uses doublespeak but civil society is strong enough to curb

a lot of its initiatives; it was forced to back down on the application of Sharia law, for example.

While the government publicly accused the Jihadists of having committed acts of violence, the opposition often criticized Ennahdha for its incompetent, lax approach with the Salafists. For its part, Ennahdha accused the opposition—Nidaa Tounes and its allies—of conspiring against the revolution in order to remove the Islamist party from power. The tensions between Ennahdha and the UGTT flared when the UGTT decided to openly take the "side of civil society and the Tunisian people in all its diversity to defend not only the working masses, but also—and especially— the Republic and its institutions." At times, the union's demonstrations in defense of civil liberties and against Salafist and police violence eclipsed its strike action. The UGTT issued a call for a national dialogue on June 18, 2012, and top union officials underlined the importance of establishing an election schedule as quickly as possible, offering further signs of the role the union intended to play at during this phase in Tunisian politics.

The same arguments put forward during the terms of the transition governments once again came to the fore. Those who backed the government reiterated their claims that the union bureaucracy had exploited and manipulated the UGTT for purely partisan ends and that the union would do better to focus on its own duties. During a televised debate on May 28, 2012, Prime Minister Hamadi Jebali spoke about the stall in public-sector negotiations, rejecting the idea of a class struggle and boasting of the government's democratic legitimacy:

> We told the UGTT that everyone had to adhere to their role and duties. We need to stop escalating the situation—the government is not the enemy of civil servants and the working class. We don't believe in this theory of a class struggle. The unemployed are not children. We don't need what they call "labor negotiations" or pressure to grant pay raises; we have other priorities at the moment. . . . Their goal is to outstrip the government. We read their political—and not at all labor-related— statements and they want to obstruct us! This government has a mandate from the election and the people. We will not back down.

In the eyes of the UGTT and opposition leadership, the union had to remain independent while playing an active role as a counterbalance in Tunisian politics. In response to the above-mentioned remarks by the Prime Minister, UGTT Deputy Secretary General Samir Cheffi went on television to defend the political role of the organization, on May 30, 2012:

> We are a major national organization that took part in the struggle for independence and social movements. The UGTT cannot accept this type of message. They are overstepping. We perform our role well and have since we were founded in 1946. We will not give up.

The same arguments are rehashed in every clash between the UGTT and Ennahdha, so what was different in this power struggle?

Ennahdha's Distrust of the UGTT

In addition to their remarks on the controversies regarding the origins and originators of Tunisia's social movements, the interview respondents stated that Ennahdha was wary of the UGTT because it was the only organized force in the country, with an impressive ability to mobilize people. Journalist Samir said:

> The Ennahdha party is very bothered by the fact that it doesn't have people inside the UGTT. The UGTT is very strong—it's the only organized force that's able to scare Ennahdha. . . . Ennahdha is insulting the UGTT because it doesn't have a presence [at the union]. They have two choices: either they create another trade union like they did with the student movement[9] or they join the UGTT.

Ennahdha officials like Houssem also confirmed this wariness or even fear of the UGTT, which may explain some of their reactions:

> It's true that at the time, in the Troika, we were in a nervous, fearful state—afraid for Tunisia and for ourselves. We were also afraid of outside elements, afraid of terrorism. That situation increased the tension and that's the reason we're afraid of the UGTT.

As fellow Ennahdha activist Mounir notes, the blurred lines between union work and politics at the UGTT pushed the party to pursue a defensive strategy:

> We have to take a look in the mirror. Ennahdha doesn't have any union experience. They were afraid of the UGTT waging a union battle because they thought that the union was mixing union affairs with politics. Ennahdha had trouble grasping how politics was played at the UGTT, which is why its leaders' reactions were out of proportion.

This distrust was heightened by the fact that, unlike the left-wing parties, Ennahdha has never succeeded in gaining any real influence in the union movement. The Islamist movement had attempted to secure a presence at the UGTT in the early 1980s, like all other political groups seeking a platform to expand their influence. There were even union delegates with Islamist ties during the UGTT congress elections in 1984 and 1989, but their support never exceeded 5 to 10% of the UGTT electorate (Alexander, *op. cit.*). In economic and social issues, the Islamists never took a clear stance on the various phases of economic liberation in Tunisia and remained silent over the structural adjustment program launched at the end of the 1980s. They never offered coherent proposals for the future of the Tunisian economy or for supporting workers. The Islamists suffered repression from the Ben Ali regime in the late 1980s, which obstructed all their attempts to gain a political presence at the UGTT. Mohamed, a former union leader, offered his analysis on what transpired:

> Believe me, the Islamists' relationship with the UGTT was similar to that of other parties. I mean by that the UGTT provided a forum for the Islamists to express their beliefs and take part in social movements but, at the same time, they tried to use the union for political ends, as did other parties, especially before Ben Ali's crackdown in the 1980s. But they never enjoyed any real influence. The Islamists obviously try to utilize figures like Fadhel Ben Achour[10] to reclaim ownership of the union movement—this was clear to see at the demonstration on May 1, 2012—but things are more complicated than that. Take the example of Fadhel Ben Achour, who was a renowned mufti, a Destourian and a member of the Destourian Liberal Party. His selection to head the UGTT was tactical. Hached and his comrades had already been unionists before founding the UGTT, while Ben Achour was the mufti of El-Zitouna [Mosque]. One aspect of the struggle for independence was a focus on defending Arab and Muslim identity, which lent legitimacy to Ben Achour as the leader of the UGTT. He didn't stay for long—two years and he was gone.

The interviewees from Ennahdha confirmed that the party had been late to join the union movement. Ennahdha activist Karim:

> Ennahdha was late to become involved in union work; the RCD had overtaken them by the time they joined UGET and the UGTT [*sic*]. As a result, they had no option but to create a parallel student union and we have always had to create other unions. It's true that we are now in an era of union pluralism and there is no shame in creating other unions, but we would have hoped to belong to national organizations. The problem is that we have always been feared and suspected of wanting to take them over.

The Islamists' ideological hostility toward unionism, which it considered one of the arms of Marxism, further complicated the situation and had long kept Ennahdha from taking part in politics at the UGTT. The Islamists even supported the regime during the events of January 26, 1978. The Iranian Revolution in 1979 greatly aided Tunisian Islamists in moving beyond Marxist terminology and turning their focus toward tension between the rich and the disadvantaged (*al-mustadh'afûn*), which enabled them to circumvent class conflict (Alexander, *op. cit.*). Mohammed, a journalist, looks back on the situation:

> Ennahdha was hostile toward union work until the end of the 1970s. The Islamists issued a recognized statement in support of the government on

January 26, 1978. But after the Iranian Revolution, they understood the importance of union work and the importance of social struggles, and they changed their position in the early 1980s. There was an Islamist list at the 1989 congress chaired by Ali Romdhane.[11]

Mohamed, a unionist with ties to Ennahdha, believes that all these factors caused the movement to commit several errors of judgment:

I tried to advise the leaders of Ennahdha but you could tell that they did not have the faintest idea about the UGTT. You have to be in the UGTT or follow it daily in order to know the union. One of their leaders told me, "The UGTT has a left-wing ideological vision, we can't work with them. . . ." I explained to him the importance of not turning our back on the UGTT, the importance of using a soft touch with them, how to use them in certain circumstances. He didn't understand what I was saying and preferred to support union pluralism.

Similarly, Khaled, a unionist with ties to the Troika government, high-lighted certain Ennahdha ministers' lack of union culture:

The health minister, Abdellatif Mekki, granted a significant pay raise to the federation without conferring with the Prime Minister or the Minister of Finance. The government learned about the agreement in the newspapers the next day and it caused a great deal of uproar. It marked the start of the mishaps. And it indicated a lack of union culture. . . . We were getting ready to start sector-by-sector negotiations, which were supposed to be centralized, which shows that they have no expertise. It's important to understand that when there are general negotiations, you don't negotiate on specific issues on the side. That's a rule that everyone knows: negotiations are centralized with the Prime Minister, even if raises for specific sectors can't be granted while general negotiations are ongoing.

How would Ennahdha, the majority party at the ANC, cope without a strategy for influencing the union movement? What attitude did Ennahdha take in its clash with the UGTT and how do unionists interpret the events?

Unionists and Ennahdha's Hegemonic Excesses

In an environment where fears of the return of the authoritarian system were ever-present, Ennahdha's distrust of the UGTT was mirrored by worries among unionists that Ennahdha would pursue the same authoritarian approach as the former regime. The interviewees believed that Ennahdha was tempted to maintain its grip on power by placing the UGTT under supervision, as had the defunct Democratic Constitutional Rally (RCD). The unionists interviewed put forward several arguments to substantiate their theory.

Their fears were heightened by the influx of new Islamist members, chiefly from the private sector. For several unionists, Ennahdha's efforts to increase its influence at the UGTT by winning over the base and intermediate unions was an old strategy that had already been used by all the other political parties, especially the RCD. Riadh, a unionist and teacher from Gafsa:

> It's interesting to take a look at the Ennahdha Facebook pages and all the virulent hostility they aim at the UGTT. But whatever people may think, Ennahdha is not planning to disband the UGTT. Ennahdha's only option is to contain [*ihtiwâ'*] the UGTT—they're going to approach the UGTT with the same style as the RCD, at the base-union level. If you look closely at what's happening with the base-union elections, you'll notice that Ennahdha's decision is clear: make inroads at the UGTT through a democratic campaign and grab as many spots as possible.

Amina, a textile worker and unionist in Ben Arous, adds:

> The UGTT is the largest trade-union organization. Whether you like it or not, no one will turn their back on the UGTT; the political parties will not turn their back on the UGTT. It's true that Ennahdha wasn't here before, but now they're trying to win over the base unions. The base-union elections are a crucial part of establishing the list of delegates who will vote at the next congress. You have to influence the base unions to change the course of events. Take the teachers' union in Tunis, for example. Before there weren't any Islamists and now they're there and threatening to withdraw support for delegates, whereas before they didn't say anything at all.

Slim, a manager in a private-sector energy company, criticized the Islamists for reviving dubious practices to win elections:

> We're noticing the same sort of cronyism. We gave permanent contracts to 50 women workers and the new union pushed for us to hire 14 contract workers so that they could vote for the Islamists, and that's how they won the elections. What was done in a totally discreet manner under Ben Ali—under the table—is now out in the open for all to see.

Some interviewees also mentioned other strategies adopted by Ennahdha to win power in the labor movement, as well as efforts by the Islamists to foster the growth of new unions, such as Ismaïl Sahbani's UTT, to weaken the UGTT:

> In my company, we can see that the new union led by Sahbani is committing the exact same abuses. Instead of defending workers' interests, the new union negotiated a quota for Ennahdha members. We also see the

same mechanisms of corruption. They officialized the abuses and hushed up corruption scandals in exchange for advantages and privileges.

(Samir, manager in the private sector)

Ennahdha's various strategies—which sometimes appeared at odds with each other—created an air of ambiguity that reinforced unionists' bias with regard to the Islamists' doublespeak:

Ennahdha follows the swing of the pendulum: at one end, they work with people to infiltrate the UGTT and gain allies; at the other, they support the UTT. Recently I heard that they want to create an Islamic union. The strategy is to be where things are going on, to be everywhere. One important point to remember is that Ennahdha is a populist movement, so it is intent on granting pay raises early on to attract followers and help out their own guys in the union. Sometimes, when a union is close with Ennahdha it gives the party privileges, the typical example being what happened at the health ministry with Mekki, Secretary General of the Health Federation, who allied with Ennahdha.

(Khaled, union activist, Health Care, Tunis)

The Islamists faced staunch political opposition, hostile news media and a lack of cohesiveness with its political allies in government. The ambiguities in Ennahdha's political stances, which were often described as double-speak, may have been further accentuated by internal dissent over how to approach the Salafists and former RCD members. One example is Ekbess (Weslaty, 2012)—meaning "turn the screw"—a large-scale campaign carried out by young Ennahdha members to urge the party leaders to break with the former regime and achieve the goals of the revolution.[12] Sfax-based unionist and postman Bilel explains:

Ennahdha is often said to engage in doublespeak. Why? Ennahdha's positions embrace the swing of the pendulum—it's like there is a spring, a spring that sometimes boomerangs back in blows up in their face! That's how all their political positions were. There is no doubt that Ennahdha are the ones behind the Leagues for the Protection of the Revolution and then you come across conflicting positions espoused by Ennahdha leaders. . . . It's hard to make any sense of it. Some people say that there are two factions within the Ennahdha movement and one always gains the upper hand over the other. Unless their strategy is to swing between two different stances. You don't know which way their compass is pointing, where they're headed. All that has resulted in the government taking an ambiguous position with the UGTT. Its approach to manage crises as they come—there is not any foresight in terms of what could happen.

The International Crisis Group report (2013) on the challenge of Salafism concurred, concluding that Ennahdha had "serious internal conflicts. The party faces a significant discrepancy between its leaders' very consensual political positions—which are regularly communicated through the media, especially the foreign media—and the profound convictions of its activist base." The report adds: "caught in the crossfire between a sometimes violent Salafi challenge and a secular opposition ready to criticise the least mistake," Ennahdha had a choice to make: "if it becomes more of a preaching and religious organisation, it will alarm non-Islamists. If it conducts itself in a more political and pragmatic way, it will alienate many of its members and push them towards the Salafis and parties to its right."

These internal tensions were not without consequence in the political battle between the UGTT and Ennahdha. The differences of opinion within the movement and disagreement over the approach to take with the UGTT can be seen in the statements made by minister and government spokesman Samir Dilou on December 6, 2012, on the power struggle between the government and the UGTT: "The government is not involved in any sort of conflict and the Ennahdha movement could have hardly imagined that one day it would enter into a power struggle with an institution of the UGTT's stature." He later specified that his "remarks do not reflect a consensus because differences of opinion exist" in (Rabaa, 2012).

How was the UGTT able to resist Ennahdha's attempts to counteract the union's political influence?

The UGTT Faces Pressure From Political Competition

The interviews conducted with unionists made evident that the UGTT was experiencing its own differences of opinion over how to deal with Ennahdha. When asked about the UGTT's political role during this period, most of the unionists stated that it was important for the UGTT to take stances in support of the opposition and to defend freedoms:

> The UGTT has always stood in solidarity with those who defend freedoms, especially during the dictatorship. The changes occurring now are clearly creating more freedoms, but as part of the transition, the UGTT has to lobby for those freedoms to be expressed in concrete form and enshrined in the constitution through laws and the ratification of international conventions. We have noticed that there are still repressive practices with regard to the media. There are still actions being taken against the freedom of religion and the freedom of assembly and the UGTT can't tolerate that kind of behavior.
>
> (Salah, union official, Higher Education, Tunis)

Other unionists took a more critical view of how the conflict interfered with the UGTT's political stances:

> The influential left-wing forces at the UGTT are playing an important role in the rapprochement with Béji Caïd Essebsi and pushing for more

radical positions with regard to Ennahdha. These left-wing forces are in favor of a front that would unite all the progressive forces, including the so-called "clean Destourians" that Béji Caïd Essebsi is seeking to represent.

(Romdhane, union activist, Mining, Redeyef)

According to the interviewees, the Executive Board hardened its stance toward Ennahdha due to the influential left-wing groups at the UGTT, which were in negotiations to form a broad-based political opposition front with Béji Caïd Essebsi. Playing a role in national politics while curbing the political plotting within the organization proved to be a particularly difficult task, as the polarization of Tunisian politics created divisions within the UGTT. Mohamed, a Tunis-based laborer and union activist, summarized the tense situation:

We base unionists are tired. Before we were fighting against the RCD and now it's against Ennahdha, instead of dealing with our own problems, like restructuring the union and offering alternative economic solutions. We're stuck between Ennahdha and a broad opposition front that could form around Essebsi, and we don't have time to offer other ways forward.

Several unionists, like Ammar, a unionist and teacher from Gafsa, asserted that the UGTT had no choice but to resist the polarization in Tunisian politics in order to maintain its power and place in the new political landscape:

The UGTT is a powerhouse that succeeded in standing up to the Ben Ali regime through its unionists' efforts. Now there is a real rift within the organization. The union activists are spread thin between politics, social issues, the union and associations. The challenge today is protecting the UGTT. The polarization is pushing people to choose between Ennahdha and Béji Caïd Essebsi, and at the UGTT, we are forced to choose between the union bureaucracy and Ennahdha. But we need a third, fourth and fifth alternative. . . . The political battle flows through the UGTT and unionists are trapped in this quandary. Unionists need to address the issue of labor negotiations, where new conditions are needed, a social and economic alternative. The UGTT has to work on a new economic and social model.

Journalist and human rights activist Fouzia stressed that the UGTT had to walk a tight line between performing its traditional role as a counterpower and fending off attempts by political parties to co-opt the union:

I was delighted to see the size of the demonstration on May 1, 2012. After that the Islamists will no longer feel like they're in the majority and

Rached Ghannouchi will stop threatening us to take to the streets. I'm happy that the UGTT is showing the Islamists that it's capable of taking to the streets. We took part in a revolution and were left faced with two outdated plans: the Islamists' plan and the RCD plan, which would deal a major blow to the revolution. I think that the UGTT would be making a big mistake if it decided to ally with Béji Caïd Essebsi.

When questioned about the conflict with the UGTT, the interviewees with close ties to the Troika offered a different perspective on the antagonistic situation. Houssem, the Ennahdha official quoted earlier:

> In my opinion, you have to make a distinction between two things. First of all, between the Troika government and Ennahdha. The Troika wasn't in a battle with the UGTT. Firstly, because the Minister of Social Affairs, Khalil Zaouia, is former unionist who is well versed in the past relationship between the government and the UGTT. Secondly, we had unionist advisors inside the Prime Minister's office who had a good relationship with the UGTT—there was a meaningful, constructive dialogue between the UGTT and the government, as evidenced by the agreement on the "social contract" signed at the ANC with many union and international figures in attendance. On the other hand, there were several crises with the opposition due to its strategy, which caused the situation to escalate. Thirdly, it was a social revolution, so it's only natural that there were social movements and the UGTT had to stand up for social causes—in a situation involving political freedoms and freedom as a union, it's natural that there would be a battle between the UGTT and the government, especially Ennahdha.

The interviewees pointed to the UGTT's ambiguous positions and the stark difference between the almost cordial relationship between the union and the Troika government and the union's public hostility toward Ennahdha. Negotiations stalled in the early days of the Troika government and their "lost year" proposal (a year with any wage increase) sparked controversy, but the union leaders were able to reach several labor agreements with the government, including a ban on temporary work in the textile sectors and others, a monthly bonus of 70 dinars (34 euros) for civil servants, and an agreement on the "social contract."[13] Khaled, a unionist with ties to Ettakatol, says that the dialogue between the UGTT and the Troika never broke down, despite their public sabre-rattling:

> The Troika government had to deal with a freshly elected UGTT leadership team that wanted to show what it was capable of, which is normal in the beginning and a tradition at all unions: you establish the balance of power. When a new [Executive] Committee arrives, it does a little display of power to make its presence felt on the ground, to demonstrate its

ability to rally its troops, to establish a balance of power with employers or the government. . . . That's what their intentions were. Another thing to remember is that we were in the midst of a revolution and protests. . . . What's funny is that the leaders of the UGTT are very attentive and open-minded during negotiations, but when it becomes public, they start repeating the same ideological slogans from the 1970s and quite simply seeking to obstruct Ennahdha.

He concludes that this oscillation between seemingly contradictory positions—head-on opposition to Ennahdha and uninterrupted labor dialogue with the government—reflects the pressure placed on the UGTT:

The UGTT, for its part, should have gotten its troops in line. Within the UGTT, there are several battles and political infighting with those who want the union to engage in partisan politics and stray from its role as an independent power that primarily defends workers' rights. The opposition—the far left, in particular—wants to turn the UGTT into a tool for attacking Ennahdha and the Troika government, hence the contradictions between the progress on labor issues and the political battle in the media spotlight. For its part, Ennahdha is pulled in several different directions: there are the moderates who want to work with the UGTT and the more radical members who conflate the UGTT with the left and want to do away with them once and for all. . . . The incident on December 4, 2012, is indicative of these ambiguities. The government and the UGTT signed a wage agreement on December 4 for the public and private sectors, which provided for a 6% raise; on that same day, violence broke out between the LPR and unionists in front of the UGTT offices.

(Khaled, a unionist with ties to Ettakatol)

What can be learned from the contradictions that surfaced at the UGTT and Ennahdha? The ambiguities observed in the stances put forward by both the UGTT and Ennahdha, which stemmed from both internal divisions and outside pressure, underscored the tensions that had arisen in the unpredictable, uncertain, fast-changing world of Tunisian politics:

The leaders of the UGTT and the government were under an equal amount of pressure. Both sides had to deal with the demands of financial organizations and manage divisions among their base and pressure from politicians.

(Mongi, union official, Higher Education, Tunis)

At the same time, the political awakening and the ensuing crisis revealed that neither Ennahdha nor the UGTT could be reduced to monolithic organizations—each had several groups of members with different beliefs and markedly divergent interests which, depending on the situation, could have led to conflict or cooperation. The intra-organizational balance between these various groups had a major impact on the political games played by Ennahdha and the UGTT. After the clash had subsided, the UGTT appeared to have overcome the tensions and maintained its political influence. Anis, a unionist and journalist, explains:

> The UGTT continues to play a significant role in Tunisian politics despite the current upheaval. It's true that before, different political forces would take refuge at the UGTT because there was no other place for political expression. But we are now in a new era where political parties can operate without any problems, and the UGTT continues to enjoy a great deal of influence, all the same. Leaders like Hamadi Jebali and Rached Ghannouchi who were around in the 1970S and 80s are only focused on one thing: how to have their say at the UGTT, as are the other left-wing leaders, Hamma Hammami and Chokri Belaïd. . . . But that's impossible because the Islamists will never be influential at the UGTT.

Fouzia, a human rights activist, adds:

> It's important for you to know that the structure of the UGTT is prestigious and there are talented people there. Unionists have always had an impact on the political situation in Tunisia. We all saw how Ghannouchi rushed to the UGTT after the incident with the garbage left in front of the UGTT offices. What ever the case may be, all political leaders—from Ghannouchi to Béji Caïd Essebsi—have to deal with the UGTT.

This period in Tunisian politics reflects tendency among the UGTT and Ennahdha leadership to pursue strategies that maintain their respective political culture. However, two new factors emerged that defined the battle between the two pugilists and made it different from previous clashes.

First, the fragile state of the country's opposition parties, which were in a rebuilding phase, made them even more dependent on the UGTT and shored up the political stature of the union leadership. Second, unlike the former regime, Ennahdha failed in its various attempts to gain influence within the UGTT and lacked expertise in unionism. Those two factors enabled the UGTT to overcome internal dissent and use its ability to unite the opposition in order to maintain or perhaps even increase its influence in the new political landscape. The role that the UGTT later played in the national dialogue further cemented its place as the leading political organization in the country. Meanwhile, Ennahdha was forced to soften its position toward the

UGTT and ended up accepting the mediator role that the union had played during the political crisis. One Ennahdha official described the shift that led to a more positive attitude toward the UGTT and the role that the UGTT played in leading the national dialogue:

> Ennahdha saw that the conflict with the UGTT was clearly going to lead to a showdown and the warning sign was the threat of a general strike on December 4, 2012. It was a powerful political message. At the time, the UGTT was involved in politics and the people weren't in favor of the fall of the government or a second revolution, especially because it was evident that the former regime was still there. During that period, the UGTT was able to push the Troika to budge on its positions while simultaneously neutralizing the movement that was seeking a counter-revolution and coup d'etat. People said that the counterrevolution was using the UGTT and, after we succeeded in installing the Mehdi Jomaa government, that Ennahdha and the Troika were doing the same. That's proof that the UGTT excels in the art of politics.

Ennahdha activist Ismaïl shared similar thoughts:

> When we took power, we noticed that the UGTT had a political agenda. When the UGTT proposed a national dialogue, we said no because at the time, we thought that a national dialogue was only a political matter for politicians. We had trouble understanding that the UGTT had always taken part in making national political decisions. In the beginning, we hadn't accepted the political role of the UGTT. Then we accepted the mission of the UGTT, which was what enabled a consensus. We now view the UGTT as a national force that manages social and union problems, as well as a stakeholder that provides input on national political decisions. In my opinion, the best way to guarantee the union struggle is successful is for the UGTT to remain the country's main trade-union force and for us not to let union pluralism, which is now a reality, disturb us. The UGTT has to play its role because although Ennahdha is in power now, it will be in the opposition in the future. If we domesticate [*tadjîn*] the UGTT, it will be a great loss for Ennahdha and Tunisia—it will weaken civil-society organizations, compromise the balance between society and the state, and foster a hegemonic central government.

After the political agreement ensured by the national dialogue, there was a certain turnaround, at least among some leaders of Ennahdha. For instance, Noureddine Bhiri, Minister-Counselor to Prime Minister Ali Larayedh, said on December 13, 2013 that "the UGTT is a school of democracy and national sacrifice, and it is impossible for it to be a putschist power one day." (gnet, 2013)

One question remains unanswered: if the UGTT was able to retain or even increase its influence as a key actor in the political transition, where did social issues fit into the new political equation?

Box 10 Mutual Distrust in the National Dialogue

The crisis between ourselves and the UGTT was the price of power. It was difficult to govern while also managing the social movement. While the UGTT is independent, by nature it is closer to the opposition than to the government. . . . When making economic decisions, we were pressured by financial organizations to take a more free-market approach, despite the fact that social and economic demands were what had led to the revolution. . . .] Ennahdha was late to learn about union work—the RCD outstripped them when it made inroads at UGET and the UGTT. . . . It's true that we're now in an era of union pluralism and that there is no shame in creating other unions. But we would have liked to be part of UGET. The only thing is, the students were afraid that we would take over UGET if we joined.

The same goes for the UGTT—they thought that if we joined, we would steal their union. They're afraid of us because our power is growing and accuse us of trying to dominate and being tempted to throw a coup ['inqilâbiya]. We have to replace this hegemonic mentality with a mentality conducive to integration—we have to integrate with the UGTT. . . . The UGTT has its regulations and laws and we're not going to change them. We need to get rid of political agendas to protect the UGTT. . . . Of course, as the moderate wing of Ennahdha, we know that we shouldn't have been impulsive, but the UGTT should have got its troops under control. Within the UGTT, there are several battles and political infighting with those who want the union to engage in partisan politics and stray from its role as an independent power that primarily defends workers' rights. The opposition wants to turn the UGTT into a tool for attacking the Troika government and especially Ennahdha. Some people at Ennahdha jumped at the opportunity to say that we had to take down the UGTT and the left. We eventually realized that all that wasn't true and we saw that the leadership at the UGTT was able to manage their internal conflicts. The UGTT is a positive force and we were able to build consensus between the UGTT and Ennahdha. The dialogue between the government and the UGTT never broke down.

Houssem, Ennahdha official

Social Pressure and the Political Calendar Weigh on the Union

The fraught political transition prompted the governing party to maintain—under other, more respectable guises—the same neoliberal economic model, while the opposition struggled to exist outside the UGTT and was unable to offer alternatives. More broadly, the continued attacks on the UGTT and social movements raised questions about the political elites' attitude toward the country's economic and social problems. In addition to their persistent tendency to criminalize protest movements, the elites had trouble placing those issues on the top of the agenda. The focus on the dispute between "Islamists" and "democrats" tended to shift attention to issues related to society or power struggles, while downplaying the importance of social matters[14] and obscuring the political elites' inability to offer a viable economic and social alternative (Hmed and Yousfi, 2012). A journalist, Souhail, noted:

> The Islamists are working with the same corrupt people from the former regime and the political parties are neglecting social issues, which are the focal point of conflict in Tunisia. If you, as a political party, do not manage strategic sectors and spend your time on the veil or the niqab, you're not a party that is capable of governing. When you look at Ennahdha's strategy for controlling the oil industry and no one is talking about it, you start wondering what's going on. Frankly, it's outrageous. Qatar made off with the largest project, Essekhira, the transaction with the government took place behind closed doors and none of the political parties is talking about it.

There is no question that the Popular Front—formed on October 7, 2012, by a coalition of far-left parties including the Workers' Party (formerly PCOT) and the Democratic Patriots' Movement (Watad) and Arab nationalists—attempted to fill that void. The Popular Front presented itself as the "third way"—an alternative to the political polarization—with the primary slogan "Neither Essebsi nor Jebali: our revolution is the revolution of the humble." However, the political assassination of its two leaders—Chokri Belaïd on February 6, 2013, and Mohamed Brahmi on July 25, 2013—resulted in the creation of the Redemption Front, which comprised the Popular Front and Nidaa Tounes. This chain of events severely restricted the scope of the third alternative in the polarized world of Tunisian politics. In the next section, I will discuss the process by which social movements were sidelined as the political calendar took precedence. I will also analyze the complex relationship between the UGTT and various social movements.

Political Battles Eclipse the Social Movements

To grasp the importance of social issues in the UGTT's action strategies, it is worth taking a step back and examining how social movements are discussed in political discourse. A review of Tunisian politics over the past three years reveals that political elites new and old alike, both in the government and the opposition, have been locked in a bitter power struggle and unable to offer viable alternatives to Ben Ali-era economic and social policy. As a result, they formed an unspoken pact to take social issues off the agenda, as evidenced by their careful distinction between political issues, their top priority, and social issues, which are depicted as obstacles that prevent the transition from arriving at its destination "safe and sound" (*barr al-amân*). Manifested in the "magic" expression "democratic transition," this distinction, whether cunningly devised or subconsciously created by the governing elite, emerged as the best means of protecting the economic interests of the dominant social classes and bringing the revolutionary process to a halt.

The conflict between politics and socioeconomic progress takes several forms in Tunisia. First, political issues are overdramatized in advance of elections in order to distract voters, pique their interest and justify the need for political organizations, which are presented as the only means of controlling the situation (Hmed, 2014). The political and media narrative focused on the importance of reaching a consensus among political actors with regard to the election schedule, while economic and social considerations were portrayed as peripheral to what were commonly called the "real issues," which had to be addressed to stabilize the political situation. Second, social protest movements led by the UGTT and others are systematically criminalized, labeled as "uncivil," and accused of impeding the economic recovery and scaring off local and foreign investors, slowing the march toward political and economic stability. The argument often put forward is, "We want a truce, let us work, be patient and you'll get what you want." Youssef, a Gafsa Phosphate Company employee and unionist:

> It is amazing to see how the three transition governments have had the same message with regard to social movements. They all tried to say that the people's demands and the goals of the revolution had not been met and, particularly in terms of employment, that this was due to the strikes, sit-ins and "chaos," which investors did not find heartening. Not only do they show disdain for the social demands that led people to rise up, they make them guilty for their own impoverishment.

Farid, a teacher and unionist from Sidi Bouzid adds:

> There hasn't been a break with the past. The expressions "economic crisis" and "difficult economic conditions" were already keywords that the government and employers used in all quarterly negotiations. Those expressions continue to be used to ostracize every protest movement.

The leader of Ennahdha, Rached Ghannouchi, is no exception to the rule. He suspected the social movements of seeking to overthrow the Ennahdha government:

> They started by blocking roads and factories, and now they're at it again, attacking the legitimacy of the government. Ennahdha is the

backbone of Tunisia. Shattering or banning it would damage the country's national unity.

(quoted in Halimi, 2013, 1–2)

Third, various political actors never cease to give solemn remarks on the importance of "reducing regional disparities," "encouraging investment" and "fighting unemployment." However, the only proposed economic alternative was to carry on with Ben Ali's economic plan—focusing all efforts to repair the economy on the fight against corruption while ignoring the country's structural economic deficiencies. The conflict at Latelec[15] is representative of this phenomenon and offers a window into an array of Tunisia's economic woes. The conflict erupted at a subsidiary of a French company that employed a qualified, inexpensive workforce. Latelec threatened to shut down when the workers struck in order to ensure their rights were met. The Tunisian economy relies on service sectors like tourism and low-value-added textiles that employ workers with few qualifications, whereas the policy focus should be on enabling the huge number of unemployed graduates to find work (Mouhoud, *op. cit.*). The Euro-Mediterranean agreements, which did much to keep these structural deficiencies in place, have been maintained without any meaningful critical review. The political showdown drew attention away from the urgent need to make economic reform a top political priority.

Lastly, the successive transition governments used police repression, a formidable weapon from the Ben Ali era, to put down various protest movements. The Troika government was no exception to the rule—it violently repressed the demonstrations held in Siliana on November 28, 2011, to demand the resignation of the governor, the liberation of prisoners held since April of that same year, and an economic aid plan. More than 200 people were wounded, many of whom sustained serious injuries to the eyes from buckshot (Puchot, 2012).

It can be surmised, then, that the only available alternatives were mass tourism, subcontracting, fairly intensive farming and infrastructure upgrades (an occasional highway or hospital). Given the situation, it is understandable that the number of social movements—led by the UGTT and others—began to rise. Workers regularly called general strikes across entire cities (Le Kef, Siliana, Ben Guerdane and Sidi Bouzid) and sector-based strikes (education, transportation, phosphates, etc.). The most determined protest movements were linked to unemployment and development disparities between the coastal cities and the rest of the country, spurred on by unemployed young people who were deeply disappointed by the government's inaction on issues related to employment and regional inequality. The movements vandalized industrial sites, blocked roads and rail lines and set up picket lines to prevent workers from getting to their jobs. These events were much more frequent and widespread than the controversies between Islamists and secularists, which received greater media attention both at home and

abroad. The young unemployed demanded jobs and worthwhile development projects in the inland regions. These social and economic campaigns
were selectively backed by activists from political organizations, but more
often viewed as a disturbance that could be exploited for political gain but
remained peripheral in relation to the celebrated "democratic transition."
For its part, the UGTT continually provided support to movements under
its banner and otherwise, but received a spate of criticism for its tendency
of ranking the protests in importance and focusing more on its political
agenda. Najiba, a journalist and human rights activist:

> The UGTT uses its history—it uses its historical legitimacy—in the
> political fight, but I haven't seen anything in social or economic areas.
> I think that the finance law tabled by Ennahdha reflects its ultra-liberal
> economic platform, which is worse than that of Ben Ali. The UGTT,
> the only political force capable of holding its own with Ennahdha, has
> forgotten its social role and focused solely on the political battle.

Moez, an unemployed graduate, views the situation along the same lines:

> We are now convinced that the UGTT is the only organization capable
> of handling economic and social issues and speaking on behalf of the
> marginalized and poor, who came out on December 17, 2010, and had
> their hopes taken from them. We noticed a change in the position of
> the UGTT, which gave more attention to the regional and UDC [the
> unemployed graduates' union] social movements, but it wasn't enough.
> The UGTT is caught up in the political fight, to the detriment of social
> and economic issues.

How did the UGTT interact with the different social movements under its
leadership and outside its control?

Using Corporatist Labor Demands in the Political Fight

After the fall of Ben Ali, the number of corporatist labor demands grew and several new unions were formed. The UGTT used these demands as an important
political weapon for negotiating its own position, but they also were a source
of instability in the inner workings of the organization. Recognizing this, all
the interviewees viewed the gains made by the union on certain employment
issues—including pay raises and a ban on public-sector subcontracting—as a
success, despite the intense conflict between Ennahdha and the UGTT. This
progress on labor issues appears paradoxical at first glance, but upon closer
inspection, one sees that the UGTT was able to take advantage of the corporatist demands to cement its influence in the political realm.

The political battle between the UGTT and Ennahdha saw the revival of
a classic union strategy: oscillating between pressure and negotiations, this

time in relations with the Troika. Certain observers may view this strategy as a sign of ambivalence or ambiguity, but it did enable the union to retain its position as a leading political actor in a period of political uncertainty. As part of the strategy, high-ranking UGTT officials would often highlight social and economic issues when speaking in public, while privately subordinating them to the quest for influence in the fast-changing Tunisian political landscape. These issues were used as a means of pressuring the government and an invaluable resource for winning union members' loyalty. The labor agreements between the UGTT and the Troika government enabled the latter to guarantee a modicum of civility in labor relations, while the union maintained its legitimacy in the eyes of its base and its ability to mobilize support. Moreover, the UGTT reached an entente with the employers' organization UTICA, which grew stronger during the national dialogue and helped the two sides find common ground on pay raises:

> With employers, however, I think that negotiations will be slightly easier than with the government. A portion of employers, at the least, are receptive to pay raises. That's clear—I heard them say so at the employers' headquarters during a negotiation preparation session. The government, on the other hand, starting playing the "lost year" card, meaning a year without any raises. Its representatives explained that employees had to make sacrifices because the country was experiencing an economic crisis. A lost year would have been unprecedented in Tunisia, and the government had to abandon the idea.
>
> (Jemli, 2012)

All these factors did much to bolster the UGTT in its battle with Ennahdha and later helped the union impose its roadmap during the national dialogue. At the same time, the UGTT's success in retaining its political role did not make it immune to bickering among its ranks. In addition to the criticism mentioned above regarding the union's political role, the explosion in company labor demands undermined the union bureaucracy, which could no longer manage all the UGTT's various organizations. There were parallels with the revolution, when certain local and regional sections had taken the initiative in ways that flaunted the union's centralized decision-making process. This crisis of authority became more severe as a huge influx of new members joined the UGTT and competition grew between the various corporatist interests. Khaled, a unionist with ties to Ettakatol, compares the decline of centralized power at the UGTT to the weakening of all government institutions due to the political rebuilding in Tunisia:

> After the revolution, all state institutions were weakened. They were weakened in terms of decision-making powers. The state grew weaker in relation to its employees and the general public, and the UGTT suffered the same thing. . . . We noticed competition between union bodies

at the UGTT. Sometimes there would be two contradictory opinions on a single issue. For example, the education ministry has nine different unions, all of which UGTT-affiliated, whose analysis and demands can be contradictory. Another telling example occurred at the airports authority, where the unions for the ground staff and the air traffic controllers are both UGTT-affiliated. The air traffic controllers said: "If you give them a raise, we're striking, unless you give us the same thing." This happened despite the fact that what they wanted was very specific; the air traffic controllers needed training in English and the others said that it was out of the question. . . . In the past, the Secretary General would take firm positions to prevent this type of event and power was concentrated in the hands of the Executive Board. Now the new members of the leadership do not take any position. You contact the members of the Executive Board and you say to them, "Is it normal that there are so many strikes in such-and-such sector?" and they tell you, "We're going to send the union official so that you can work that out with him." . . . And you wonder, "But what is the Executive Board's position?" It doesn't do anything.

Mohsen, a postman and unionist from Sfax, had similar thoughts:

The union leaders are playing a leading role on the national political stage but in strictly union matters, they don't have the same influence. They're unable to enforce their decisions for several reasons, such as the excesses of the base, the lack of unionist culture among new UGTT members, the inability to revise union regulations, and the organizational structure at the UGTT. At the Tabarka Congress, they said that a national congress would be held a year later to change the union statutes; it's now been three years, which says a lot about the difficulties they've had. They had planned to make large unions. Now they're moving in the opposite direction, increasing the number of Administrative Commission members, creating other unions, and making plans to split the postal and telecommunications union in two, whereas in the past it has been a single union. All that is being done to serve the interests of certain groups—[Workers' Party leader] Hamma Hammami's supporters want more influence in the Administrative Commission. They are already influential at the postal service but, as there are more UGTT members in telecommunications and a lot of companies with about the same statutes, like Orange and Tunisiana, the postal service was in the minority. The telecommunications companies are privately owned and pay high wages; the postal service is more politicized, with Hamma supporters pushing to split the union in two in order to secure their own existence. There are also very small unions with 40 to 60 members that have a place in decision-making bodies. Mohamed Trabelsi proposed restructuring to form a sort of board of directors and representation for the major sectors, in order to have general overall policy. The way things are going now, the more we divide the union the more difficult it is to have consistent policy, which weakens us. The people at the UGTT are aware of the issue but they are under pressure.

It is eminently clear, then, that the corporatist demands and the political battle obscured what should have been the top priority, namely implementing the reforms required to improve Tunisia's social system and resist the free-market directives of international financial organizations. Sami, a doctor and union official, explains:

Ennahdha and the UGTT were equally opportunistic in their handling of social issues. They settled for negotiations on pay raises and neglected social projects, such as reforming the status of the public sector and the status of state-run companies, which were put on hold. . . . We knew that they were in a disastrous situation. . . . No, the UGTT leadership couldn't see the purpose of it all. They could've done it but they said no and it wasn't something that the base could challenge. . . . It was a decision that they were able to enforce. There are major problems: the state's coffers are empty. The UGTT has to take responsibility. There is a structural deficit in government funds due to demographic change—especially in the pension fund. . . . Reforming the social security fund is also key—the government is currently funding the deficit. The CNRPS [pension fund] deficit is rising slowly but surely. The same goes for the CNSS [social security fund]—if nothing is done by 2017, we may have a colossal deficit. And most private-sector employees—the lowest earners—use the CNSS, so it will be a disaster if we don't do anything.

Mohamed, a textile worker and unionist, said:

The political battle wore us out. The financial organizations' neoliberal offensive is very serious—the few social benefits we have could disappear overnight, we continue to add fuel to the fire with quarrels between Islamists and modernists, and at the UGTT we keep the unionists quiet with a few pay raises. The UGTT has to take responsibility and move beyond the political battle to be able to offer a real economic and social alternative.

The combination of the union leadership being locked into the political process and the crisis of central authority at the union led the base to embark on more unauthorized initiatives. Two camps emerged: those in favor of centralized, offensive actions capable of causing the government back down, and those who backed initiatives led by the base, which could be very organized but were necessarily less supervised. The latter type of initiative was more focused on defending individual, local, regional or professional interests, or bringing about change. The UGTT appears to have maintained an often-fragile balance between stopping out-of-control initiatives when needed and winning concessions that, while viewed as unreasonable by some, were key to cementing the union's power. Several protest movements and demonstrations were led locally by the unemployed. How did the UGTT interact with these movements? The next section focuses on the relationship between the UGTT and UDC.

The Hot-and-Cold Relationship Between the UGTT and Unemployed Graduates

During the revolution, members from the unemployed graduates' union worked side by side with unionists to coordinate various mobilizations. After the fall of Ben Ali, the UDC led several initiatives in support of the right to employment and regional development, for which the UGTT regularly provided logistic and political assistance. This partnership between unionists and the unemployed dates back to the dictatorship, when UDC activists were still often working in secrecy. Sabra explains:

> Before January 14, they [the unionists] were the only ones who gave us a little support. We were underground without authorization, so we couldn't work. With the UGTT, we had a little room for maneuver. None of the political parties supported us—the unionists were the only ones who defended the right to employment. We remain in touch to this day through individual contacts in certain industries.
>
> (Chaïfa and Hamdi, *op. cit.*)

This partnership did not have the blessing of the union bureaucracy, which, according to some interviewees, resorted to force in order to halt protest movements.

> In 2006 when the UDC was created, no one would give us the time of day—not parties, associations or civil-society organizations. What is more, we were often assaulted by the union bureaucracy's militias on Place Mohamed Ali Hammi. That said, there are unionists who have supported us from the beginning, even if they didn't have very much power at the time.

Unemployment once again became a central concern after the December 17, 2010 uprising and the unemployed began to demonstrate in greater numbers across Tunisia. However, the post-January 14 political climate and successive attempts to halt the revolutionary process led to widespread efforts to disparage all social movements in political discourse and the media, making the unemployed the prime target of political repression. The interviewees often spoke about the violent crackdown on the UDC rally on April 7, 2012, during which several people were injured.

> There was a major crackdown on April 7 but it wasn't the first of the sort. We never gave up during Ben Ali's reign of torture and we won't back down now. We are always in conflict with the government, no matter who is in power, because of our cause and the fact that we're primarily a social movement. We have been attacked by all the governments: Ghannouchi, Essebsi and Jebali. Under the Béji Caïd Essebsi government, one of our activists was beaten violently. He was unemployed so he didn't have the social security coverage needed to receive adequate treatment, so we paid for it out of pocket to help him.
>
> (Maher, UDC activist)

For the first time, the UGTT officialized its support for the UDC and victims of repression through a statement of solidarity with the unemployed and medical treatment for the wounded (Ben Tarjem, 2012).[16] Maher confirms:

> The UGTT issued a statement on April 8 after we suffered police violence on April 7. We found the UGTT's reaction to be revolutionary—it was the first time that the UGTT had released a statement that supported our demands, condemned the assaults we had suffered and placed the blame on the government.

The UDC was recognized as a major national organization in terms of membership[17] and various political parties began to set their sights on the organization due the country's financial problems and instability plaguing the nation's unemployed. Like the UGTT, the UDC was victim to political sniping and horse-trading, as UDC activist Amine explains:

> The UDC's problem is financial and that financial problem may make the UDC an easy mark. The UDC has to find a suitable organizational structure—they have to act democratically amongst themselves. They don't have the financial capacity to hold a congress and there aren't any powers capable of helping them to get organized. The UDC could be a major organization—as powerful as the UGTT—it's the country's second-largest organization in terms of membership. . . . I can assure you that we received a lot of phone calls from political parties in the run-up to the ANC elections. They offered us colossal sums and we refused because we value our independence. The UDC is a group of people who are threatened by instability and poverty, which helps them keep their fighting spirit. It's extraordinary to be able to resist in that way, especially when there is a large influx of foreign money from Freedom House and others, which threatens the integrity of civil-society

associations and threatens our young people, who are in precarious situations.

Further criticism came from Salah:

> The UDC is an organization for people who are marginalized and in precarious situations. Back when we were the only ones demonstrating, certain political parties accused us of needless escalation. After January 14 and the influx of new UDC members, the same parties are now trying to use us. The cause of the unemployed has become an attractive cause for investing political capital and we have to resist these attempts at exploitation. . . . The irony of it all is that the political parties that rejected the UDC's platform are now sending their members to join. . . . Their strategy is to push us onto the front lines of the clash with the government, so that they can come in afterwards and reap all the rewards of our efforts. It's disgraceful to use the unemployed and their poverty to strike bargains.

The political tug-of-war during the post-January 14 surge in protest movements impacted relations between the UGTT and the UDC. Interviewees from the UDC mentioned both the friction between corporatist labor demands and unemployment issues and criticized the UGTT for using the plight of the unemployed to pressure the government into accepting the union's agenda:

> The UGTT has always had an ambivalent relationship with the unemployed. The union has often used their cause to its own ends. The UDC is an activist organization and people saw the fight led by its members in 2006. They don't even have enough money to rent an office. The UGTT used the UDC in several political fights. Many UDC activists joined with the UGTT in several initiatives. The UGTT uses the UDC as a lobbying card to play with the government in order to win concessions for itself. What social issues motivate the UGTT? It often demonstrates for pay raises in labor negotiations, and that's it.
>
> (Hatem, UDC activist)

The lack of understanding between the UGTT and the UDC was exacerbated by the priority given to the election schedule over social issues. Those most critical of the UGTT felt as if competing political actors had used them as "cannon fodder." Class relations played out between the UGTT—representative of the organized middle class—and the unemployed. Unemployed graduate and UDC activist Hakim explains:

> We have always supported the UGTT, despite our past problems with the union bureaucracy. We want to protect our independence while

continuing to coordinate with the UGTT, in particular with regard to demonstrations on social issues. There has not been a single UGTT demonstration without us. But the UGTT continues to look down on us. At the municipal employees' strike [February 2012], we were surprised to see that the UGTT had invited representatives from associations and political parties, who were on the balcony when Houcine Abbassi gave his speech. No one had invited us, despite the fact we are much greater in number than all those associations and political parties combined. People are often very condescending with us and I don't understand why. Are they afraid of us? Is it because they can't pin us down? I don't understand.

Unemployed graduate Salah recognizes the UGTT's legitimacy in economic and social issues but finds it regrettable that the unemployed have no representation on decision-making bodies related to unemployment:

We have trouble coordinating with the UGTT. We have made several requests to form an organization for national dialogue aimed at finding solutions to Tunisia's unemployment problem. It's true that the UGTT and certain political parties do present proposals to help the unemployed, but we want to be included in the efforts to develop solutions because, as the Tunisian saying goes, "you can only feel the embers [al-jamra] if you put your feet on them." We are the ones most affected by the unemployment problems. We have statistics, we have experts, we are capable of tabling proposals, but unfortunately, no one listens to us. The unemployment problem has to be treated as a national problem relevant to all associations and parts of civil society, led by the UGTT, in order to find a solution to the problem, which is destroying society. Remember, the slogan of the revolution—"Employment is a right, pack of thieves!"—was initially an unemployed graduates slogan. It's a slogan that became popular and did much to radicalize the December 17, 2010 protest movement.

Despite their critical views, the UDC members continued to look to the UGTT as the only actor capable of influencing the country's economic and social policy. They defended the independence of the UDC but sought to develop joint solutions together with the trade union.

We hold an outstretched hand in their direction and feel confident that we will find solutions that can facilitate our joint duties. We are not going to stop or settle for support that, on the whole, only covers the essentials.
(Moez, unemployed, UDC)

We have always said in our speeches and statements that we are counting on the UGTT. That means that, in spite of the errors of the bureaucracy and the errors of certain individuals, the UGTT is still a leading organization that is assuming its responsibilities. We will always continue to count on the UGTT. There wasn't really any coordination during the Ben Ali era and after January 14, the relationship with the UGTT remained tense, so the process of building a relationship really only began after the Tabarka Congress and the statement issued on April 7, 2012.

(Maher, unemployed, UDC)

The new political climate in Tunisia ushered in new political and social challenges for the UGTT. While many acknowledged that the UGTT had lent political support to protest movements originating inside and outside the union, political jockeying appears to have established a hierarchy favoring the social strata affiliated with the UGTT and elevated political aims above socioeconomic considerations. Within the UGTT, tensions continued to rise between a desire to make every effort to reach a national agreement acceptable to the political class and some unionists' support for social movements. At the same time, the turmoil at the UGTT over the prioritization of politics did not in any way signify a sign of weakness or a split with the base, which was fairly skeptical about the union's political interventionism. Rather, it denoted a willingness to negotiate a balanced relationship with the government. As the leaders of the UGTT were the only stakeholders capable of acting with the moderation required to prevent a flare-up related to social issues, they were in a comfortable negotiating position.

To what extent, then, would the UGTT continue to walk the tightrope between the continually dashed hopes for negotiation with the government and the acts of social revolt and significant divisions within the organization? To what extent would the UGTT be able to control popular unrest and mitigate the risk of watering down its principles in the seemingly never-ending negotiations with various political actors? After two years of conflict between UGTT and Ennahdha, Tunisia's political stakeholders successfully established a national dialogue that resulted in a nationwide agreement. What role did the UGTT play in the national dialogue? Was the union able to incorporate its social and economic aims into the final agreement?

Box 11 The Political Battle Expands the Divide Between the Political Class and the Social Sphere

Tunisia's political powers—organizations such as the UGTT and political parties—need to realize that new political and social forces emerged with the revolution that must be reckoned with. There are leaders who need to understand that they didn't carry out the revolution they had been dreaming of for decades; the Tunisian Revolution was carried out by the Tunisian people—the famished and the marginalized without political ties—outside any sort of political framework. They need to understand that the political parties and their representatives are not the ones who led the revolution. . . . They need to understand that as things stand, the revolution was served to them on a gold platter but they haven't been able to take advantage, to carry it forward or complete it to achieve the aims of the revolution.

The problem today is that the country's elite, the political powers, hold the most responsibility for the failure of the revolution. They have to recognize this failure. The People—who Bourguiba called a "scattering of people"—cannot organize . . . individuals cannot organize without political leaders who can rally them together. It's clear to see. Today, the failure that we've experienced is due to the fact that we haven't been able to organize as a people. The tragedy of the Tunisian people is that the political leaders are the ones who lost the revolution for us, the political parties caused the revolution to fail. Thank you to the people who set the revolution in motion and shame on the political parties that made it fail. . . . The People "cut off the serpent's head" and the political powers—who call themselves revolutionaries—should have taken up the mantle to see the process through. The problem is that the People cannot remain in a perpetual state of revolution. We let the street cool down like iron—the blacksmith heats the iron before forging it and it has to be done hot. You then have to strike it, and if the iron isn't hot enough or malleable enough at the start, you can't forge it anymore. Today, we've left those on the street behind and the Tunisian people are cooling down. People have lost confidence in the political elite—we can no longer dream of bringing the streets back to life or reviving the spirit of the revolution. It's all over because the counterrevolutionary forces—RCD partisans and their allies—that's it, they've gained momentum. They were frozen at the beginning, they were scared and confused. We never dealt them the fatal blow; now they're back out and stronger than before. Whether we like it or not, the political powers in the current transition phase need consensus [*wifaq*]—now is not the time for partisan scheming. If we want to rebuild the country, we need councils or frameworks for managing the transition. The time is not to split up the "*mouhassassa*" pie. . . . There has to be a plan, there has to be trust and a platform on which an agreement can be reached that is in the country's best interest.

There is no legal government today—the only form of legitimacy that exists is that of the revolution and the struggles. That's the only form of legitimacy that allows you to win people's trust, the only one that commands people's respect, that prevents people from telling you to "get lost." That's what the politicians need to understand. You see them now, battling it out for a place on the municipal council or the revolutionary council. They all think that they deserve a place because they are such-and-such party, but none of them stops to think about what they have done for the Tunisian people, for the country, to deserve that place. Most of the parties were formed after the revolution. The people who used to support the regime and cheer it on are now find ways to seek out a place in the new political landscape. It's shameful!

> The political powers and the revolutionary forces that have campaigned throughout Tunisia's history, the people who were imprisoned, tortured, insulted, who went through unemployment, poverty and misery . . . those people are known, everybody knows them. The people who gave everyone freedom, the people who gave them the freedom to organize and take part in politics, those people's reward is an indecent battle among politicians to win power. That's what the problem is.
>
> Adnene Hajji, union leader, Redeyef

The UGTT Crafts the National Dialogue

The different crises that took place after the election made the period a critical phase for negotiations to allocate power among the various political and social stakeholders. The period served as a unique testing ground for potential methods of redefining the issues at stake and the conventions of Tunisian politics. This was due to the fact that the ANC elections on October 23, 2011, lacked the democratic legitimacy required to buttress political decisions and foster the emergence of rules of practice with widespread support. The legality of the elections did little to cement the legitimacy of the government or the ANC, which was regularly contested and called into question (Yaalaoui, 2012). In practice, this legal foundation was far from the only source of power and proved incapable of curbing the political crisis. The instability of the "democratic transition" created several competing sources of legitimacy that gradually developed a new political lexicon and brought new issues to the fore in the debate over the new institutions to be established. Three groups of stakeholders emerged that drew from three forms of legitimacy as they engaged in a fierce battle for power: Ennahdha, the Islamist party that dominated the coalition government and sought electoral legitimacy to remain in power; the political opposition, dominated by Nidaa Tounes, which opposed Ennahdha head-on and sought consensus-based legitimacy to return to managing the country's affairs; and lastly, the defenders of the revolutionary ideal demanded direct power for the People in the name of revolutionary legitimacy. Throughout the term of the Troika government, each group of actors depicted their respective legitimacy as sacred, unsurpassable and untouchable, while launching exclusionist jabs at their adversaries.

These competing sources of legitimacy coincided with a political competition in which Tunisia's intermediate power structures and traditional systems of allegiance between the state—the administration, in particular—and individuals remained intact. The arrangement inherited from the former regime was termed by some as the "deep state," referring not to its more common meaning—dispersed ex-RCD members—but to the networks of businessmen, politicians, policemen and informants that comprised the economic system which governed the country for more than 50 years. These networks, which continued to exert a significant influence in Tunisian society and wanted to prevent their interests from being jeopardized, fiercely resisted all attempts to bring about change. The survival of these longstanding practices saw the coexistence of different systems that exploited, competed and clashed with one another at various intervals.

The political system during the transition was further weakened by the fact that it was caught in a vice between the authoritarian past and democratic institutions that still lacked solid footing. A perfect illustration of the situation is the battle for power between Ennahdha and Nidaa Tounes, which both attempted to co-opt the networks from the former regime into the state apparatus (Krichen, 2013). The gap between the power enshrined in law and the real power behind the scenes led to the shelving of initiatives on the martyrs and wounded of the revolution and delays in implementing a justice system during the transition. This political tension exacerbated both the crisis of authority at government institutions and Tunisians' distrust of the political class (Naccache, 2013). Naima, a human rights activist, offered her perspective:

> There is a real crisis of confidence in the political parties. People now have an aversion to anything related to power, politics, unionism—any form of power—and, as soon as they see that you belong to an organization, they associate that setting with hegemonic power. I don't know what we're going to do, how the relationship with politics is going to change. There is no magic solution and I hope that the distrust will last a bit longer, because we can't write the politicians a blank check. People have to pressure the political parties so that they understand that they're here to satisfy our needs.

Finally, foreign interference in the form of speeches on the importance of the "democratic transition" (Perez, 2012) and foreign countries serving as an intermediary (Mandraud, 2013) in political negotiations created another source of power that competed with the elected government. The interviewees sometimes spoke about the geopolitical aspect of the transformation of Tunisian politics, but this was often limited to criticism of the networks of arms dealers that fueled terrorism or the warm welcome given to the international powers that praised the revival of the national dialogue.[18] The influence of foreign powers vying for influence in Tunisian politics was rarely analyzed.

The UGTT, which boasted having independent, impartial legitimacy, found itself at the center of interactions between the various other sources of legitimacy and power systems. What was the outcome of these interactions? What role did the UGTT play in forging a relatively legitimate political solution that was accepted by all stakeholders?

Political Crises Serve as a Catalyst for a National Consensus

The polarization of Tunisian politics and the controversies targeting the UGTT held the union leadership back from establishing an alternative to the country's two dominant political forces. However, the union did launch a "political initiative" (UGTT, 2012) on June 18, 2012, which sought to rekindle consensus among political powers, the government and civil society on the main bones of contention: the key principles of the constitution, election dates and the members of the electoral commission. The initiative proposed the creation of a national council on dialogue that would meet periodically to resolve disagreements and establish a consensus. This forum for dialogue would become a source of new ideas but did not in any way replace the government or its existing constitutional, lawful institutions. Lamjed Jemli (*op. cit.*), coordinator of the private-sector UGTT sections, explained the concept:

> The UGTT launched a "political initiative" in June that aims to rekindle a national consensus. The government explained that it had achieved a majority in the elections and that this gave it the right to do as it pleased. But it doesn't work that way in practice. Firstly, because the Troika won a majority in seats but not in votes. Secondly, having a majority at the Constituent Assembly doesn't mean anything if the government is not able to apply the decisions it makes. All that does is increase tension and dissent at a time when we need to unite all key stakeholders behind common goals, which must be the goals of the revolution. . . . The UGTT initiative falls along those lines. It calls for the creation of a national council on dialogue that would bring together civil society, the opposition and the parties in power. . . . The idea is to achieve a consensus—the opposite of what the government is doing when it says, "We have the majority so we're going to put our decisions to a vote," and wants to arrogate the right to have sole control over appointing the members of the electoral commission. . . . The UGTT started getting in touch with the political parties, and everyone they have met with so far is on board. The same goes for the Prime Minister, although other Ennahdha members have stated that the UGTT shouldn't get involved in the issue. If the council never gets off the ground, the democratic transition will reach an impasse. Personally, I think that the initiative is important. If it comes together, everyone will be better for it. If it doesn't come together, the UGTT will have to think of something else, but it will be able to say, "I proposed a dialogue and you refused." Everyone will have to come to terms with their responsibilities.

However, the UGTT struggled to bring the initiative to fruition and gain acceptance for its role as a political mediator in the crisis. Ennahdha and the CPR expressed reservations about Nidaa Tounes taking part in the dialogue and decided not to proceed with the proposal, on the basis that it amounted to defying the will of the people and creating a parallel forum for debate alongside the Constituent Assembly, in a venue more advantageous to the opposition (Gharb, 2012). This failure raised doubts about the UGTT's ability to unite parties with such different ideologies and motives behind a single goal.[19]

In addition, some observers viewed the UGTT's plans for a general strike on December 5, 2012—later canceled after the union reached an agreement with the government—as another aborted attempt to assert its centrality in Tunisian politics (Brésillon, *op. cit.*). Two of the main demands behind the strike were the creation of a roadmap setting forth the subsequent steps in the transition and the resumption of the national dialogue. The UGTT wavered with dramatic intensity between two necessities: taking a conciliatory approach while continuing to dialogue with the government, and not backing down in order to satisfy large swathes of unionists and government opponents. Viewed from this perspective, the cancelation of the strike served two purposes. First, it was a reminder of the union's clout and ability to mobilize. It also was an act of good faith that demonstrated the UGTT's efforts to channel unionists' indignation and defuse the outcry breeding among the opposition.

On July 25, 2013, the day on which the left-wing nationalist MP Mohamed Brahmi was assassinated (following the murder of Chokri Belaïd that February), Tunisia plummeted into a serious political crisis that opened the door to another period during which the legitimacy of the country's institutions was contested (Yousfi and Hmed, 2013). The opposition called for the Islamist-majority government to step down and for the dissolution of the National Constituent Assembly, but without offering a viable alternative.[20] The Troika government and Ennahdha, in particular, clung to their electoral legitimacy and refused to leave power. Khalid, a unionist and Ettakatol sympathizer, noted:

> It's important to realize that before Brahmi's assassination, the UGTT and the government had a great relationship. We were supposed to hold a meeting between the government and the UGTT on July 26, to establish a roadmap for the main issues at hand—we had held a preparatory meeting on July 24. . . . All systems were go but the assassination put a halt to everything and killed all our momentum.

The UGTT held a series of meetings in a bid to find a solution to the crisis. The union no longer presented itself solely as a platform for dialogue, but as a proactive participant. For the first time, the UGTT sought out three national organizations to lend credence to its initiative: the Tunisian Union for Industry, the Order of Lawyers and the Tunisian Human Rights League. The UGTT and the National Dialogue Quartet developed an initiative to end the crisis that included a joint roadmap with three main focuses: maintaining the ANC, forming an apolitical government of technocrats and establishing an election schedule. After a series of political negotiations, the UGTT's consensus-based approach surmounted the disagreement over legal legitimacy and revolutionary legitimacy, enabling the parties to complete the constitutional process and end the crisis.

Tunisian gendarmes and armed underground fighters died in clashes in Sidi Ali ben Aoun, in the Sidi Bouzid region, on October 23, 2013, two years after the first free elections were held. The tragedy occurred just as the Quartet sponsoring the national dialogue succeeded in establishing the conditions for new talks by drafting a working document that officially recognized the political parties' desire to end the three-month-old political crisis (UGTT, 2013). The tragedy revived the same political tensions sparked by the assassinations of Chokri Belaïd and Mohamed Brahmi in February and July, respectively, which were attributed to "Jihadists." In this climate of serious security concerns and a resurgence of acts of terrorism, politicians' appeals for unity among all Tunisians against terrorism restored law and order as the country's top and only priority.[21] After a few false starts, the national dialogue began on Friday, October 25, 2013, following Prime Minister Ali Larayedh's written statement in which he undertook to step down within three weeks and be replaced by an "independent" cabinet led by a new head of government to be named within a week.

The crises that had hit Tunisia heightened the need to come to an understanding and avoid political violence. Reaching a consensus was no longer a matter of speeches on the steps in the transition (Perez, *op. cit.*) or vague hopes expressed by the UGTT, but a prerequisite for the state to function and guarantee civil order. The UGTT's authority was embodied in the creation of a regulatory body. What, then, were the terms of the agreement and how did it reshape the political landscape in Tunisia?

A Consensus-Based Approach to Conflict Resolution

The roadmap drafted by the UGTT and the three other mediators, which was signed by 21 of the 24 invited parties on October 25, 2013, established a general framework for the national dialogue.[22] The plan set forth a carefully devised set of three processes. First, a governmental process that required political actors to agree on an "apolitical" government and an independent prime minister, following which the Troika government would resign. Second, a constitutional process that would result in the adoption of a new constitution within four weeks, at the most, with the aid of a committee of experts to speed up decision-making. Third, an electoral process aimed at creating an independent election commission charged with organizing the upcoming legislative and presidential elections. The competing sources of legitimacy that had fueled the political battle gave way to coexisting and even complementary mediation systems that provided a modicum of political stability. Houcine Abbassi delivered a very insightful rebuke to critics who had accused the national dialogue authority of betraying the government's legitimacy as an elected body:[23]

> What has somewhat muddled things is that some people at the ANC think that the national dialogue is an alternative to the Assembly, which is not at all the case. It's merely a grouping of the parties represented at the ANC within the framework of the national dialogue. The parties taking part in the Quartet's initiative represent a source of ideas, support and contribution—in no way a replacement for the ANC, which remains the country's sole legitimate government. There is no ambiguity or ambivalence with regard to the situation—the work done as part of the national dialogue is separate from but complementary to that of the ANC. As such, in order to speed up the work of the committee for [the election commission] ISIE, representatives from the national dialogue may intervene in the event of a conflict in order to find a solution.

He later added:

> Our roadmap plans to establish ISIE in the first week after the national dialogue begins. The commission will take two weeks to adopt the schedule for the legislative and presidential elections. To avoid wasting time and creating an institutional vacuum, things will be done simultaneously—a new government cabinet will be formed to address economic, financial, social and security issues. The cabinet will be overseen by the ANC, which will be able to issue a motion of no confidence by a three-quarters vote.

During the national dialogue, negotiations were held on both the conditions for political stability and the role of the UGTT in Tunisian politics. Salah explains:

> It's understandable that there are divisions within the UGTT with regard to its political role. What Abbassi did truly is a historic exploit and that's why I believe that it was intelligent for him to say that the national dialogue had to succeed, because if it had failed that would have been a great loss for the UGTT. Abbassi never lost sight of the goal, which was not just to save the country but also to save the UGTT's place in the new political configuration.

What are the consensus building process mechanisms? First, the UGTT and the National Dialogue Quartet defended the idea of a national government comprising individuals recognized for their expertise instead of based on political criteria. The government was not supposed to make strategic decisions that would affect the Tunisia's future, but to prepare for the elections and manage the country's routine business. It was striking to see how several political figures in the opposition and the Troika government proposed a technocratic government—sometimes also called an "expertise-based government"—every time the crisis intensified, to the point that it was constantly on the table (S.T., 2012; Dahmani, 2013). What was so appealing about the idea of "technocrats"? For a start, the tensions caused by the political rivalry fostered the belief that apolitical, independent expertise was the only guaranteed means of stabilizing the country and quelling the unrest spurred by the social movements.[24] Faced with a political crisis that required a political solution, Tunisia resorted to a technical solution which maintained the illusion that a country can be governed independently of its political discord and political system (Naccache and Abdessalem, 2012). It is remarkable to see how that logic dovetailed with the UGTT's frequent rhetoric on "independence." The union kept its distance from the political parties but continued to play a leading role in politics, which it secured through tactics to influence other political and social stakeholders.

Furthermore, this solution seemed to be the only means of helping the opposition to regain a role in managing the country's affairs. For Ennahdha, the solution provided a means to remain in government while avoiding the risk of dissolving the ANC. Finally, the never-ending negotiations over the figures to select for the government exposed the myth of technocratic independence—each party did its utmost to defend technocrats who would be loyal to them. The IMF (International Monetary Fund), which gave its blessing by releasing 560 million dollars in loans the day that the Jomaa government took office, did nothing to allay fears that the political neutrality of the new team of "experts" was synonymous with deference to the diktat of international institutions and their capitalist ideology (Leaders. com.tn, 2014).

Second, the guiding principle during the national dialogue was a unified commitment to save the country from terrorism and the risk of chaos. This commitment led the UGTT and the employers' organization UTICA to form a coalition of employees and business owners to lead the dialogue—a grouping that has precedent in Tunisian history. A few days after Tunisia gained independence (March 20, 1956), the UGTT formed a national coalition with Neo-Destour and UTICA for the 1956 constituent elections and the 1959 legislative elections. In the name of unity, President Bourguiba stated that campaigns to reduce inequality should not develop into a situation where the poor pressure the wealthy—the primary goal was to build the Tunisian state. The same rhetoric had also been used earlier to rally the labor movement behind the struggle for independence. During the political crisis in July 2013, the pact between the UGTT and UTICA bolstered the labor union's authority in the political negotiations and its ability to gain support inside and outside the organization for its role as a leader in the national dialogue. One participant in the national dialogue spoke of Houcine Abbassi in these terms: "He facilitated discussion. Sometimes he imposed his decisions. He would even require representatives from political parties to stay in the room after the meeting if no decision had been made (quoted in International Crisis Group, 2014, 4). For its part, UTICA (Hibou, *op. cit.*, 152), which presents itself more as a network of businessmen than as an influential, organized force, lacked the historical legitimacy of the UGTT. Yet the employers' organization was able to completely change tack almost overnight. What was once an organ of the Ben Ali regime representing coinciding economic and political interests became an influential organization that had a say in forming the new government which resulted from the national dialogue. The employers' group emerged as a key stakeholder in the advancement of democracy in Tunisia, as doctor and unionist Raouf explains:

> The UGTT launched the first national dialogue initiative all on its own and it ended in failure. The alliance with the Order of Lawyers, the Tunisian Human Rights League and UTICA lent more credence to its roadmap. What's more, on a symbolic level it was good for international institutions to see employers and the working class together. It's clear that UTICA has never had the same ability to mobilize people as the UGTT and gained a lot of influence through the alliance. The UGTT, on the other hand, lost a little bit more credibility in the eyes of those who found that it lacked dedication to social causes.

All these factors led certain critical unionists to describe the national dialogue as a class consensus reached between the rich and the middle class to the detriment of Tunisia's poorest citizens, which they say benefitted from the weak position of the revolutionary forces. Ridha, a unionist and rail worker based in Sfax, pointed to the strong ties that continued to bind the UGTT to the interests of the governing class, despite criticism from the union's intermediate bodies:

> As an organization, the UGTT has close ties with the governing party; socially and politically, its goals are bound to those of the single-party state and the governing class. The negotiations on wages and laws primarily aim to subjugate [*adjîn*] union work to aid the exercise of power. And at the same time, you find activist sectors at the UGTT whose goals run counter to those of the governing class.

The top priority for UTICA was to reassure investors, as UTICA President Widad Bouchamaoui stated at a press conference on September 28, 2013: "The country is in a very serious economic crisis and the pace of investment will only recover if a secure, stable environment is established." Certain UGTT officials seemed to take a similar stance, including Nasreddine Sassi, director of the UGTT research and documentation department:

> The UGTT doesn't have hostile, gratuitous prejudices against the IMF. The Secretary General has met with Christine Lagarde and several World Bank delegations in this very place. We are aware that the country cannot survive outside of the global system, but we try to guide policy. We told the World Bank, "You supported Ben Ali. Now you have to demonstrate, via pilot development projects in disadvantaged regions, your desire to support democracy."
>
> (Halimi, *op. cit.*)

The pact that united the UGTT and UTICA demonstrated yet again the primacy of political issues over economic and social considerations in the union's strategy, while also establishing the principle of unity as a core concept in what was considered "good government" in Tunisia. Indeed, Tunisian politicians and protest movements both constantly referred to the idea of unity. The unity/division dichotomy was commonly used as a key to interpreting various aspects of Tunisian politics. The political parties employed the concept in their strategies, via slogans such as "United against Ennahdha," "United against RCD holdovers," "United behind Tunisia" and "United behind the general interest." Unity was also prominent within the UGTT—"United against the government." The lines thus blurred between uncritical unanimity and pluralist unity that encompassed the Tunisian society in all its diversity. Houcine Abbassi made the following remarks on the Tunisian national television station Wataniya 1, on October 28, 2013:

> UTICA and the UGTT share a common destiny—they will support each other—and have been building a partnership since immediately after the revolution, when the social contract was established. What brings them together today is the best interests of the country. . . . For the trade union, it was no longer possible to remain impassive due to the country's economic nosedive, and towards the end of the national dialogue, each party will resume its role on the national scene.

Third, while the national interest was held up as the beacon guiding the national consensus, partisan politics was readily apparent in the process leading to the agreement. Ennahdha and Nidaa Tounes dominated the process, ensuring that the system built on compromises based on partisan interests would endure:

> In my opinion, the Jomaa government is the political bare minimum that we were able to agree on—it's not a government that represents the will of the people, but rather a government that represents

the political consensus, in particular between Ennahdha and Nidaa Tounes.

(Houssem, Ennahdha official)

Consequently, when the interviewees described the consensus, it was often in terms of *tanazûlât*, meaning awarding concessions rather than reconciling views or contrasting differing opinions. One Ennahdha official commented:

> In my view, a consensus is a set of political concessions [*tanazûlât*] in Lenin's sense of the term: two steps forward, one step back, to move forward more quickly. We reached a critical situation in which blood was going to be spilled. Ennahdha is not the only one that made concessions—all the political powers made concessions. It's true that there is real hostility in Tunisia between politicians, but people have to understand that the politicians are the ones who enabled us to avoid the catastrophic scenario that occurred in Egypt and Syria. We have achieved this situation thanks to the lucidity of the Tunisian political class as a whole.

Box 12 What Is a "Good" Dialogue?

Speech Given by Houcine Abbassi on October 28, 2013

We form judgments about others that sometimes originate from a misunderstanding or an inability to listen. That is why having patience with others and listening to them, to understand their expectations and assess their fears while expressing our own needs and expectations with clarity and accuracy, those are the only conditions by which any battle or conflict—as tense as it may be—can be transformed into a calm, constructive, credible dialogue. We have to rid ourselves of the winner/loser mentality, admit that we cannot achieve everything we want in the current situation, and accept the necessary concessions in order for the dialogue to be effective and for it to take place in an atmosphere of trust and responsibility. It is no secret that the credibility of the dialogue depends on a certain number of qualities that the stakeholders have to demonstrate and I think that you have them: goodwill, respect for the parties and respect for the right to defend one's point of view.

The dialogue requires self-control and tolerance for others and for positions that may be unshakeable or cause tension. This tolerance is a source of strength and self-control that can influence the parties and move them to adjust their attitude. We stress this point, in particular, because we are intent on ensuring that the discord that has dominated the political scene and actors up to this point does not interfere with our plans to address the economic, social and security situation.

Everyone needs to remember that we are on the same ship and that what could be decisive in our relations with each other is love for the nation, dedication to serving it, caring about its prosperity and the sacrifices made for its security and sovereignty. All of us have to make the nation our top priority, before any party, alliance or personal ambition.

Houcine Abbassi also used the term "concession" when describing the stalemate in the national dialogue:

> Since the start of the crisis, Ali Larayedh, the head of state, has stated that the government would not step down before the end of the constitution process, setting a deadline of two months. However, the constitution process has been stalled for several weeks and the country is nearly paralyzed. So we have launched this initiative—the most serious of any put forward—to reconcile the stances of the key stakeholders on the political scene. We have started to observe progress. Yet it is apparent that when the Ennahdha movement prizes concessions from others, it gives nothing in exchange. The opposite is true—when that happens they ask for more. And so we're back where we began. During their conference on Monday morning, the three leaders of Ennahdha asserted that they had made concessions during the two months of consultations. I don't see where or in what area! And then the Salvation Front put a damper on their demands—they ended up accepting that the ANC continue to pursue its work and are no longer seeking the immediate resignation of the government.[25]

Was the import of unity and consensus merely a discursive strategy that stemmed from an old "technology" of power from Ben Ali and Bourguiba (Hibou, 2006, 244) that aimed to restore the former political order and re-establish consensus-building as a mode of government? Would the national dialogue only amount to an exercise in power sharing among the different political camps?

The various interviews conducted revealed that, with the disappearance of centralized power, consensus shifted from rhetoric disconnected from actual practices to a real conflict mediation mechanism. The successive political crises and the crises of authority impacted all the country's institutions, cementing a long-term consensus and institutionalizing the process as the preferred method of reconciling differing interests and points of view. Three elements are indicative of how the new approach to consensus factored in to the reconfiguration of Tunisian politics.

First, the opposition, dissent and disagreement during the process leading to a national consensus during the interim phase demonstrate how consensus, rather than discursive rhetoric, is the preferred method of conflict mediation in Tunisia. References to consensus—whether used as part of an old strategy employed by the former regime or in the terminology of political transitions—appears to be rooted in a local political culture. The emphasis on a "baseline" consensus reflects the interaction between consent and enduring differences of opinion or divergent interests in the development of agreements. Consent, which is part and parcel of the consensus-building process, coexists with other forms of defending one's interests and protest; the different moments when the dialogue broke down are a perfect illustration of this. Consensus was no longer the enshrinement of a supreme power; it became a means of neutralizing the political parties' designs on hegemony:

> The UGTT may have the same message as the Popular Front on economic issues but it would have been an error to confuse the UGTT with the Popular Front. Ennahdha's attitude was "everyone who is against us is from Nidaa or the Popular Front," but that wasn't true and that's what led Ennahdha to pursue entrenched positions and democratic excesses. . . . But the Islamists later learned about the UGTT's approach; by spending time with the unionists, they succeeded in establishing a consensus that protects the country from single-party hegemony.
>
> (Foued, unionist with ties to the CPR)

Nevertheless, certain analyses criticized the elite for taking control against the will of the people. Critics pointed out that the various bodies created by the Quartet, the "sponsor" of the national dialogue—including the commission of experts for the drafting of the constitution and the commission for the governmental process—and their members closely resembled the High Authority for Realization of the Objectives of the Revolution, Political Reform and Democratic Transition, which prepared for the October 2011 elections (Hmed, 2013). Yet, while the final national consensus somewhat concealed the full extent of the national leaders' domination over their base and expanded the divide between the political elite and the people, the fact that it was constantly mentioned in even the most critical or partisan speeches attests to its place as the preferred mechanism for conflict resolution. UDC member Ghassen, for example, criticized the partisan approach that governed consensus-building at all the national organizations but did not reject consensus as a negotiating method. Rather, he called for the inclusion of new political and social forces in the consensus-building process:

> All congresses lead to a political consensus. The UGET and UGTT congresses led to a consensus between the political parties. It's a fact that the UDC has become a fertile recruiting ground for the parties. And of course, it's fertile ground for the left-wing parties. For the congress, at a meeting I defended the idea that the interim executive committee shouldn't run at the next congress. We need new faces, new activists to take over, especially among those from outside Tunis. Tunisia's entire

political world is focused on the Tunis metro area, despite the fact that most of the revolutionary activists come from other areas like Sidi Bouzid and Thala. The new political forces have to be included in the process for reaching new consensus-based solutions.

Meanwhile, CGTT Secretary General Habib Guiza stated that his organization had proposed a crisis-exit roadmap to the government a few days after the assassination of Chokri Belaïd and lamented not being included in the national dialogue:

> An initiative dated February 21, 2013, which is very similar to that of the UGTT, went unacknowledged. . . . That said, despite being victim to exclusion, we firmly support the Quartet's initiative. . . . In addition, organizations shouldn't replace political parties—that would be a major mistake because the organizations are supposed to serve as a counterweight to the government.
>
> (quoted in Kefi, 2013)

The CGTT released a joint statement with the Confederation of Tunisian Citizen Enterprises (CONECT) and the Union of Tunisian Workers (UTT) in which they called on the authorities to observe union pluralism by including their organizations in the national dialogue. They asserted that without pluralism for political parties, unions and associations, the democratic transition would be devoid of purpose and only a pipe dream (Y. B., 2014).

Lastly, the emergence of consensus-building as the conflict-mediation mechanism at the ANC and in the national dialogue appears to have resulted from the various institutional experiments conducted after the fall of Ben Ali. As mentioned earlier, the UGTT established the Council for the Protection of the Revolution (CNPR), which officialized and structured discussions between the government and the opposition, resulting in the decision to create the National Constituent Assembly. The CNPR was succeeded by the High Authority for Realization of the Objectives of the Revolution, Political Reform and Democratic Transition. The authority was formed strictly in an advisory capacity and received substantial criticism, but nonetheless played a major political (oversight of the government and election of the Independent High Authority for Elections) and legislative (key pieces of legislation such as the election law) role. Sana and Rafâa Ben Achour (2012) believe that this second interim period was rooted in a "consensual" form of legitimacy because it took place outside any type of constitutional framework.

Other political actors mentioned other group protest experiences during the Ben Ali era in which consensus was the watchword, such as the October 18, 2005 Collective for Rights and Liberties: "The collective defines itself as a space for coming together; it remains open to all activists, political organizations and associations that endorse the founding platform.

It promotes transparency, collegiality and consensus-building" (Collectif October 18, 2012). This marked the first time that Islamists and defenders of the secular state decided to sit down together to devise a joint initiative aimed at breaking with the authoritarian regime and strengthening freedom and democracy. The same guiding principles for managing diverse viewpoints and interests appear in the initiative's founding document, as the following sections illustrate:

> Further to the goals that the initiative sets, cohesiveness and trust among its members must be achieved through unified political action. Members must clearly and explicitly endorse a set of fundamental principles. This also provides a means of ensuring a credible approach to reconciling elements with different and sometimes contradictory policies and platforms. The following goals form, in our opinion, part of the minimum requirements for effectively ending the dictatorship and have been met with consensus on our part.

According to Kamel, an Ennahdha official, the October 18, 2005 experience facilitated the national dialogue during the interim period:

> Ennahdha was in the opposition and ended up in the government overnight—it was completely unexpected. There was a group within Ennahdha that was seeking a confrontation with the UGTT and, in the same way, there was a group within the UGTT that was seeking a confrontation with Ennahdha. But our history of resistance with the left against Ben Ali, our history of dialogue with the left and progressive forces—in particular our experience with October 18—enabled us to see through the dialogue and reach a consensus on the constitution and to deliver the country from the crisis.

These experiences mirror the organizational process at the UGTT, which, due to its structure and sociology, has always relied on a precarious balance between sector-based interests, regional considerations and political priorities (cf. Chapters 1 and 4). It is not so much the ideological or partisan divide that dictates the union's decisions as the need to reach compromises between divergent interests in multiple sectors. The positions, hand-wringing and tensions that shaped the UGTT's history are the product of a political culture based on a modus operandi that combines pressure and negotiations to blunt conflicts. It is this same political culture that enabled the UGTT to moderate the national dialogue between the various stakeholders in the political sphere and to absorb the blows that were dealt. There are undoubtedly certain political groups that are more influential than others at the UGTT, such as the left and the remnants of the RCD/PSD, which pressure the leadership politically through the union's intermediate bodies. However, the UGTT's history and membership shield the union from partisan excesses because the organization is required to maintain its unity. This tightrope act also dictated the UGTT's position in the political arena, explaining the recurrent misunderstandings with regard to the union's political positions.

As Tunisia lacked firmly established democratic institutions, consensus-building subsequently became a tool for handling political crises. Social stakeholders—including the National Council for the Protection of the Revolution, the High Authority and the National Dialogue Quartet—stumbled and made missteps as they attempted to manage the transition period, revealing the complexities of translating universal democratic principles into rules that reflected local expectations as to the relationship between individuals and society. Consensus-building provided a basis for the symbolic aspects of government and imparted the established institutional solutions with a certain degree of legitimacy. Abstract and sometimes demagogic discourse on consensus and the cohesiveness of Tunisian society gave way to consensus-based institutions rooted not only in rhetoric, but also in local practices that were regularly tested by political crises. The consensus ideal was more than ideological window dressing or a strategy for domination— it represented a collective sense of purpose and helped define the interplay between legitimacy and legality. The concept was a vital part of the stakeholders' acceptance of the legitimacy of the government. Tunisians' willingness to recognize and take ownership of these institutions and respect their authority hinged on this acceptance.

This point comes into focus if one looks to other countries recognized as democratic, whose respective visions of the relationship between the individual and the collective greatly influenced the manner in which democratic ideals were put into practice. Consider, for example, the owner-centric market regulation in the United States, or the French devotion to government regulation and the figure of the noble, which are both rooted in different social and cultural traditions and have made a lasting impact on each country's respective institutional framework (Iribarne, 2003b). Governments draw legitimacy from cultural, social and mythic elements related to a group's view of and vision for authority and itself. What occurred in Tunisia serves as yet another example of how government practices evolve over time in relation to social structures. The interpretations and meaning attributed to the practices by the stakeholders, which are often shaped by the individual and collective psyche, serve as the foundation that legitimizes a mode of government and enables it to take root.

In Conclusion

While the national dialogue did run into some stumbling blocks, it successfully established the conditions for a certain degree of political stability and resulted in a consensus among political actors. Ennahdha avoided the risk of being permanently removed from power and losing all legitimacy in government, through the continued existence of the National Constituent Assembly. The opposition, under the controversial, imposed leadership of Nidaa Tounes, was finally able to force the Islamists to step down. The opposition was then able to secure power by taking part in appointing the new "technocratic" government under conditions that were clearly more favorable from their perspective.

As the events unfolded, the opposition strongly urged the UGTT to take political action, but the union succeeded in remaining within the boundaries it had set and avoided shifting toward a biased position by calling for the dissolution of the ANC. The union's most hardline members were compelled to clash intensely with the Troika government, while the more moderate unionists increasingly felt that the union was in danger of overstepping its role. During this tense period at the UGTT, the union's desire to negotiate a balanced agreement with the government consistently won out. Social pressure mounted and could have caused the UGTT to implode, but instead of destroying the union, it helped lend credence to those who were seeking a political and institutional breakthrough. Now firmly entrenched in politics, the UGTT drew strength from the protest movements, which gave the union both a unique means of rallying support and an invaluable resource for negotiating with the sitting government. In this way, the UGTT was able to cement its place as a central stakeholder in Tunisian politics despite the turbulence inside and outside the union.

What is more, the UGTT, a singular forum for collective action that was spared the worst of the dictatorship, developed various institutional experiments that it was able to implement in a makeshift manner in order to effectively mediate internal and external political conflicts through consensus-building. This approach was also a stepping stone to the drafting of the constitution, which led to an entente between the Islamists and the modernists. However, this consensus was achieved largely through political maneuvering, remained confined to the political and economic elite, and suffered from a lack of viable political and economic plans.

Finally, while the UGTT continued to initiate sector-based demonstrations and appear to protect the interests of the unionized middle class, the national dialogue's exclusive focus on political issues created conflicts within the union. The traditional divide within the UGTT during the dictatorship was between the base, which sought independence from the Ben Ali regime, and the Executive Board, which was more or less subjugated by the single-party state. This division was replaced by a new split that affected the entire organization, over the approach to be taken with regard to social issues such as the privatization of the civil service, debt relief and unemployment problems. The gap widened between those who supported limited action negotiated step by step—gradually pushing back the government without ever overthrowing it—and those who believed in the power of the social movement and sought a firmer stance that would lead to a break with the past, due to the worsening economic crisis and their dwindling confidence in negotiations with the government.

The UGTT, the main architect of the national dialogue, succeeded in saving the country from the real or imagined risk of following in Egypt's footsteps, by establishing a consensus between the old elites from the regime and the newly elected elites. However, social movements do not play out over the same timespan as political battles. The major challenge that remains for the UGTT and political parties is to re-incorporate social and economic issues into the heart of politics, in order to prevent the political sphere from becoming even more disconnected from the social sphere.

Notes

1. In support of the general strike and the UGTT leadership, left-wing activists from *Al Amel Ettounsi* proclaimed the fateful day "Red Thursday," in reference to the blood spilt by workers and the general population. Others termed it "Black Thursday" in condemnation of the UGTT leadership.
2. Chokri Belaïd, Secretary General of the Democratic Patriots' Movement and leader of the Popular Front coalition of left-wing parties formed on October 5, 2012, was assassinated on February 6, 2013. Mohamed Brahmi, a left-wing nationalist member of parliament who joined the Popular Front after the assassination of Belaïd, was assassinated on July 25, 2013.
3. Minister of the Interior in the Hamadi Jebali government, Layaredh was named Prime Minister on February 22, 2013, following the political crisis triggered by the assassination of Chokri Belaïd and the resignation of Hamadi Jebali.
4. The quotations in this chapter are from interviews conducted in 2012, 2013 and early 2014.
5. Leagues for the Protection of the Revolution (LPR) are the successors to the neighborhood protection committees formed after Ben Ali suddenly fled, on January 14, 2011. Unionists and activists with ties to far-left movements joined the newly established LPRs, followed by Ennahdha members. The National League for the Protection of the Revolution was created on June 14, 2012, providing legal cover for the committees. The members of the national league did not hesitate to disrupt rallies and demonstrations held by the UGTT and the opposition parties. The LPRs attempted to "cleanse" and "purify" the UGTT of its "counterrevolutionary residue," one of their main hobby horses. Cf. Hédia Baraket (2012).
6. Nine centrist and center-left parties, including the Progressive Democratic Party (PDP), led by Ahmed Néji Chebbi, and Afek Tounes (Horizons de Tunisie), led by Yassine Ibrahim, merged to form the Republican Party on April 9, 2012.
7. Formed via the merger of the Ettajdid Movement, Tunisian Labor Party and independents from the Democratic Modernist Pole.
8. A coalition of former members of the RCD and other "democratic" parties united behind former Prime Minister Béji Caïd Essebsi.
9. Islamists were unable to gain representation in the General Union of Tunisian Students (UGET), which has been dominated by left-wing groups since the 1970s. In 1986, Islamists created the General Tunisian Union of Students (UGTE).
10. Sheikh Mohammed Fadhel Ben Achour, a Tunisian theologian and intellectual, was elected President of the UGTT in 1946. Sheikh Cheikh Muhammed Salah Enneifer, an ally of the Muslim Brotherhood, was also present at the first UGTT

constituent assembly in 1946. Beginning in early July 1946, tensions began to mount between Farhat Hached and Fadhel Ben Achour over the role that religious matters should be granted. Cf. Ahmed Khaled (2007).

11. Current leader of the Tunisian Labor Party. The rumor that Romdhane, a redoubted Achourist, sympathizes with or adheres to Islamism is as enduring as it is regularly denied.

12. Cf. the official website of the movement: www.ekbes.net/

13. The new social contract was signed on January 14, 2014, at the National Constituent Assembly. The contract comprises five main policy planks: "economic growth and regional development," "employment policy and vocational training," "labor relations and decent employment," "social welfare" and "the institutionalization of the three-party labor dialogue." The document, which was signed by the government, the UGTT and UTICA, which essentially seeks to establish labor relations based on "the institutionalization of a permanent, ongoing, comprehensive three-party labor dialogue" on concerns relevant to the three signatories.

14. Identity-related issues dominated discussion in politics and the media, resulting in the re-emergence of the same points of discord present during the development of post-independence Tunisia. A division re-emerged between two conceptions of Tunisian identity: an Arab/Muslim identity that claimed Ben Youssef's legacy and a Tunisian "modernist" identity in the mold of that defended by Habib Bourguiba. Cf. Nicolas Dot Pouillard (2013).

15. SEA Latelec, a subsidiary of the French company Latécoère and an Airbus subcontractor, moved part of its cabling manufacturing operations to the Tunis suburb of Fouchana in 2005, in order to take advantage of Tunisia's qualified, inexpensive workforce. However, workers began to organize in 2010 in order to stand up for their rights, demanding an end to excessive overtime hours and compliance with employment law. This was systematically met with anti-union repression: layoffs, bribery attempts, insults, unjustified punishment, isolation of union workers, sexist remarks and death threats. Cf. Comité de soutien aux syndicalistes de SEA Latelec de Fouchana (2013).

16. Cf. www.leconomistemaghrebin.com/2012/04/08/les-diplomes-chomeurs-ont-brave-linterdiction-de-manifester/

17. The organization now has more than 10,000 members.

18. Cf. the televised interview granted by Ennahdha leader Rached Ghannouchi to Nessma TV on August 24, 2013.

19. Prime Minister Hamadi Jebali and Moncef Marzouki launched other initiatives for a national dialogue after the assassination of Chokri Belaïd on February 6, 2012, and on April 15, 2013, respectively. Both initiatives ended in failure.

20. Organized by the opposition, the Bardo sit-in called on the government to resign, a government of technocrats to be appointed, the constitutional process to be completed by a specialized commission, and for elections to be held in the fall. Ennahdha held its own sit-in at the same place to defend the government against the "risk of a coup d'etat." This is how the Bardo came to become the epicenter of the political crisis following the assassination of Mohamed Brahmi.

21. This is reminiscent of language from the Ben Ali era. Any attempt to criticize or express dissent was considered "immature" or, worse, "unpatriotic." Ironically, the law and order embodied by the army and the interior ministry, which Tunisians had risen up against during the revolution, became the sole guardian of the "democratic transition." What is more, the National Union of Internal Security Forces (Syndicat national des forces de sécurité intérieure; SNFSI) issued

a statement on October 25, 2013, publicly demanding that the SNFSI officers fired and convicted after the revolution be freed and ventured to add, "with all due respect to the martyrs' families."

22. The main parties were represented, except for the Prime Minister's party, Congress for the Republic (CPR).

23. Exclusive interview granted to the national station Wataniya 1 on October 28, 2013.

24. The appointment of Ennahdha sympathizers to public-sector posts made questions about the public administration's neutrality and relationship with politics a central concern in the debate.

25. Interview with Houcine Abbassi published in the newspaper *La Presse* on September 25, 2013.

6 Conclusion
Lessons Learned From the UGTT's Role in the Revolution

The powerful trade union played a role in Tunisian politics over this three-year period that continually elicited passionate debate, to say the least, between those who benefitted from the UGTT's actions, those who criticized the union and especially its central leadership for failing to meet its duties as a union, and, finally, those who purely and simply picked a fight with an organization they thought embodied the surviving wing of the former ruling power. All these debates highlighted the influence of the UGTT—the country's oldest and largest national organization—on the transformation of Tunisian politics and contrast with the narrative that depicts the revolution as the abrupt, untimely advent of a new political and social order. At the same time, this debate came at an opportune moment as it raised questions about the media's focus on controversies between Islamists and secularists and the theory that Tunisia's political challenges boiled down to constitutional reforms or simply achieving a positive outcome in the elections.

This state of affairs leads one to attempt to answer a recurring question: what was the UGTT's role in the revolutionary process and why does the union evoke such passionate reactions? This work, the fruit of a three-year journey inside the UGTT at a crucial juncture in Tunisian politics, enabled me to hone my own knowledge of Tunisian unionism and the union's lasting yet labile role in the political sphere. Fieldwork is the only excuse for bold claims, so I will venture to submit the following conclusions:

First, while the central challenge for the UGTT in the fast-moving political situation was to fight for the political conditions that would enable it to retain power or expand its purview, the changes that Tunisia underwent did little to fundamentally alter the union's core identity at the nexus of unionism, politics and social issues. The UGTT does not mobilize union members solely to defend their interests as workers—the union has always been and will continue to be a much broader forum for political action that aims to combine socioeconomic aims with individual and collective political liberties. The various political crises that occurred after December 17, 2010, greatly strengthened this unique identity. Looking back at the union's history, it is easy to see how the UGTT represents both a union movement and a political actor on the national stage—two roles that are inextricably linked—and to show how the organization integrates and unifies highly diverse social and political components. It is much harder, however, to demonstrate that in spite of the successive crises, all the groups within the UGTT—as incompatible as they may appear—together form potential combinations of constituent elements that unite at different times and places, defining the union's actions and identity.

The UGTT's role on the Tunisian political scene from the beginning of the uprising to the adoption of the constitution shows how the union continually shifts its focus between national political considerations and union affairs. At times, the union takes the offensive and clashes with its adversaries; at others, mediation and negotiation are its favored methods. The UGTT has mastered two approaches, which sometimes come into conflict. The union charted a path that enabled it to rein in internal conflicts and overcome challenges to fulfill its dual roles in unionism and politics, by constantly moving towards negotiations and institutional solutions through a commitment to consensus-building. The UGTT draws strength from precisely this synthesis of unionism and politics. It would not be more effective if it concentrated all its efforts in one of those two areas. The opposite is true—the UGTT would become isolated and weakened, whereas it is currently an organization for everyone that unites hundreds of thousands of Tunisians who have differing political opinions and interests.

This distinction between the two dimensions to the UGTT's actions yields an analysis of the union's post-December 17 trajectory in three phases. The organization first provided political and logistical support to the popular uprising. Then, after Ben Ali fled, the UGTT's political action grew in scope and the union combined its role as a refuge for social movements with its desire to assert its political heft by contributing to the institutional mechanisms established to structure discussions between Tunisia's political and social actors. In the third phase, a period during which doubt was cast on the legitimacy of the post-election institutions, the UGTT reacted to the urgings of its own movement and the worsening economic and political crisis by making a more direct foray into politics and leading the national dialogue that resulted in a breakthrough in the political stalemate. Throughout these crises, the union was able to appease the movement within the union pushing it toward more social endeavors while protecting its power in the new political landscape. The UGTT demonstrated its commitment to social causes but still managed to exert the pressure required to establish an election schedule, calling for elections to be held as quickly as possible but acting with the knowledge that its scope for political action was limited by its ability to secure social demands.

Second, the UGTT provided an innovative laboratory for exploring Tunisians' expectations for a legitimate mode of government acceptable to all. The union was instrumental in establishing institutional experiments to exit the crisis, against a backdrop of resurgent tensions caused by competing sources of legitimacy and power systems. This is how the union came to take part in instituting consensus-building as the preferred conflict-mediation method. As a unique space for organized collective action, the UGTT remained shielded from the total domination of the Ben Ali regime, enabling it to develop a unique organizational culture. This, in turn, provided the conditions for the union to withstand internal and external pressure and make a major contribution to the solutions that defused the national political crises. Due to its sociology and membership, the UGTT has always depended on an often precarious balance between sector-based interests, regional considerations and political affiliations. The need to maintain this balance is what elevated reaching a consensus between groups with divergent interests over ideological and partisan divides in the UGTT's decision-making process.

The proceedings at the 22nd UGTT Congress served as a stark demonstration of how misguided one would be to believe that a formal, stringent democratic system could triumph over the social constructs that govern relations between unionists. Unionists followed the formal, impersonal rules that governed the proceedings meticulously, while interpreting and employing them based on developments in the web of social relationships that bind the union's different social and political components. Here again, the institutionalization of consensus-building as the preferred means of conflict mediation enabled the UGTT to maintain cohesiveness while retaining its power. Knowing this, the positions, prevarication and tensions that have defined the UGTT's path take on a new light. These elements are the product of a consensus-based political culture that mediates conflicts through a combination of pressure and negotiations. It is this political culture that enabled the UGTT to provide the December 17 uprising with the organizational and political resources that hastened the fall of Ben Ali. And it is this political culture that enabled the UGTT to moderate the national dialogue between the various stakeholders in Tunisian politics and blunt mounting tensions. At that point, the union's close ties with Tunisia's social movements gave it the means to influence the government's choices and major political decisions. In exchange for securing certain concessions from the ruling class for the protest movement, the UGTT avoided risking a direct clash between the old and new political powers. The union's critics assert that these actions also curbed the potential for a radical break with the former regime. More than a traditional trade union and different from a political party, the UGTT became a key stakeholder in the political transition through its ability to forge compromises between those seeking a clean break from the Ben Ali era and those who advocated a more reformist line.

The UGTT demonstrated throughout that it was fully aware of its power to rally support and challenge the successive governments, which had been greatly undermined by the weakening of Tunisia's institutions. At the same time, the union did not behave like a political outfit seeking to take power or as a revolutionary union capable of reversing the governing elite's economic and social policies. At times, the UGTT was overwhelmed by the scope of its own political action, but nevertheless made clear that it did not want to become a political party. The union's self-proclaimed identity as a "counterbalance"—a stakeholder that exerts pressure and initiates negotiations—meant that it was not resigned to the purely defensive stance of a counterweight but did not have to take sole leadership of the political transition, either. The UGTT's stability during the process was a testament to its refusal to engage in direct confrontation. While all unionists who accepted the UGTT had to take action that went beyond criticism of the government and represented a central role in establishing new democratic institutions, they recognized that certain lines should not be crossed—including that of a direct clash with the government. In fact, apart from solemn declarations that were not followed up with actions, the UGTT leadership continued to resist the revolutionary movement, which continued to gain momentum as the events unfolded.

It was not surprising, then, to see the UGTT declare in increasingly clear terms that only consensus-based solutions between the country's political and social forces could put an end to the crisis. At each juncture, the cost of avoiding a descent into chaos was a long, ongoing dialogue that had to gradually incorporate the entire spectrum of interests and perspectives in order to forge a compromise acceptable to all parties on each issue. Paradoxically, this role as a counterbalance—which primarily consisted in building consensus among Tunisia's political actors—enabled the union to retain its power and take part in leading the political transition, but it also created adversaries for the UGTT among these same actors. The UGTT became a target for those who held it responsible for the economic and social crisis and accused the union of co-opting the revolutionary process. In the end, however, the union was able to strengthen its position in Tunisian politics despite the rifts inside and outside the union.

The process by which political and social actors adjust their positions to reach a consensus is even more important in Tunisia, where democratic institutions lack the solid footing required to govern power relations—a situation in which what must be done and how do to it are constantly being redefined. Compromises on "interests" are a prerequisite for a government to be accepted in all countries, but individuals' conditions for entering into a lasting, trust-based relationship vary from nation to nation. The case of Tunisia demonstrates that political and social actors formulate criteria when accepting the legitimacy of a government, which draw from the fundamental tenets of democracy, but also from an ability to establish an ongoing dialogue between the parties—the only means of guaranteeing a consensus. The trial-and-error process and missteps encountered during the three years of institutional experiments revealed complexities of an unprecedented initiative: translating universal democratic principles into legitimate, functional rules that reflected local expectations as to good government. The empty talk about consensus and the cohesiveness of Tunisian society gradually gave way to consensus-based institutions backed not just by rhetoric, but by local practices that were frequently put to the test by political crises.

When the authoritarian central power disappeared, consensus shifted from a concept disconnected from reality to the predominant method of conflict mediation, in order to meet concrete expectations for good government in Tunisia.

Yet while the UGTT, the main architect of the national dialogue, managed to allay political tensions through a laboriously negotiated agreement, the outcome was a power-sharing arrangement between the former governing elite and the newly elected elite. This widened the gap between two rival visions of democracy: the idea that the representativeness of political parties and elections form the core of democracy; and the belief that there can be no viable democracy if social issues are not a central priority in the political alternatives on offer. The UGTT, which accepted to join forces with employers to negotiate a balanced solution among the country's political and social actors, took the risk of weakening its ability to pursue social action. What is more, the union showed a willingness to accept a new wave of economic liberalization proposed by international financial organizations—not for the first time—in exchange for paltry pay raises for its members. Challenges now stand before the union that are undoubtedly even more formidable than those past.

First, the union is finding it more difficult to maintain its place in between the social movements, which represent marginalized groups such as youth and the unemployed, and as the protector of the interests of the unionized middle class—a role from which the UGTT derives its strength and ability to rally support. The traditional divide within the union during the dictatorship was between the base, which sought independence from the Ben Ali regime, and the Executive Board, which was more or less subjugated by the single-party state. This division has been replaced by a new split that affects the entire organization, over the approach to take with regard to social issues such as the privatization of the civil service, debt relief and unemployment problems. The gap has widened between those who support limited action negotiated step by step—gradually winning concessions from the economic elite without ever upending the economic and social order—and those who want the UGTT to take a firmer stance, due to the worsening economic crisis, their dwindling confidence in negotiations with the political elite and growing faith in the effectiveness of social movements.

The course of events over these three years shows that the UGTT's top-down structure enabled the union to maintain cohesiveness and withstand political crises—highlighting the importance of spaces for organized collective action in influencing politics—but the union's need to restructure its organization is more pressing than ever. The UGTT must adapt to Tunisia's new economic and social environment and the evolution of the working class, by establishing more democratic processes that dovetail with the political transformation underway in the country. A survey of the new coalitions and social movements that are emerging underlines this urgent need to restructure. A new vision of politics is forming that marks an intellectual and structural departure from traditional political organizations. The central goal of these groups is to redraw the line separating the challenges of democratic change from social struggles by doing away with the top-down organizational model. For example, demonstrations in support of the unemployed will join forces with the solidarity movement backing those wounded during the revolution. The defense of individual liberties will be closely intertwined with activism to promote social justice. The movement in support of migrants' rights will pair with criticism of the Euro-Mediterranean partnership agreements. These mass movements are sowing the seeds of a new type of socio-political movement whose message is a clear rejection of the neoliberal model and its disciples inside and outside Tunisia. They are questioning the relationship between economics and politics, leadership and spontaneity, traditional and emerging forms of collective organized action, and class struggles and individual rights. In so doing, they lay bare the urgent need for the union to restructure.

The UGTT is once again torn between its desire to play a leading role and politics and its duty to stand in solidarity with social struggles, between its conservative instincts and pressing needs, namely to meet new organizational challenges. The union runs the risk of losing the balance between its unionist and political components—its major strength—and seeing its power to act erode. The path that will be charted by the next government remains unknown and it would be pointless to speculate, but one thing is sure: the single-party state's monopoly on power is finished. New economic forces and a new type of social movement are developing outside the hands of a single-party state, fostering new social dynamics. The UGTT is heir to a great tradition of social activism and a rich heritage of memories that have secured its place in history. Today, the UGTT is at a crossroads—it can only manage its own shifting identity and continue to defend its place in the new political and economic playing field if it is able to move forward as a union and place social justice at the center of its efforts toward political emancipation.

Still, the question remains: What general lessons can be drawn from the example of the UGTT that deepen our understanding of the relationship between trade unionism and Arab revolutions?

The first step to answering this question is assessing the trade union situation in the Arab world. What is commonly called the "Arab world" has not had a uniform trade union history; one may even say that trade unionism has yet to emerge in some countries. This disparity is explained by the history of capitalism, industrialization and colonialism in the region as well as the nature of the political regimes in place. One can distinguish three groups: countries where trade unionism is still non-existent or embryonic, such as the Gulf monarchies, where the overwhelming majority of workers are foreigners who do not have the right to organize. Second, countries in which trade unions are totally submissive to the single-party state such as: Syria, Iraq, Yemen and Libya. Third, countries where unions are monitored in relations characterized by compromise, resignation, allegiance, as part of an ongoing struggle with the ruling power such as: Tunisia, Morocco and Egypt.

While the historical trajectory in each country is unique, on a broader scale, the Arab labor movement emerged at the beginning of the 20th century as a result of the spread of wage labor by Western colonialism. Thus, the development of Arab trade unions was inseparable from anti-colonial struggles for national independence. anti-colonial struggles shaped the founding principles of Arab trade unionism that distinguish it from the main European Union movements. After these countries gained independence, their trade unions succeeded in obtaining official recognition of their existence. Post-independence constitutions enshrined the right to assembly in law, including the right to form trade unions, political parties and associations. However, the forces that took power in independent Arab states quickly launched operations to subdue the unions and secure workers' loyalty. Whenever possible, the regimes imposed a unified national trade union that was primarily composed of public-sector workers and financed via compulsory membership. Thus, trade unions transformed into bureaucratic state apparatuses that served to advance the hierarchy of power. The trade unions were used to prevent the emergence of collective organized action that could challenge both the economic and social policies implemented during the successive waves of economic liberalization imposed by aid donors and the privileges and corruption of economic and political elites. The trade unions—which, admittedly, were not always entirely submissive—participate to a certain extent in maintaining the social equilibrium critical to the survival of the authoritarian regimes.

Without going into the finer historical and political details, it is possible to put forward the theory that is in the countries where trade unionism has been present, active, demanding and part of the revolutionary movement that we have witnessed the fall of dictatorships, the denunciation of the neoliberal order and the corruption of the elite. By comparison, in countries where the trade union movement was absent or co-opted by the ruling regime—Syria, Yemen, Bahrain, Libya, etc.—social movements have been stifled by tribalism or military intervention. The lack of structural organizations and opposition groups such as trade unions could undermine the ability of social movements to overthrow authoritarian regimes. With the UGTT in Tunisia, the possibilities for and limitations on workers' agency and their influence on the political landscape were largely the product of the union's ability to organize and its longstanding relationships with political parties, the economic elite, NGOs, the unemployed and State institutions, as well as changes in the local and global political economy. These factors explain why and how the UGTT decisively influenced the post-Ben Ali political landscape.

More generally, while the successive waves of economic liberalization in the region have perpetuated old forms of domination, they have also fostered new employment models as well as new control mechanisms and configurations of labor and power relations. Recent uprisings in the Arab world remind us that, faced with the diversification of forms and seats of power, new types of political opposition, activism and collective resistance are emerging in the form of local social movements. At the same time, the case of UGTT shows that in each specific context, power relations are affected by multiple dialectics between existing repertoires of action and domination, existing institutions and established strategies of resistance, on the one hand, and the emergence of new forms of dominant power, contentious politics and collective action, on the other. The interconnections between established actors and organizations, and those between the social movements and challengers, offer a promising avenue for exploring the emerging dialectics between old and new forms, construction and deconstruction, and strategies and counter-strategies.

For instance, although unemployed young people played particularly a important role in Cairo, Tunis and elsewhere, by leading the way in the use of social and citizen-run media, organizations such as the UGTT in Tunisia and the Muslim Brotherhood in Egypt are crucial to understanding the dynamics of the so-called "spontaneous" uprisings as well as the political transformation currently underway. They illustrate the importance of established organizational structures and traditional partisanships and leadership as well as the connections between formal and informal institutions. These organizations, which are dialectically affected by the emergent social movements and the arrival of a new political elite, are playing a growing role in mediating the so-called "political transitions" (constitutional assembly or legislative elections, development of transitional justice, etc.), but they also played a part in the authoritarian consolidation as in Egypt. They are the key players converting primary revolutionary situations into revolutionary outcomes and institutionalized processes by leading transactions between state, social movements and formal/informal institutions. Paradoxes, contradictions and interactions—between the new approaches to collective mobilization and repertoires of action in the Arab region and longstanding organizational structures—could represent one of the key issues for social science in the years to come.

Finally, the challenges faced by the UGTT in meeting the economic and social demands championed during the revolutionary process should lead the Arab labor movement and its unions to reconsider a number of fundamental questions about their role in society and their relationship with the state, political parties and new social movements. It should also lead them to question their role in shaping economic and socio-political decisions, as well as to re-examine their identity, structure and organizational resources, in order to cope with the fast-moving political and economic environment. What is happening today on the ground—in workplaces and public spaces in Arab countries—represents a historic opportunity for the labor movement to reconnect with its emancipatory social and political mission and to support the opportunity for the region to reinvent its politics.

Postface

The Tunisian National Dialogue Quartet—the powerful Tunisian General Labor Union (UGTT); the Tunisian Union of Industry, Trade and Handicrafts (UTICA, an employers' union); the Tunisian Human Rights League (LTDH); and the Tunisian Order of Lawyers—was awarded the Nobel Peace Prize in 2015 for "its contribution to the democratic transition in Tunisia since the 2011 revolution." The prize was meant to serve as recognition of the exemplary nature of the Quartet's work. However, more than a year later and six years after the outbreak of the popular uprising, it must be said that being stamped as a model of democracy (after being seen as a model of economic success under Ben Ali) has not always made it possible to satisfy the social and economic demands of the inland regions and the unemployed. By reassuring the political and economic elite and backing a new wave of economically liberal reforms led by aid donors, the Nobel Peace Prize might as well have been one for "social peace at all costs." The Nobel Committee's celebration of the political role played by the alliance of "employees and employers"—represented by the collaboration between the UGTT and UTICA—sounds, in effect, like a warning to all the fractions of the working and unemployed classes who hope for a more just and decent life.

Faced with the alarming erosion of Tunisian state institutions, national political leaders and their international counterparts keep clinging to the notion of "civil society," which they claim is the bulwark against general chaos. The Nobel Prize awarded to Tunisian civil society is a form of recognition of its increasing power. But what are the political implications of this enthusiastic support for civil society?

In January 2015, the government appointed a minister in charge of relations with the constitutional institutions and civil society—a clear indication that the latter has become a key actor on the political stage. Civil society is no longer merely a countervailing force; it is now a central partner in the political decision-making process that has been relatively successful in stabilizing the political climate and brokering a power-sharing arrangement between the newly elected leaders, Ennahdha, and those from the former regime, partially reunited in Nidaa Tounes. However the transformation of Tunisian politics is still in full swing and there are many disagreements over the limits of civil society's role. Proponents of a broad role for civil society believe these organizations are the best avenue for reaching a compromise between the government and social movements, thereby ensuring political stability. Their opponents are critical of the exclusive priority granted to civil-society organizations on issues related to individual liberties, the cooptation of social movements, and the fact that new social and economic dynamics are not represented in organized civil society.

Furthermore, the massive influx of international NGOs, mostly based in the US or Europe, which intervene directly or indirectly by financing local associations, continues to weaken the influence of longstanding civil-society organizations such as the UGTT or the Tunisian Human Rights League (LTDH). Most of these NGOs, which are richly endowed and professionalizing the work of activists, are promoting a neoliberal mindset that is destined to transform the relationship between the state and the citizen into one of supplier and consumer. This is turning Tunisia into a free market for commodities and identities with little room left for the notions of general welfare and national sovereignty. These new international NGOs are competing not only with the social movements but also with elected bodies such as the Assembly of the Representatives of the People.

New challenges have emerged for Tunisia's longstanding associations, which were originally created to resist the stranglehold of the single-party state and campaign for a democratic society built on new foundations. The new civil society, financed by international NGOs, aims to create autonomous spaces outside state control, or to replace government completely on issues such as the vital task of decentralization. The NGOs' rise has been made possible by the lack of serious debate on the role of the state; the competition between the old guard embodied by Nidaa Tounes and the new elite associated with Ennahdha; and the general weakness of political parties as such. The new NGOs have secured their grip on power by becoming the main intermediaries between international aid donors, who demand increased economic liberalization, and local players in search of a place in the sun. Finally, this international support for the new civil society has also resulted in a de facto exclusion of informal associations and those deemed not to be civic bodies, such as religious and political associations. This has created a defective vision of civil society as it actually exists, blind to the various forms of opposition to the power of the state and economic and political elites, as well as non-conventional forms of political activism (e.g. the Salafist movement, small employers' associations and football clubs).

There are a number of issues that organizations such as the UGTT must contend with, namely the role of government in post-January 14 Tunisia and the allocation of roles between the state, elected officials, political parties and civil society; ensuring new social and political dynamics achieve the recognition they deserve, and resistance to the neoliberal agenda imposed by the international aid donors. The traditional organizations of Tunisian civil society will have to make progress on all these fronts if they wish to recover their ability to emancipate the people and neutralize financial back-ers' attempts to sweep aside with the social and economic demands of those who initiated the Revolution of Dignity (and not the "Jasmine Revolution," as the Nobel Committee put it). The actors leading these new social dynam-ics have not yet had their last word.

Appendix A
Acronyms

ANC	National Constituent Assembly—Assemblée Nationale Constituante
ATFD	Tunisian Association of Democratic Women—Association tunisienne des femmes démocrates
CGT	General Confederation of Labor—Confédération générale du travail
CGTT	General Confederation of Tunisian worker—Confédération Générale Tunisienne du Travail
CGTU	Unitary General Labor Confederation—Confédération générale du travail unitaire
CNLT	National Council for Freedom in Tunisia—Conseil national pour les libertés en Tunisie
CNPR	National Council for the Protection of the Revolution—Conseil national pour la protection de la révolution
CONECT	Confederation of Tunisian Citizen Enterprises—Confédération des entreprises citoyennes de Tunisie
CPR	Congress for the Republic—Congrès pour la République
EU	European Union
FDTL	Democratic Forum for Labor and Liberties—Forum démocratique pour le travail et les libertés
FTCR	Tunisian Federation for Citizenship on Both Banks of the Mediterranean
IMF	International Monetary Fund
ISIE	Independent High Authority for Elections—Instance supérieure indépendante des élections
ISROR	High Authority for Realization of the Objectives of the Revolution, Political Reform and Democratic Transition—Instance supérieure pour la réalisation des objectifs de la révolution, de la réforme politique et de la transition démocratique
LPR	Leagues for the Protection of the Revolution—Ligues pour la protection de la révolution
LTDH	Tunisian Human Rights League—Ligue tunisienne des droits de l'Homme

MTI	Islamic Tendency Movement—Mouvement de la tendance islamique
PCOT	Tunisian Communist Workers' Party—Parti communiste des ouvriers tunisiens
PCT	Tunisian Communist Party—Parti communiste tunisien
PDP	Progressive Democratic Party—Parti démocratique progressiste
PSD	Socialist Destourian Party—Parti socialiste destourien
RCD	Democratic Constitutional Rally—Rassemblement constitutionnel démocratique
SFIO	French Section of the Workers' International—Section française de l'internationale ouvrière
SNJT	National Union of Tunisian Journalists—Syndicat national des journalistes tunisiens
UDC	Union of Unemployed Graduates—Union des diplômés chômeurs
UGET	General Union of Tunisian Students—Union générale des étudiants de Tunisie
UGTT	Tunisian General Labor Union—Union générale tunisienne du travail
UNAT	National Union of Tunisian Farmers—Union nationale de l'agriculture tunisienne
UTICA	Tunisian Union of Industry, Trade and Handicrafts—Union tunisienne de l'industrie, du commerce et de l'artisanat
UTT	Union of Tunisian Workers—Union des Travailleurs de Tunisie

Appendix B
UGTT Decision-Making Bodies

National Congress   The union's highest decision-making body and authority of last resort. Meets every five years or on an extraordinary basis at the request of two-thirds of the National Council members.

National Council   The second-highest decision-making body after the congress. Ordinarily meets every two years or on an extraordinary basis at the request of the majority of its members.

National Administrative Commission   The third-ranking body. Makes decisions based on proportional representation and is convened by the National Executive Board, normally every three months, or on an extraordinary basis at the request of two-thirds of its members.

National Executive Board   Thirteen members elected by the National Congress sit on the committee, which meets every three months and, if needed, on an extraordinary basis at the request of two-thirds of its members.

Extended Executive Board   The 13 members of the Executive Board and the 24 secretaries general of the regional unions sit on the committee, which meets once per month.

National Sector Council   The secretaries general of the federations and general unions sit on the council, which meets once per month.

Secretary General   The top UGTT official and spokesperson, who manages union business both within and outside the trade confederation and coordinates the union bodies alongside the members of the Executive Board. Serves as editor-in-chief of the union newspaper *Echaab*.

Sector-Based and Regional Bodies

Federations and general unions   Workers in the same sector belong to federations and workers from one or several fields in a sector belong to general unions.

Regional unions   Established in the capital of each governorate, regional unions oversee local unions, federal sections, regional sector-based unions and the regional discipline commission.

Local unions   Established in the capital of each delegation (the second level of administrative divisions in Tunisia, below the governorates), local unions are responsible for all the workers and retirees in their delegation.

Federal branches and regional sector-based unions   Regional organizations that are responsible for all the workers and union sectors in a specific sector.

Base unions   The grassroots organizations at the UGTT that represent workers at their place of employment. May be established by a group of at least 50 workers. The unions' ordinary congress meets once every three years or, if needed, at the request of at least two-thirds of its members.

Union branches   Established in all workplaces or delegations that have at least 50 members in a given sector.

Permanent Commissions

National Internal Organization Commission   Oversees the application of and compliance with UGTT statutes and regulations. Elected by the National Congress.

National Financial Control Commission   Oversees the financial management of the UGTT and all its organizations, as well as its business and social undertakings. Elected by the National Congress.

Advisory Commissions

Women's Commission   Elected every four years. Advances the causes of women in the workplace, defends women's rights, provides guidance and promotes the role of women in unionism.

Youth Commission   Provides guidance to young workers and encourages their participation in union activities.

Sector-based groups   The public-sector group, state-run company group and the private-sector group.

Union University   A scientific institution that studies topical issues.

Hached Institute   A union establishment that provides training and vocational education in a wide variety of areas.

Union library   The UGTT operates a national union library and regional libraries.

Communication and information   The UGTT publishes a tabloid weekly entitled *Echaab* (The People), which covers all aspects of union activity.

Appendix C
UGTT Chronology (1946 to January 2014)

1946	The UGTT is founded and Farhat Hached named Secretary General. The UGTT leadership concurrently sit on the Néo-Destour Political Committee.
1952	Farhat Hached is assassinated.
1953	The General Union of Tunisian Students (UGET) is founded in Paris.
1954	Ahmed Ben Salah is elected UGTT Secretary General.
1955–1956	The UGTT leadership supports Bourguiba over Ben Youssef, who is expelled from the party and later assassinated in Germany.
1956	The UGTT and Néo-Destour establish the Tunisian Union of Industry, Trade and Handicrafts (UTICA) and the National Union of Tunisian Farmers (UNAT), a "national front" that runs in the 1956 constituent elections and 1959 legislative elections.
1963	Professional groups obedient to the ruling power are established in workplaces to compete with the UGTT. Habib Achour, UGTT Secretary General and a member of the PSD Political Committee from 1964 to 1966, opposes the devaluation of the dinar and cooperativist policies.
1964	The UGTT campaigns for pay raises.
1965	Béchir Bellagha replaces Habib Achour as leader of the UGTT following intervention by the government.
1966	Habib Achour is imprisoned by the regime.
1970	Facing a severe crisis, the ruling power asks Achour to reclaim his position as secretary general. The union immediately becomes embroiled in disputes between clans within the regime.
1974	A wave of social movements and strikes hits Tunisia amidst the global economic crisis.
1978	The UGTT calls a strike on January 26, during which hundreds are wounded and killed. Several unionists, including Habib

	Achour, are arrested. The ruling power installs figureheads to lead the union and "legitimate" unionists are thrown in prison.
1981–1982	New wave of worker and student movements.
1984	The "bread riots" erupt from December 29, 1983, to January 6, 1984. The ruling power instigates a split within the UGTT that results in the creation of an offshoot, the UNTT, on February 18, 1984. PSD militia seize union offices to provide to the new organization, which continues to exist until April 1989.
1985	Habib Achour and other union leaders receive harsh prison sentences and a new leadership team takes office that is loyal to the regime.
1989	The UNTT merges with the UGTT. Ismaïl Sahbani becomes UGTT Secretary General, signaling the reunified union's subservience to Ben Ali.
1993	Sahbani and his allies decisively marginalize the heirs to Achourism, who are led by Ali Romdhane.
2002	Sahbani, who has become a burden to the ruling power, is accused of embezzlement and imprisoned. Abdessalem Jrad replaces Sahbani at the helm of the UGTT Executive Board, where he would remain until 2011.
2008	A revolt breaks out in the Gafsa mining area that lasts over six months and is violently put down by the Ben Ali regime. The UGTT leadership condemns the protest movement, which is supported by several regional unions and sector federations.
2010	A rally is held outside the UGTT headquarters on December 17 in support of the Sidi Bouzid uprising, which is publicly condemned by the Secretary General.
2011	On January 4, the UGTT National Administrative Commission distances itself from the regime. On January 11, the Commission allows regional unions to call general strikes. Ben Ali flees to Saudi Arabia on January 14.
2011	The left-wing "consensus" list wins the elections at the 22nd UGTT Congress, held from December 25 to 28. Houcine Abbassi is elected UGTT Secretary General.
2012	On December 4, as the UGTT is preparing for the 60th anniversary of the assassination of Farhat Hached, the UGTT headquarters on Place Mohamed Ali Hammi is attacked by Committees for the Defense of the Revolution, which are rumored to have ties to Ennahdha. The UGTT Administrative Commission announces a general strike on December 13 as a form of protest. Following pleas from several politicians and negotiations with the government, the union calls off the strike on December 12.
2013	On June 18, the UGTT announces the creation of a council for the national dialogue aimed at establishing a consensus

between political and social actors, the Troika government and civil society regarding the major issues that had led to political disputes, namely the constitution, the election schedule and the individuals who would sit on the election commission.

2014 The government, the UGTT and UTICA sign a "social contract" at the National Constituent Assembly on January 14, which provides for labor relations based on "the institutionalization of an ongoing, permanent, comprehensive three-party dialogue" pertaining to the concerns of the three signatories.

Bibliography

Abdessamad, Hichem. 2012: « Le peuple et ses masques », site Nachaz.org, juillet. 2012.

Afaya, Kacem. 2012. "À propos du pluralisme syndical." *Solidaires International*, vol. 8: 67–8.

Alexander, Christopher. 2000. "Opportunities, Organizations, and Ideas: Islamists and Workers in Tunisia and Algeria." *International Journal of Middle East Studies*, vol. 32, no. 4: 465–90.

Allal, Amin. 2010. "Réformes néolibérales, clientélismes et protestations en situation autoritaire. Les mouvements contestataires dans le bassin minier de Gafsa en Tunisie (2008)." *Politique Africaine*, vol. 117: 107–25.

Amami, Mongi. (2008). "Les syndicalistes Tunisiens à l'épreuve des changements. Quelles représentations? Pour quels enjeux identitaires? (Observations du Congrès de Monastir 14–15 et 16 décembre 2006)." Master's thesis, Institut Supérieur des Sciences Humaines de Tunis.

Ayari, Michael Béchir. 2009. *S'engager en régime autoritaire: Gauchistes et islamistes dans la Tunisie indépendante*. Aix-en-Provence: Institut d'études politiques.

Baraket, Hédia. 2012. "Tunisie: que veulent les ligues de protection de la révolution?" *La Presse*, November 4.

Ben Achour, Rafâa and Ben Achour, Sana. 2012. "La transition démocratique en Tunisie: entre légalité constitutionnelle et légitimité révolutionnaire." *Revue française de droit constitutionnel*, vol. 92: 715–32.

Ben Achour, Yadh. 2011. "Rien ne sera plus comme avant en Tunisie." *jeuneafrique. com*, June 7. www.jeuneafrique.com/Article/ARTJAJA2629p050–054.xml0/

Ben Gharbia, Sami. 2011. *Borj Erroumi XL, voyage dans un monde hostile*. Tunis: les Éditions du patrimoine.

Ben Haj Yahia, Fathi. 2010. *La gamelle et le couffin. Fragments d'une histoire de la gauche tunisienne*. Tunis: Mots passants.

Ben Hamida, Abdesslem. 2001. "La ville lieu de transition entre solidarité d'origine et solidarité syndicale: le cas de Tunis et de Sfax à l'époque colonial." *Cahiers de la Méditerranée: ville et solidarité en Méditerranée*, vol. 63: 69–77.

Ben Hamida, Abdesslem. 2003. *Capitalisme et syndicalisme en Tunisie de 1924 à 1956*. Tunis: Faculté des Sciences Humaines et Sociales.

Ben Hamida, Abdesslem. 2012. *Habib Achour, le timonier de l'UGTT*. Tunis: Self-Published.

Ben Hammouda, Hakim. 2012. *Tunisie. Économie politique d'une revolution*. Louvain-la-Neuve: De Boeck.

Ben Othman, Nejia. 2011. "Tunisie. Pourquoi l'UGTT n'implose pas?" *kapitalis. com*, March 5. www.kapitalis.com/politique/2928-tunisie-pourquoi-lugtt-nim-plose-pas.html.

Ben Romdhane, Mahmoud. 1982. « Mutations économiques et sociales et mouvement ouvrier en Tunisie de 1956 à 1980 », *Annuaire de l'Afrique du Nord*, Paris, CNRS-Editions, Vol. 21: 259–284

Ben Romdhane, Mahmoud. 2011. *Tunisie, État, économie et société*. Paris: Publisud.

Ben Salah, Ahmed. 2008. *Pour rétablir la vérité. Réformes et développement en Tunisie. 1961–1969*. Tunis: Cérès éditions.

Ben Tarjem, Khansa. 2012. "Manifestation de l'Union des diplômés chômeurs (UDC): les diplômés chômeurs ont bravé l'interdiction de manifester."

Bessis, Juliette. 1974. "Le mouvement ouvrier tunisien: de ses origines à l'indépendance." *Le Mouvement Social*, vol. 89: 85–108.

Bessis, Sophie and Belhassen, Souhayr. 2012. *Bourguiba*. Tunis: Elyzad.

Brésillon, Thierry. 2012. "Tunisie: L'UGTT renonce à sa grève générale après un accord avec le gouvernement." *blogs.rue89.nouvelobs.com*, December 12. http:// blogs.rue89. nouvelobs.com/tunisie-libre/2012/12/12/tunisie-veillee-darmes-dans-lattente-de-la-greve-generale-229166.

Camau, Michel, ed. 1987. *Tunisie au présent. Une modernité au dessus de tout soupçon?* Paris: CNRS éditions.

Camau, Michel and Geisser, Vincent. 2003. *Le Syndrome autoritaire. Politique en Tunisie de Bourguiba à Ben Ali*. Paris: Presses de Sciences Po.

Catusse, Myriam; Destremau, Blandine and Verdier, Eric. 2008. *L'Etat face aux débordements du social au Maghreb, Formation, Travail et protection sociale*, IREMAM, Ed. Karthala.

Chaïfa, Sabra and Hamdi, Maher. 2012. "Les relations entre l'UDC et les partis." *Solidaires International*, vol. 8: 93–4.

Chater, Khalifa, 2006, Le temps politique d'un syndicaliste in *Mélanges au professeur Dominique Chevallier*, Académie Beit al-Hikma, Carthage:195–210.

Cherni, Amor. 2011. *La révolution tunisienne, s'emparer de l'histoire*. Tunis: Editions Abouraq.

Chouikha, Larbi and Geisser, Vincent. 2010. "Retour sur la révolte du bassin minier. Les cinq leçons politiques d'un conflit social inédit." *L'Année du Maghreb*, vol. VI: 415–26.

Collectif du 18 Octobre Pour Les Droits Et Les Libertés. 2012. "Documents sur le Mouvement du 18 Octobre." *Nachaz Dissonances: revue numérique tunisienne*. www. nachaz.org/index.php/fr/textes-a-l-appui/politique/102-2012-09-11-12-11-20.html.

Comité de soutien aux syndicalistes de SEA Latelec de Fouchana. 2013. "Appel du Comité de soutien aux syndicalistes de SEA Latelec de Fouchana." May 14. www.facebook.com/ComiteSoutienSyndicalistesLatelecFouchana/posts/538244802884405.

Dahmani, Frida. 2013. "Crise en Tunisie: le coup de poker de Hamadi Jebali." *jeuneafrique.com*, February 11. www.jeuneafrique.com/Article/JA2717p016.xml0/.

Dakhlia, Jocelyne. 2011. *Tunisie: Le Pays Sans Bruit*. Paris: Actes Sud.

Dobry, Michel. 2009. *Sociologie des crises politiques, la dynamique des mobilisations multisectorielles*. Paris: Presses des Sciences Po.

Dot Pouillard, Nicolas. 2013. *Tunisie: la révolution et ses passés*. Paris: L'Harmattan.

Ferchichi, Kamel. 2012. "La Centrale syndicale à l'épreuve de la restructuration." *lapresse.tn*, January 5. www.lapresse.tn/02072014/43101/la-centrale-syndicale-a-lepreuve-de-la-restructuration.html.

Gantin, Karine and Seddik, Omeya. 2008. « Révolte du "peuple des mines" en Tunisie », *Le monde diplomatique*, juillet.

Ghaith, J. 2011. "L'UGTT conteste la nomination du Premier ministre Béji Caïd Essebsi." *tixup.com*, February 28. www.tixup.com/international-politique/3449-lugtt-conteste-la-nomination-du-premier-ministre-beji-caid-essebsi.html.

Gharb, Imen. 2012. "L'initiative de UGTT au centre des débats." *L'économiste maghrébin*, October 17.

Gnet.tn. 2013. "Tunisie; l'UGTT est une école de démocratie (Noureddine Bhiri)." *gnet.tn*, December 16. www.gnet.tn/actualites-nationales/tunisie-lugtt-est-une-ecole-de-democratie-bhiri/id-menu-958.html.

Gobe, Eric. 2008. "Les syndicalismes arabes au prisme de l'autoritarisme et du corporatisme." In *Autoritarismes démocratiques et démocraties autoritaires au XIXème siècle*, Convergence Nord/Sud, edited by Olivier Dabène, Vincent Geisser and Gilles Massardier, 267–84. Paris: La Découverte.

Gobe, Eric. 2013. *Les avocats en Tunisie de la colonisation à la révolution (1883–2011)*. Tunis-Paris: IRMC-Karthala.

Guerfali, Riadh. 2011. "Tunisie: Quand Abdessalem Jrad louait éhontément Ben Ali." video, *nawaat.org*, April 16. http://nawaat.org/portail/2011/04/16/tunisie-quand-a-jrad-louait-ehontement-ben-ali/.

Halimi, Serge. 2013. "Islamistes au pied du mur." *Le monde diplomatique*, March 1–2.

Hamza, Hassine Raouf. 1994. *Communisme et nationalisme en Tunisie, de la libération à l'indépendance*. Tunis: Université de Tunis.

Hamzaoui, Salah. (2013). "Pratiques syndicales et pouvoir politique: pour une sociologie des cadres syndicaux (cas de la Tunisie)." PhD dissertation, Université Paris 7, Paris.

Hermassi, Abdelbaki. (1966). "Mouvement ouvrier en société coloniale. La Tunisie entre les deux guerres." PhD dissertation, EPHE, Paris.

Hibou, Béatrice. 2006. *La force de l'obéissance: économie politique de la répression en Tunisie*. Paris: La Découverte.

Hmed, Chokri. 2014. "Le temps de la complexité." In *Fragments d'une révolution*, edited by El Kasbah, 48–73. Tunis: Imprimerie Simpact.

Hmed, Choukri. 2013. "Tunisie: le salut par le dialogue national?" *Libération*, December 18.

Hmed, Choukri. 2012. « Réseaux dormants, contingence et structures. Genèses de la révolution tunisienne », *Revue française de science politique*, Presses de Sciences Po, vol. 62, n° 5–6, Paris: 797–820.

Hmed, Choukri and Youfsi, Hèla. 2012. "Pour la chute du régime de Tunis." *Libération*, May 29.

International Crisis Group. 2011. "Popular Protest in North Africa and the Middle East (IV)." *Tunis-Brussels, International Crisis Group*, April 28.

International Crisis Group. 2013. "Tunisie: violences et défi salafiste." *Rapport Moyen-Orient/Afrique du Nord No. 137*. Tunis/Bruxelles, International Crisis Group, February 13.

International Crisis Group. 2014. "L'exception tunisienne: succès et limites du consensus." *International Crisis Group*, June 5.

Iribarne, Philippe (d'). 2003a. *Le Tiers monde qui réussit, nouveaux modèles*. Paris: Odile Jacob.

Iribarne, Philippe (d'). 2003b. "Trois figures de la liberté." *Annales. Histoire, Sciences Sociales*, vol. 5, 58th year, Paris: 953–78.

Iribarne, Philippe (d'), Henry, Alain ; Segal, Jean-Pierre, Chevrier, Sylvie and Globokar Tatjana 1998. *Cultures et mondialisations, Gérer par-delà les frontières.* Paris: Seuil.

Jemli, Lamjed. 2012. "L'initiative de l'UGTT." *Solidaires International,* no. 8, Fall: 65–6.

Kefi, Chiraz. 2013. "Tunisie: 'les organisations ne doivent pas remplacer les partis politiques'." *gnet.tn,* October 7. www.gnet.tn/temps-fort/tunisie-les-organisations-ne-doivent-pas-remplacer-les-partis-politiques/id-menu-325.html.

Khaled, Ahmed. 2007. *Farhat Hached, héros de la lutte sociale et nationale, martyr de la liberté (itinéraire, combat, pensée et écrits).* Tunis: Editions Zakhâref.

Khiari, Sadri. 2003. *Tunisie, Le délitement de la cité, Coercition, consentement, résistance.* Paris: Karthala.

Krichen, Azyz. 2013. "La seule issue honorable." *Post on Personal Facebook Page,* August 5. www.facebook.com/notes/el-kasbah/la-seule-issue-honorable/616157468423824.

Lamloum, Olfa. 1988. « Janvier 84 en Tunisie ou le symbole d'une transition », in *Emeutes et mouvements sociaux au Magreb, perspective comparée,* sous la direction de Didier Le Saout et Marguerite Rollinde, Karthala, Institut Maghreb Europe, Octobre 88: 231–242.

Leaders.com.tn. 2014. "Jomaa au FMI et la Banque mondiale: plus de soutien, plus de souplesse." *leaders.com.tn,* April 4. www.leaders.com.tn/article/jomaa-au-fmi-et-la-banque-mondiale-plus-de-soutien-plus-de-souplesse?id=13747.

Liauzu, Claude. 1977. "Salariat et Mouvement ouvrier en Tunisie." PhD dissertation, Université de Nice, Nice.

Mandraud, Isabelle. 2013. "Tunisie: un nouveau Premier ministre nommé sous la pression occidentale." *Le Monde,* December 13.

Meddeb, Hamza. 2011. "L'ambivalence de la 'course à el khobza'." In "Obéir et se révolter en Tunisie." *Politique Africaine,* vol. 1, no. 121: 35–52:Karthala.

Mejri, Ouejdane, and Hajji, Afef. 2013. *La Rivolta Dei Dittatoriati.* Messina: Éditions Mesogea.

Mestiri, Ahmed. 2012. *Témoignage pour l'histoire. Des souvenirs, quelques réflexions et commentaires sur une époque contemporaine de la Tunisie, accessoirement du Maghreb (1940–1990).* Tunis: Sud Editions.

Morel, Léon. 1949. *Les mineurs de Gafsa, mémoire du contrôleur civil adjoint.* (n.p.; n.d.).

Morrisson, Christian and Talbi, Béchir. 1996. *La croissance de l'économie tunisienne en longue période. Etudes du Centre de Développement, "Croissance à long terme."* Paris: OCDE.

Mouhoud, Mouhoub El. 2011. "Économie politique des révolutions arabes: analyse et perspectives." In "Les révolutions dans le monde arabe: un an après." *Maghreb-Machrek,* vol. 4, no. 210: 35–47.

Mouterde, Perrine. 2011. "Le syndicat UGTT se cherche une nouvelle légitimité." *france24. com,* March 5. www.france24.com/fr/20110304-tunisie-syndicat-ugtt-corruption-revolution-legitimite-jrad-ben-ali/.

Naccache, Gilbert. 2009. *Qu'as-tu fait de ta jeunesse? Itinéraire d'un opposant au régime de Bourguiba (1954–1979).* Paris-Tunis: Cerf-Mots Passants.

Naccache, Gilbert. 2013. "Vers la Démocratie? chapitre 4: La classe politique et la Révolution après le 14 Janvier." Interview with A. Bisquerra, *Nawaat.org,* January 28. http://nawaat.org/portail/2013/01/28/vers-la-democratie-entretien-avec-gilbert-n-chapitre-4-la-classe-politique-et-la-revolution-apres-le-14-janvier/.

Naccache, Gilbert and Abdessalem, Tahar. 2013. "Gouvernement politique ou gouvernement de technocrates." *Authors' Personal Facebook Page*, January 31. www. facebook.com/notes/gilbert-naccache/gouvernement-politique-ou-gouvernement-de-technocrates/10150514744167749.

Ould Aoudia, Jacques. 2006. "Croissance et réformes dans les pays arabes méditerranéens." *Alternatives Économiques*, no. 253.

Perez, Déborah. 2012. "Être député en situation révolutionnaire. La fabrique du politique à l'Assemblée nationale constituante tunisienne." Master's thesis, EHESS, Paris.

Puchot, Pierre. 2012. "Siliana la répression des tunisiens se fait à la chevrotine." *mediapart.fr*, November 28. www.mediapart.fr/journal/international/281112/siliana-la-repression-des-tunisiens-se-fait-la-chevrotine.

Rabaa, H. 2012. "Tunisie: Samir Dilou 'Ennahdha n'aurait jamais pensé rentrer dans un bras de fer avec l'UGTT'." *tunisienumerique.com*, December 6. www.tunisie-numerique.com/tunisie-samir-dilou-ennahdha-naurait-jamais-pense-rentrer-dans-un-bras-de-fer-avec-lugtt/155998.

Slateafrique.com. 2011. "Tunisie—Affrontements sanglants à Metlaoui." *slateafrique. com*, June 9. www.slateafrique.com/2531/bilan-du-carnage-de-metlaoui-tunisie.

S. T. 2012. "Marzouki appelle à la création d'un gouvernement de compétences et à l'organisation d'élections avant l'été 2013." *businessnews.com.tn*, November 30. www.businessnews.com.tn/Marzouki-appelle-%C3%A0-la-cr%C3%A9ation-d%E2%80%99un-gouvernement-de-comp%C3%A9tenceset-%C3%A0-lorganisation-d%C3%A9lections-avant-l%E2%80%80%99%C3%A9t%C3%A9-2013,520,34865,3.

Tabbabi, Hfaeidh. 2006. "Le fait colonial et la problématique du mouvement syndical dans un milieu rurale et bédouin: le cas des mines de Gafsa." In "le Sud Ouest tunisien." *Rawafid*, vol. 11: 157–71.

Thedrel, Arielle. 2011. "À Tunis, la "révolution du jasmin" se radicalise." *lefigaro. fr*, March 3. www.lefigaro.fr/ international/ 2011/03/03/0100320110303ART-FIG00768—tunis-la-revolution-du-jasmin-se-radicalise.php.

Timoumi, Hédi. 1983. *Naqabât al-âraf ettounissyin (1932–1955)*. Tunis: Ed Mohamed Ali Hammi.

Tlili, Ahmed. 1966. *Lettre à Bouguiba (janvier 1966)*. Tunis: Imprimeries réunies.

Touraine, Alain; Dubet, François, Wieviorka, Michel and Strzelecki Jan. 1982. *Solidarité, Analyse d'un mouvement social, Pologne, 1980–1981*. Paris: Fayard.

UGTT. 1956. *Rapport économique du VIe Congrès de l'UGTT*. Tunis: UGTT.

UGTT. 2006. *Vers un renouveau syndical: diagnostic quantitatif de l'UGTT par ses cadres*. Tunis: Département des études et de la documentation, "Opinions syndicales."

UGTT. 2012. "L'initiative de l'UGTT sur le lancement d'un conseil de dialogue national." *ugtt.org.tn*, June 18.

UGTT. 2013. "Initiative du Quartet parrain du dialogue national pour la résolution de la crise politique." *ugtt.org.tn*, October 10. www.ugtt.org.tn /fr/2013/10/10/initiative-du-Quartet-parrain-du-dialogue-national-pour-la-resolution-de-la-crise-politique/.

Weslaty, Lilia. 2012. "Ekbess, campagne des partisans d'Ennahdha: diversion ou véritable contestation." *nawaat.org*, September 11. www.nawaat.org/portail/2012/09/11/ekbess-campagne-des-partisans-dennahdha-diversion-ou-veritable-contestation/.

Yaalaoui, Abderrahmane. 2012. "Légitimité électorale et légitimité révolution-naire." *La Presse de Tunisie*, October 3.

Y. B. 2014. "Dialogue national, Connect, UTT, CGTT, demandent à en faire partie." *l'Economiste maghrébin*, April 18. www.leconomistemaghrebin.com/2014/04/18/dialogue-national-conect-utt-cgtt-demandent-faire-partie/.

Yousfi, Hèla. 2007. "Gérer en Jordanie: une coexistence problématique entre système hiérarchique et idéal religieux d'une communauté d'égaux." *Revue Française de Gestion*, vol. 171, no. 2: 157–73.

Yousfi, Hèla. 2008. *Culture et gestion au Liban, Gestion en contexte intercultural.* Québec: Presses de l'Université Laval.

Yousfi, Hèla. 2010. "Le climat d'investissement en Égypte, les conditions d'une réforme durable: institutions ou relations? Une approche ethnographique." *Gérer et Comprendre*, no. 101: 72–83.

Yousfi, Hèla. 2012. "Ce syndicat qui incarne l'opposition." *Le Monde diplomatique*, November 17–18.

Yousfi, Hèla. 2014. "Rethinking Hybridity in Postcolonial Contexts: What Changes and What Persists ? The Tunisian Case of Poulina's Managers." *Organization Studies*, vol. 35, no. 3: 393–421.

Yousfi, Hèla and Hmed, Choukri. 2013. "Non à l'assassinat de la révolution tunisienne." *Le Monde*, July 31.

Yousfi, Mohammed Lamine. 1983. *Alharaka Ennaqabia fitounes 1900–1981*. Sfax: Editions Coopi.

Zeghidi, Salah. 2001. "UGTT: à quand le véritable renouveau?" *Alternative Citoyennes*, no. 1. www.alternatives-citoyennes.org/num1/actu-syndicalisme-w.html.

Zghal, Riadh. 1998. "Nouvelles orientations du syndicalisme tunisien." *Monde Arabe, Maghreb-Machrek*, no. 162: 6–17.

Index